sex,
society,
and the
Disabled

Sex, Society, and the Disabled

a Developmental Inquiry Into Roles, Reactions, and Responsibilities

ISABEL P. ROBINAULT

Project Director, Research Utilization Laboratory, ICD Rehabilitation and
Research Center, New York, New York

Harper & Row, Publishers
Hagerstown, Maryland
New York, San Francisco, London

78 79 80 81 82 83   10 9 8 7 6 5 4 3 2 1

Library of Congress Cataloging in Publication Data

Robinault, Isabel Pick.
  Sex, society, and the disabled.

  Bibliography: p.
  Includes index.
  1. Sex instruction for the handicapped.
2. Handicapped—Sexual behavior. I. Title.
HQ54.R6   613.9'5'0240816   77–28196
ISBN 0–06–142274–6

CONTENTS

Appendices

PREFACE

We have, because human, an inalienable prerogative of
responsiblility which we cannot devolve, no, not as once
thought, even upon stars. We can share it only with each
other.

—Sherrington

Ours is a multiculture society. "From sea to shining sea" more people, able and
disabled, live longer, live differently, and live in closer juxtaposition to one another. A rapidly interacting and poorly understood variety of cultural forces have
concurrently produced a sexual revolution which expresses itself haphazardly in
literature, in entertainment media, and in some of the overt behavior of youth
and adults. It is the premise of this book that a developmental perspective, discussed in easily understood terms, may prove to be a connecting thread through
this confusion. Therefore, the sexuality of individuals with chronic disability (con-
gential or acquired) is presented in the sequence of the life-cycle from infancy
through older ages. The challenges at each stage are pointed out from the perspective of how individuals and their advocates in the helping professions balance
innate and acquired capabilities with realistic interpersonal experiences, with confusing social cues, and in spite of the limitations of present-day knowledge and
technologies.

Samples are chosen from real life experience and research reports to illustrate, at
each stage, what the disabled share with their able-bodied contemporaries, where
adjustments have to be considered, and what realistic options exist. We present
options in terms of the possible reactions to them and the responsibility of attendant
decisions. This book's purpose is to stimulate productive inquiry among professions
that concern themselves with the sexuality of the disabled, and to relate existing
professional resources to the needs of people with disabilities. A comprehensive
bibliography on the sexuality of the disabled encourages this.

There are times when, as quoted in Green Pastures, "everything nailed down is
comin' loose." This is one of those times in the field of human sexuality. Solutions must
be sought in terms of developing individuals and their life styles, rather than offering
quick prescriptions or laundry lists. Therefore, the emphasis in this book is on the
growing relationships between people—between the able and disabled, as well as the
disabled and other disabled. How these relationships in various social contexts (such
as home, camp, clinics, school and work) foster growth and development, and how
they subsequently mold the sexuality of persons who are disabled, or become disabled, will be followed through the major life stages. This approach is not offered as
a comprehensive or definitive work. Rather, it presents a current state-of-the-art,
inviting inquiry and further research into the sexuality of persons who are disabled.
And, possibly, just possibly, the outcome may be a prototype that shows how a more

general population may be wisely educated and more wisely counseled for responsive and responsible sexuality.

Robert Tanton has drawn the illustrations, and for the many helpful suggestions and criticisms regarding this endeavor, I am indebted to Dr. Eric Denhoff, Dr. Ralph Hanna, Helen Wallen and Dr. Arthur Zitrin. However, none of them are to be held responsible for value judgments taken by the writer on issues where valid differences of opinion may have arisen.

sex, SOCIeTY, and the DISaBLeD

1 EARLY PSYCHOSEXUAL DEVELOPMENT: I'm A Boy—I'm A Girl

When one tugs on a single thing in nature, he finds it attached to the rest of the world.—John Muir

Our National Parks

EXPECTATIONS AND REALITIES

Mrs. Smith is "expecting" . . . Mrs. Jones is "expecting" . . . Mrs. Green is "expecting" . . . Miss Brown is "expecting." All Mrs. Smith wants is a girl, while Mrs. Jones, with her three girls, wants a boy so Mr. Jones will have "his son." Mrs. Green, on the other hand, didn't expect this baby at all. At her age, she will be satisfied as long as it is healthy and as long as Mr. Green stops grumbling over rising prices and drinking himself into resignation. Miss Brown is frightened; she's expecting hard times ahead.

These fragments of general attitudes reveal how often each baby, healthy or in jeopardy of disability, is born a product of many expectations. At the same time, this baby is also a product of biologic heritage and prenatal environment. Actually, any disability in a baby adds a threatening complication to the already imposing list of parental expectations. A baby's sex, its temperament, its looks—or the discovery of its disability—are hard realities that produce an effect upon all the people with whom it comes in contact. In turn, it is affected by these reactions. Eventually, however, this new biologic organism, full of poorly coordinated initiative, is transformed by a spiraling interactive developmental process into a human sexual person (397). In early formative years, the baby evolves from what it seemed-to-be to others into what it believes itself to be: a boy or a girl person. In the long pull of growth, he or she, excitable or placid, intact or impaired, joins the family of man in striving to be human (118). The eventual objective of these strivings may be "love and work" (Freud), "identity" (Erikson, Rogers, May), "competence" (White, Piaget), or "self-actualization" to realize one's highest potential (Maslow). Whatever the goal, the basic threads of healthy development and of human sexuality are related to many interwoven factors of biologic, physical, emotional, social, and intellectual functionings (92).

BASIC DEVELOPMENTAL FACTORS

Everyone, whether he or she has full or impaired competencies, shares a hard-earned heritage of information about human sex and sexuality (270). The whole story has not yet been deciphered, but an earnest group of medical and social scientists of this century have changed the whispers about sex into an exchange of opinions. They have examined the biologic bases of sexuality, the old wives' tales, the ways of different cultures, and the choices of different personalities. A thumbnail sketch of these new learnings will throw better perspective on our developmental view of the maleness and femaleness of disabled individuals.

CHROMOSOMES: CONTRIBUTIONS AND COMPLICATIONS

The most significant advances in medicine during the past 25 years in Swinyard's opinion have been made in the field of human genetics (420). He lists these in the following chronological order: a) Recognition by Barr in 1949 that the sex of an individual can be detected by microscopic inspection of somatic cells. b) The number of chromosomes in man were correctly identified in 1956 by Tijio and Levan. c) The chemical and physical characteristics of human hereditary material (deoxyribonucleic acid [DNA]) were identified by Kornberg in 1950; Lederberg in 1951; Watson and Crick 1953; Ochoa 1955 and Wilkins 1956. d) Recognition by Lejeune in 1959 that human abnormality can be produced by abnormal numbers or malformations of whole or parts of chromosomes. e) Development of techniques by Nadler in 1968 for prenatal detection of genetic disease by biochemical or cellular study of samples of a pregnant woman's amniotic fluid. All of these advances have provided practical assistance to genetic counseling.

Biologically, each human being is part of the animal world in which sex is determined at conception by an X chromosome from the mother and an X or Y chromosome from the father. A father–mother XX combination makes a new girl, a father–mother XY combination starts off a new boy. At the same time, a small percentage of new embryos may receive unusual number or combinations of sex chromosomes (XXY or XXX or XYY) which require—and are getting—more research to determine whether they impose disability by contributing to unusual behavior or biologic variations (459). There also are a number of these chromosomal anomalies which are related to disabilities associated with atypical sexual function in adolescence and early adulthood. Klinefelter's syndrome (47 XXY), usually in a male with small or dysfunctioning gonads, sterility, and mild retardation, is the most common. Turner's syndrome in females (45/XO or 46 with breakage), characterized by primary amenorrhea, shortness of stature, and multiple somatic defects, is another variant which contributes to sexual maladjustment. The syndrome also occurs in males. There are other anomalies such as Tetra-X Syndrome (XXXX) or Penta-X (XXXXX) where the female is sterile and often retarded, while the male is sterile and often retarded in Tetra-XY Syndrome (XXXXY). In what is called the XY female, the individual is sterile but female in all respects, due to inability of the uptake granules in the cytoplasm of the embryonic cells to use those hormones that usually produce maleness in normal XY combinations. "Supermales" or "superfemales," i.e., those with extra X or Y chromosomes, also present varying personality problems, the significance of which is still unclear (87). Still other inherited defects are not chromosomally selected, but involve sex and genelinked abnormalities within the cell (212, 316).

Fortunately, the number of defective fetuses that come to term (are born) is lower than the number conceived, since nature is the first censor of inadequate life via spontaneous abortion or miscarriage (459). Actually, about one in ten pregnancies end in spontaneous abortion—which is a conservative estimate, since those occurring in the first month are not easily recognized. While a fertile woman has about 360–400 ovulations (one a month) during the reproductive period of her life, researchers claim that she produces 10–20 ova with abnormal chromosomal complement. Thus, chromosomal aberrations are by no means rare, but . . . most of them are aborted; very few reach the end of gestation (459).

In view of increasing knowledge of the high genetic or infectious risks often resulting in stormy pregnancies, the struggle to help women carry to term is due for reconsideration. This greater knowledge opens up a horizon of value judgments which may put the physician's attempt to save life (a life which nature may have censored as unfit) in conflict with the wishes of informed parents. The actual "right" to decide this issue has never been settled and is one of those human problems under critical appraisal in the ever-growing considerations of medical, legal, and human ethics (242).

HORMONES: CONTRIBUTIONS AND COMPLICATIONS

Hormones (those glandular secretions into the blood which activate some distant organ) also play a part in the biologic determination of sex, as well as in occasional sex dysfunctions. In the normal development of a fertilized egg, an embryo with XY chromosomes develops testes, while an embryo with XX chromosomes develops ovaries. Within the early prenatal months, the testes of a male fetus start secreting a form of male hormone that triggers the development of accessory male organs. In the absence of this hormone, the XX fetus develops female apparatus. Thus, although embryos of both sexes possess basic tissues which can develop into male or female accessories, the presence or absence of testicular hormones influences the differentiation in one of a male epididymis, vas deferens, and seminal vesicle, and in the other of female fallopian tubes, uterus, and median vagina.

Unfortunately, there are hormonal as well as chromosomal aberrations which may cause physical confusion of sexual anatomy. Money, one of the outstanding researchers in this area, explains that when a baby is born with sexual anatomy improperly differentiated, the baby is, in other words, sexually unfinished.

If the external genitalia are involved, then they look ambiguous . . . an incompletely differentiated penis may be indistinguishable from an incompletely differentiated clitoris, irrespective of genetic and gonadal sex. Moreover, a genetic female may be prenatally androgenized (subjected to androgen hormone) to such a degree that the baby is born looking like a boy with undescended testes. Conversely, a genetic male may be born with a genital appearance indistinguishable from that of a normal female (279).

In former times, these unfortunate baby victims of biologic sex developmental deficiencies were social outcasts or silent sufferers. But active research and a better educated population are laying the foundation for better understanding, for preventive efforts, and for rehabilitative techniques (442). Medical centers all over the country now have specialized clinics for early rehabilitation of these unfortunate babies and their families.

In normal prenatal development, hormones have increasingly important biologic roles during the 9 months. By the second trimester of fetal life, additional developments are taking place, such as the beginnings of the glandular system which will eventually influence puberty. In addition, the neural and muscular systems that will make sexual responsiveness possible in later life and the brain centers that will eventually send and receive sexual messages are also being laid down in this second trimester of prenatal life.

BIOLOGY AND BEHAVIORS

Because biology is the active determiner of anatomic sex development, the extent, if any, to which it is a general determiner of behavior should also be considered. From studies in comparative zoology and psychology, we learn that sexual behavior in animals below the level of primates is *biologically* impelled. It is strongly dependent upon the action of sex hormones on certain centers deep in the midbrain. As a result, sex is tied to reproduction at the specific times when an animal is "in heat"—the times optimal for reproductive capacity. However, going up the evolutionary scale, as the cortex of the brain increases in size and complexity, so does *cortical control* over behavior increase. As a result, *monkeys, apes, and man need education in sex behavior.* In these primates, the actual act of coitus is not instinctive, as it is in birds and in lower animals. It must be determined by trial and error, or it must be learned from another experienced member of the same species. To repeat: monkeys, apes, and man need education in sex functions.

In man (men and women) sexual behavior and reproductive behavior are no longer synonymous. Poets and humorists have been saying this in many ways for many ages. Elizabeth Browning has sighed, "Men do not think of sons and daughters when they fall in love." And Heyward Broun (56) chuckled, "The ability to make love frivolously is the chief characteristic which distinguishes human beings from beasts". Because man's desire for sex is not seasonally geared to a reproductive period, human beings need to learn both control of relationships as well as contraceptive techniques in order to ensure the separate freedoms of sexual desire and desired reproduction. Since many disabled individuals have special problems associated with the requisites for these freedoms, these will be dealt with in appropriate developmental sections. Add to this man's need for education in *love* related to sexual behavior (102). Unfortunately, the word *sexual* is "narrowed in many Western adult minds to cover only the act of coitus, as though the sexual relationship were confined to that act alone and successful marriage sprang ready-made out of no previous experience of loving" (444). Actually, another necessary learning related to the maturity of mankind is an education in that love of humanity which is related to generalized sexuality: that noncoital, interpersonal interaction subsumed under a caring charm, an empathetic charisma, or being "simpatico," by which each culture recognizes what it designates as a warm *masculinity* or *femininity*.

SOCIETY, SEX, AND DISABILITY

In addition to the psychobiologic aspects of sex and sexuality our human heritage is weighted with social contributions. At birth, each society looks between the legs of the newborn and says, "It's a boy" or "It's a girl," and proceeds to define those characteristics of masculinity or femininity peculiar to its own cultural interests (139). In addition, each society still counts the baby's fingers and takes a long look at whether the rest of the child is "well made" or "questionable."

Historical Perspectives

History has dealt variously with the decision. Ancient and primitive civilizations often killed the physically imperfect. At times it was done to ensure survival of the group and at other times from superstition leading to human sacrifice. The Middle Ages tolerated the "different," making them jesters of the court or general objects of ridicule and fear. With the Renaissance came the start of asylums, and the eighteenth century saw the first concept of modern care begin in Switzerland. The nineteenth century brought the beginnings of education for the physically disabled, the retarded, and the emotionally ill. Then the twentieth century initiated total rehabilitation for civilian populations after pioneering efforts for military casualties. Finally, the most recent generations started considering "personhood," with its concomitant sexuality, as an integral part of total rehabilitation. It has been a long pull. So it is wise to keep in mind the sweep of these changes and to work patiently and constructively to overcome some of today's recognizable social lags.

Cultures (social aggregates) tend to crystallize the attitudes and roles of their participants, no doubt holding onto those that have enabled survival during the precarious times of mankind's 80,000 years of acculturalization. Today, instead of surveying the panorama of role possibilities for both men and women that technologic communication has recently brought into the reach of every part of our planet, different cultures continue to grasp for superficial polarizations. Some hail man-the-agressor, the prototype of "masculinity," in comic strips, paperbacks, and audiovisuals. On the other hand, man-the-cooperator, the "womanly," "nurturing" prototype, is hailed by rural communes, isolated philosophers, and hopeful religionists. These roles descend from departmentalization of labor by early man during prehistoric times. Actually, as Montague has been trying to tell us, it must have been organization plus consistent masculine and feminine cooperation, even within the primitive hunt and gathering times (280), that enabled man to survive against the mammoths and the mastadons with only a pitifully few crude hand tools. Then, again, how literally or how pervasively should we be taking the heritage of the ancient rivalry between prehistoric *matriarchal* societies and those later developing *patriarchal* ones that finally outnumbered them during historical times? The myths, the sagas, and the poetry are treasuries of male and female experience and creativity. However, the extent to which blind acceptance of these ancient rivalries should be taken as universals is being challenged by our present day social sciences (viz. the Oedipus–Electra competition).

Modern Perspectives

In the twentieth century, serious inquiry using a wide horizon of scientific approaches has given broader vision to mankind's social heritage and to the varieties of living potentials. Ford and Beach provide a truly insightful view of man's nature and patterns of sexual behavior (140). These researchers consider humanity's place in animal evolution, in differing societies around the world, and in the light of the relationship between sexual behavior and the physiology of brain and body capacities. They point out that the higher the degree of cortical development in the evolutionary sequence, the more variable will be behavior and the more behavior will be open to modification through experience. Mankind's variability and learning capacity is borne out through cross-cultural studies which reveal that no one society can be regarded as representative of the human race as a whole (140). While some universals do exist, there is a wide range of accepted interpersonal experiences of designated male and female roles and of accepted sexual behavior in cultures that are now in existence around the world. Ford and Beach also direct our attention to the universal human chronology (hereditary underlying drive) for sexual responses that appears in an immature person before he or she is capable of fertile copulation. Some societies condone or encourage early sexual experimentation, while others forbid and punish it. Societies also differ in their attitudes toward such sexual behaviors as masturbation, homosexuality, types of foreplay prior to coitus, as well as the means of sex education (26).

In addition, societies differ about male and female roles, dress, and what is considered admirable physique or beauty. Societies also differ in their tolerance of the differences of those individuals who vary in physical, mental, or emotional capacities from the accepted norms. For example, a representative to a recent international health conference said that, even today, some rural tribes of the Third World demand that disabled babies be left at the outskirts of their territory for come what may. Compliance, even within that tribe, varies from literal obedience to secretive forays by a baby's family to bring it scraps from an all too meager larder. Although Margaret Mead, time and again, has indicated that the character of a culture can be judged by the way it treats [its lame, its halt, and] its disabled, our culture, for example, has wide variations. True, great strides have been made in Western rehabilitation. True, up to 20% of the population will be working in "helping" professions during this decade. True, professionals come from all over the world to study medical, educational, and technical advances in the United States. Yet, we still have to ask ourselves how many disabled can claim to be living in the mainstream of society; how many children in residential facilities have gone without a family visitor from one year to another; what are we doing about more than a million cases of battered or neglected children annually where one in five are dying and many will grow up emotionally if not physically disabled (443)?

Much of our cultural heritage disposes many of us to respond negatively (if not with fear) to ugliness, difference, disfigurement, and disability (215). This immediate primitive reaction is too often left in its raw state due to lack of contact with the capabilities of disabled persons. Separations in school, work, or even religious gatherings do nothing to correct superficial surface impressions. Children who are separated by race, sex, disability, etc., cannot be expected to understand themselves, much less one another. Taking cues from research, we find that sustained interpersonal relationships can effect more positive attitudinal changes than all the lectures in the world. Other constructive cues come from a typical American product, mutual help societies. In the past, these were often started by parents of the disabled. However, more and more the disabled themselves are taking leadership in outreach efforts. These private volunteer efforts, in concert with more social legislation, are beginning to make a dent in the cultural alienation of people who differ, but who have contributions to make to a human society. In fact, at the rate that medical science is saving people from acute sicknesses and prolonging life, more and more of us will have to learn to live with chronic body changes, giving less emphasis to perfect bodies and intensifying the search for meaningful ways of life—quality of life.

Since more of us may be living with impairments, let's look at some of the problems of the disabled population in our society: lack of adequate functional housing, unavailability of public transportation, the excessive cost of special transportation without adequate tax relief, the high cost of artificial aids and the difficulty in getting adequate and prompt repairs, as well as the lack of jobs for those willing and able to work but not able to keep up with the pace assigned to minimum wages. The chronically disabled are also constantly required to face the unreasonable public belief that absolute cure is just around the corner, so needed social steps are often delayed. The chronically disabled are also generally looked upon by others as asexual—or, just as erroneously, it is believed that they should be so preoccupied with rehabilitation that sexuality should not detour them.

In actuality, modern rehabilitation includes sexuality among its remediation. The disabled do not ask to be objects of pity, fear, or laughter. They correctly resent a classification (17) which does not give consideration to their emotional, social, and sexual needs. In summary, without negative community attitudes, disabled individuals and their families could deal more easily with their actual limitations (219). But the stigma of negative attitudes and the social barriers that still pervade our society restrict the life space of our disabled fellow man and often contribute to their problems of personal, social, and vocational adjustment (123, 180).

INFANCY: GROWING A NEW PERSON

Infancy is that initial developmental stage of biologic, psychologic, and social interaction which extends from birth to the onset of appropriate language use (62). Biologically, the normal infant retains residuals of the reflex sexual physiology of the animal species. For example, it is common for baby boys to have erections of the penis, especially when the bladder is full or during urination. Today, most child specialists consider this strictly a neuromotor response occurring at a time when sexual impulses are unformed (102, 406). Physically speaking, very little development takes place until puberty. In contrast, a growing body of research indicates that the *psychosexual* development which is actively initiated in infancy is the cornerstone of future sexuality (362). Interpersonal interactions are the building blocks of this psychosexual development. They are cemented into the personality by the baby's active responsiveness and sensitivity to the surrounding world. In this, even normal infants vary from one another (68, 92). However, in our fragmented society, where the extended family is taking a back seat, too many adults still look upon infants as sleeping or eating blobs of life. A short survey of the biologic bases of love in normal infancy will explain why the present day professional seeks to give top priority to infants and families at risk— disabled infants or those that may be saved from the ravages of disability or alienation by specialized techniques and family counseling.

Each infant has its own personality and distinctive cry (21). Yet all have a need for consistent, affectionate mothering and for enriching experiences, alternating times of peace and privacy with periods of quiet play and excitement. While Erikson refers to the mouth as the historic focus of the first general approach to life (oral stage in psychoanalysis), he speaks of the "incorporate approach" where a baby is receptive in many respects, not only in an overwhelming need for food. That is, the baby "takes in with his eyes whatever enters his visual field . . . his senses, too, 'take in' what feels good" (128). In fact, most infant studies of recent years point out that from the very first weeks of life an infant's visual, auditory, olfactory, pain, and gustatory sense organs are capable of responding to appropriate stimuli.

Holding and cuddling of the infant plays an important part in a child's subsequent sexual development. During close body contact, the newborn develops a strong sense of enjoyment as the nurturing adult tries to establish eye contact, finger contact and as the heartbeats are felt and heard. As Money (277) so aptly puts it, "Dogs turn on sexuality with their noses, but humans do it with their eyes, their ears, and their touch." A youngster who has felt the intimacy of a warm adult embrace has an experience that will later be sought in self-elected intimacies and that he or she will be able to demonstrate in later life to anyone loved. Interestingly enough, some researchers hypothesize that the greater tactile stimulation received by girl babies may account for the "American female's tendency to be so much less uptight about tactuality (feeling and touching) than the American male" (167).

The particular importance of tactile and soothing contactile experience at this time of life is brought out dramatically by Harlow's clever experiments with baby monkeys whose subsequent social development was influenced constructively by dummy wire surrogate mothers wrapped in soft terry cloth, as against cold wire models. Harlow refers to the contactually satisfying infant monkey experience as the "biologic bases of love," and social learning studies of infants reflect this insight (21, 92, 184). It is from these biologic bases of love that human infants learn a sense of trust or mistrust as the environment or other people respond, or fail to respond, to the baby's physical, mental, emotional, and social needs (288). This basic balance between trust and mistrust, starting with mother or a loving, competent mother-substitute, is nurtured by positive interpersonal experiences which gradually include significant others until young adulthood when one other becomes sexually significant. Eventually, another generation to cherish becomes significant and brings to maturity the full cycle of mankind's sexuality, inclusive of love.

THE "DIFFERENT" BABY

But what about babies who bring biologic variations to the initial developmental stage? Statistics indicate that the 3,559,000 babies born in a recent year (of which 1,826,000 were male and 1,733,000 female) may look forward to a life expectancy of 67.4 years for the male and 74.9 years for the female (408). Of this number, about 14% will have a major or minor neurodevelopmental disability. In actual numbers, this means that at least 250,000 babies are born each year with major and obvious defects (92). Among these are a particularly unfortunate few infants with visible genital differences due to prenatal endocrine conditions that have produced developmental deviations. For example, in girl babies what is called the androgenital syndrome causes clitoral enlargement to such a degree that gender is doubtful. In fact, the genitalia may appear male and are often mistakenly accepted as such in less sophisticated medical times or locations. Conversely, a baby boy, having male chromosomes, may be born with external genitals that are ambiguous —the phallus could be mistaken for an enlarged clitoris just as easily as an imperfectly formed penis. Fortunately, modern surgery and hormone therapy can minimize these initial genital defects. In fact, as a result of Money's years of study and writing, there are resources for these problems in the major medical centers of the United States (279).

Among the problem babies born each year with nongenital malformations are many whose major and obvious defects bring initial shock to their families. Only if a girl had been hoped for in an all boy family, or the converse, does the baby's sex add to the misfortune of the presenting disability. More often, sex is not only forgotten, it is practically rejected in the face of unexpected deviations of the baby's make-up. A touching illustration of this is given in the records of a public health nurse who visited the home of a couple whose newborn baby boy was grossly deformed and almost certainly severely mentally retarded. During the nurse's initial visit, the depressed young mother constantly referred to the baby as "it" and kept a physical distance from the crib (208). It took a great deal of supportive help on the part of the nurse to guide the young couple through their grief to a recognition of this baby as a person—a person for whom society offers several caring alternatives. Personhood is the threshold of sexuality.

Other infants have such subtle deviations that certain conditions are suspect but do not reveal their real nature or yield to treatment during the early months. Pinpointing infant abnormalities is difficult without repeated examinations at regular intervals (101). Some of these subtleties take months to clarify, as when a flabby baby turns rigid and only months later develops the writhing motions of athetosis. Other subtleties may take years to decipher, if their course is erratic and they show specific characteristics only at later developmental periods (89). Some subtleties remain subtle. For example, only the accumulated lag, shown up by period evaluations, reveals the slow developmental pace of a mildly retarded child.

MEANINGFUL EXPERIENCES

The severity of a child's disability or the subtlety of it is not as relevant to a child's eventual sexuality as the child's participation in those experiences that are generic to the early sexual development of all human beings. The Perskes, who have contributed for many years to the rehabilitation of retarded children, outline these earliest experiences as (323):

1. Being held close in a mother's arms and being fed
2. Being tickled and bounced on a father's knee
3. Being hugged and shoved around by brothers and sisters
4. Feeling the relief of giving up body wastes at the right time in the right place
5. Having curiosity about all the parts of one's own body

One must be careful to grasp the spirit, rather than the specific wording, of this message: joyful interaction with people and body control.

Even a most wanted baby may find that differences cause family strain due to factors such as a) a conflict between the child's constitutional predisposition and a parent's expectations of what a child should be like, b) a circular conflict where neither responds as expected and the gap of misunderstanding increases; or c) the fact that the child presents young parents with a test of their abilities and of their capacity to adjust in the face of great difficulty (392). Although the casual baby observer may find it hard to believe, experienced clinicians find that some babies with problems seem to reject their mother's affectionate contacts in various ways. For example, they may respond minimally or not at all, their continual and intense crying may not be comforted, they may become rigid upon contact or struggle against being held, and some may exhibit bizarre behavior. In fact, many infants with developmental delays or other neurologically based impairments respond in ways sufficiently deviant to make mutually pleasurable interaction between an adult and the infant difficult to achieve (24, 51).

Interestingly enough, parental reaction to a colicky crying infant has parallel in the animal world. Bell, psychologist at Northern Illinois University, reports that the inconsolable mewlings of a malnourished rat pup eventually frustrated its mother who tried everything but nothing worked. "She can't shut the pup up no matter what she does and she races around the cage distractedly. Eventually, she acts more at random, becomes less responsive or not responsive at all" (29). This "caged feeling" is well known to young human parents who may not find the support and resources needed to work through this problem. This is corroborated by many child development studies of recent years which illustrate how the newborn child, a social being by biologic origin, *socializes others* more than he is socialized! The young mother of an impaired child "is experiencing shock, deep sadness, depression, guilt, anger, embarrassment, revulsion, personal responsibility, uncertainty about personal worth and about managerial ability because her creative products are defective" (24). These emotions extend to immediate family and friends, influencing normal socialization patterns of visiting, religious observances, family celebrations, etc. Unfortunately, the strain and drain of a severely defective child who so disrupts normal socialization needs may in some instances also disrupt marriage ties. In such households, with a live-in tragedy and few resources to cope with the condition, "either the couple stayed together in the same household and went their separate ways —the mother into chronic, continuous depression and the father into drink or an 18-hour-a-day job—or they actually separated" (257).

NURTURING—A LEARNED SKILL

Unfortunately, developmental approaches to mothering and fathering have not been incorporated into the basic education of recent generations. As extended families break up and couples scatter around the country, even a young couple with normal children enters parenthood with inexperience, misconceptions, and few resources. Couples with babies who vary from the normal have little satisfaction in early diagnosis, if it is not accompanied by emotional and constructive suggestions for the care of their baby. Fortunately, growing public recognition of developmental disabilities and of the need for early stimulation of babies at risk has called for action. Developmental centers for parental guidance, relief, and counseling have been initiated by such care-oriented agencies as Easter Seal, United Cerebral Palsy, and the National Association for Retarded Citizens (51, 101, 337). The child with developmental lag or a frank disability is no longer kept in cotton batting, lying around until he's "ready." If at all possible, readiness is encouraged by sensorimotor stimulation during interpersonal contact (314). The baby is rocked, rubbed, and carried around for good kinesthetic input and circulatory stimulation. If he isn't breast-fed, he's held during some feeding and loving periods. Every trick in and out of the book is used to encourage oral neuromotor maturation so that optimal rooting, sucking, and swallowing reflexes are obtained, and primitive reflexes are extinguished in time. Mysak considers this push on orality as only one-half of the delightful "Love–Dove" theory. He points out that a baby with enough opportunity to nestle in mothering arms finds the rhythm of the mothering heart so favorite a pattern that he eventually imitates it in sound. What the physicians hear as lub–dub, the baby translates into "mamma, ma–ma" or "da–da" (294). This, then, is the "eureka experience" of basic trust which is soon tied to conscious interpersonal recognition. As Erikson points out, "The amount of Trust derived from earliest infantile experience does not seem to depend on absolute quantities of food or demonstrations of love, but rather on the quality of the maternal relationship" (128). Maternal, in the experience of a disabled infant, may be translated into mothering, which in turn may mean the earliest socialization (by mother, father, nurse, or any significant others) which nourishes the roots of lifetime sexuality.

PRESCHOOL: BECOMING A BOY; BECOMING A GIRL

The preschool years of a normal child are the time when interaction with particular people and things assume prevalent patterns, and the child builds up a response repertoire that characterizes him or her as a particular individual boy or girl. Normal children are reaching out, running ahead, returning in doubt, rushing and stumbling only to be shamed by their own inadequacies. However, they push on into that autonomy which is theirs alone. The child with developmental lag, emotional difficulty, or frank motor or sensory disability may have to take much longer to assert himself and free himself from protection. He may have to break bonds of smothering care, which are more illness oriented than growth oriented. For example, a child may escape athetosis as a result of early exchange transfusion but may not escape neuroses if all contacts with him are made on the basis of his being "delicate." For healthy development the disabled child may need contrived sensorimotor experiences of more prolonged duration (101) and may need to extend his relationships beyond his immediate family to some significant others in his social radius.

BUILDING BLOCKS OF SEXUALITY

While the normal child may be controlling his bowels between 18 months and 2 years and is ready for potty training when able to hold urine for several hours during the day, it may be unrealistic to expect this from some disabled youngsters during preschool years. But personalities should not be made in bathrooms. A mind can grow, a heart can love or hate, whether or not the fanny is in diapers. A far more important concept is that of physical activity geared to emotional and social growth. Within this developmental context, preschool sex education for children who are different follows the normal guidelines, reaching beyond the facts about reproduction to encompass all of sexuality (191). This includes expressing feelings about being male or female, developing the ability to trust and to love, becoming aware of one's attitudes toward family and new relationships, and getting some idea of where one fits into relationships among all living things (335). Children who are merely regarded as "outpatient" may get their limbs better aligned through braces or therapeutic exercises, may get their hearing aids and eyeglasses adjusted, and may get proper dosage of their medication for seizures. However, in special nursery programs where the therapy is brought to the child (rather than the reverse) and remediation of defects is handled within a developmental group framework, the disabled child participates in a slice of real life. There, the child sheds his outpatient label. There the child stands a chance of becoming a boy or a girl—a real person.

Emotional responsiveness is a requirement for healthy sexuality and is a learned and relearned experience. At birth, each child's level of excitement is laid down by individual temperament . . . all other feeling tone is learned (68). About 3 months later, a child feels the experience of delight or distress. Emotional awareness continues to expand until at the age of only 2, a child can be said to have a repertoire of some 11 major emotional responses: fear, disgust, anger, jealousy, distress, excitement, delight, joy, elation, affection for adults, and affection for children (20). This sequence may take longer than 2 years for the disabled child, but these are the building blocks for future responses; experiences, not time, should become the measure. As Caplan so pertinently states, there are no rigid prescriptions for successful personality development. Whether the child should be breast-fed, given early or late toilet training, disciplined by spanking or not are some of the things that have different meanings in different families, according to their personalities and culture (66). Healthy parent–child interaction and relationships are characterized by the parent's sensitivity to the child's individual needs at any particular moment and the attempt to satisfy those needs in a way appropriate to the child's particular state of development (92).

Many adults, professional as well as parental, who pride themselves on sensitivity to a child's needs are particularly uptight about some of the erotic pleasures of the young child. Toddlers of both genders tend to touch their genitals and express pleasure when the genitals are stimulated in the course of diapering and washing. Both little boys and little girls stimulate their penis or clitoris as soon as they acquire the necessary coordination (221). Children with disabilities are no different. A visit to a nursery for blind, deaf, cerebral palsied, mentally retarded, etc. will confirm this, although perhaps not always as expected. Instead of the coordinated approach of the normal child, one may see some rocking motions or a child rubbing his thighs together—accomplishing much the same purpose. Among disabled children who have pleasurable play activities geared to their developmental capacities, there is no more erotic "pleasuring" than among a normal preschool population. As with normal children, it is the adult's reaction that makes a difference. It is well for the adult observer to keep two things in mind. First, the actual stimulation cannot be harmful to the child, either physically or mentally. Second, this activity is socially unacceptable in our culture, and a child with a disability doesn't need another social strike against him. *How* the adult handles this is important. Shaming a child or punishing him only leads to future inhibitions and sex-related anxieties. The preschool child is better distracted by other interests and play activities. The older child may be helped to discriminate between what is permissible and what is taboo behavior in group or public situations. In other words, what may be done in the privacy of one's bed is not always welcome elsewhere.

BASIC SEX IDENTITY

Many people do not realize that a normal child's awareness of sex identity (I am a boy—I am a girl) begins early in the second year of life. It is part of a complex sequence of male and female biologic development which interrelates with masculine and feminine attributes. Only in recent years has sophisticated research probed the mysteries of normal sexuality, its horizons, and its variations (25, 178, 279, 298). The little person who decides "I am a boy" or "I am a girl" has already had a dynamic sexual history and will continue to develop within a stream of sexuality. For simplicity's sake, the sequence (Fig. 1–1) may be listed as follows (279, 298):

1. *Genetic or chromosomal sex.* At conception a new girl (XX) has an X chromosome from her mother and another X from her father. A new boy (XY) has an X from his mother and a Y from his father.
2. *Gonadal sex.* The male fetus develops testes while the female fetus develops ovaries.
3. *Hormonal sex.* Internal secretions of the testes and/or ovaries have masculinizing and feminizing effects during critical periods of prenatal development and puberty. Some researchers believe the brain is also masculinized or feminized.
4. *Body sex.* prior to birth
   a. *Internal.* Hormones cause the male fetus to develop a vas deferens and the female to develop a uterus.
   b. *External.* Hormones also cause a male fetus to develop a penis and scrotum while a female fetus develops a clitoris and labia.
5. *Delivery room sex.* At birth, someone looks between the legs and says, "It's a boy!" or "It's a girl!"
6. *Legal sex.* This is what is on the birth certificate.
7. *Sex of rearing.* This is when the parent says, "My son" or "My daughter," and others call the child boy or girl. The infant or toddler is concurrently unconsciously developing a body image (42, 279).
8. *Gender identity.* The personal feeling of "I am a boy," "I am a girl," or "I wonder" makes its first appearance in early childhood and has its second major appraisal after puberty ("I'm a man!", "I'm a woman!", or "I'm Ambivalent!").

Fig. 1–1. Sequence of identity and role

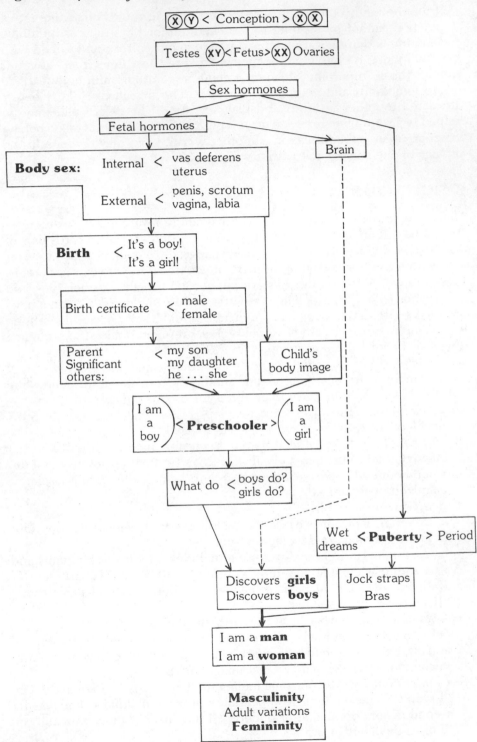

9. *Gender role.* Everything a person says and does to indicate to others or to self the degree that one is either male, female, or ambivalent (279).

Today, it is generally recognized that a person's sexual direction has a lifelong history. A child's concept of body image and awareness of sex identity are essential precursors and components of his or her adult sexuality (42). Freud's general contention that normal heterosexual *behavior* is more influenced by a child's family and social relationships than by simple biologic factors is no longer refuted. In fact, modern psychiatry has evolved many new hypotheses of human sexuality from the Freudian stages of psychosexual development (oral, anal, genital, oedipal, etc.). However, the Freudian school of developmental theory and early twentieth century emphasis on the role of fundamental drives and drive reduction in sexuality are being challenged as unnecessarily complex by educators, psychologists, and anthropologists. These groups see people more as "information-processing" creatures whose emotions, fantasies, dreams, and self-concept are part of a search for certainty, balance, and novelty in interaction with one's environment (289). Kohlberg and Zigby believe that basic sex identity is the *result* of self-categorization as male and female, made early by bright children, and that imitation of an adult proceeds from this self-categorization rather than causes it. Heatherton, on the other hand, frees sex roles from identification with a parent of the same sex. Her hypothesis of sex–role learning is closer to aspects of parental dominance. In brief, masculine sons as well as feminine daughters are the products of families where the father is dominant (138).

Irrespective of theory, it is a fact that the normal 3–5 year old child attains increased awareness of sexuality and of his or her identification as male or female. While the actual age of a child who is retarded or who has a disability may exceed this normal time span, the sequence within developmental experience still holds. In many ways, the preschool child who is different leads an asexual and nonpersonal clinic life. A busy mother has to fit clinic schedules and home therapy prescriptions into family life. A busy father, if it is a two-parent family, has added financial burdens to meet and often, reasonably enough, cannot visualize an adult role, vocationally or interpersonally, for this very different child. Boyishness or girlishness seem irrelevant in the face of more urgent problems. However, extremes are not unusual at this time. Clinic personnel are well acquainted with the fussily dressed disabled little-girl-doll who is literally a feminine clotheshorse, unable to derive satisfaction in other ways. Then there is the preschool sportsman who may not be able to move a muscle, but carries in full football regalia and all small talk revolves around a falsified sports life.

In contrast is the institutionalized child who, before senior citizen volunteers thought of proxy grandparents, may never have had a visitor or who is surrounded by constantly changing adult caretakers. What members of the helping professions have to keep asking themselves is: how do we reach these little people who are being treated as nonpersons; how do we find satisfying solutions to the needs of disabled children during this critical period in the child's development of gender identity—a time when adult expectations

(including parental expectations) and interactions with youngsters are especially important? Furthermore, how do we program experiences for these
children to meet the three conditions outlined by researchers as necessary
for normal heterosexual development? (313)

1. The same sex parent or parent substitute must not be so punishing or so
   weak as to make it impossible for a child to identify with that person.
2. A parent or a parent-substitute (therapy or institutional personnel) of the
   opposite sex must not be so seductive as to make it impossible for a child
   to trust members of the opposite sex.
3. Parents or their substitutes must not systematically reject a child's biologic sex or attempt to teach cross-sex behavior.

TABLE 1-1. EXEMPLARY PROJECTS—EARLY CHILDHOOD*

HEW's Office of Education has cited 7 early childhood projects that deal with education for
handicapped children as "exemplary and suitable for use by school systems" that wish to set up
such programs. These projects have been funded by the Bureau of Education for the Handicapped under the new Education of the Handicapped Act and they are said to demonstrate how
handicapped children can be reached at an early age to reduce some of the negative effects on
the handicapped.

    Projects cited are

The Rutland Center
Dr. Bill Swan
698 N. Pope Street
Athens, Georgia 30601
(404) 549–3030

PEECH
Dr. Merle B. Karnes
Colonel Wolfe School
403 East Healey
Champaign, Illinois 61820
(217) 333–4890

Comprehensive Training Program
Dr. Michael J. Murnane
10437 West Watertown Plank Road
Milwaukee, Wisconsin 53226
(414) 257–5100

UNISTAPS
Dr. Winifred H. Northcott
Minnesota Department of Education
St. Paul, Minnesota 55101
(612) 296–5605

Model Preschool Center
Dr. Alice Hayden
University of Washington
Seattle, Washington 98195
(206) 543–7583

Portage Project
Mr. David E. Shearer
412 East Slifer Street
Portage, Wisconsin 53901
(608) 742–5342

    The Seattle, Washington Center has two projects: 1) a communication program (2–6 years);
2) a Down's Syndrome Program (birth to 6 years). The Rutland Center treats emotionally
disturbed children (birth to 14 years). The Minneapolis program is a family-oriented, non-
categorical program for severely handicapped children (birth to 5 years). The Champaign,
Illinois program is for "Precise Early Education for Children with Handicaps (3–6 years)." The
Milwaukee program is a comprehensive training program for infants and young cerebral palsied
children (3 years and under). And the Portage, Wisconsin enterprise is "a home approach to the
early education of handicapped children (birth to 6 years)."

*American Academy for Cerebral Palsy and Developmental Medicine: NEWSLETTER, Vol.
28, No. 3. Bulletin No. 93, November, 1976.

MEANINGFUL INTERACTIONS

It would be unworthy of the valiant efforts of many fine people to assume that the wheel must be reinvented. There are institutions providing simulated extended family life where children live in small groups with cottage "parents." There are group therapy and preschool nursery experiences augmenting some of the major medical pediatric clinics. There are special education courses in major universities that teach fine developmental principles for disabled preschoolers and special techniques for reaching the blind, the deaf, the retarded, the emotionally deprived, the physically disabled. The national agencies established to help children with special disabilities have information related to all of these resources.

The major problem that *now* confronts impaired preschool children is the dwindling number of available experiential resources. This is due not only to recession budgeting, but also to the false concept that it is all right for a disabled child's education to wait until regular school starts at 6, 7, and sometimes 8 years old. Fortunately, there are some notable efforts in progress which demonstrate how to reduce the negative impacts of disability by supplanting them with abilities via preschool education.* These exemplary projects can be very helpful for constructive planning and for facing up to realistic budgetary needs. They provide the building blocks of personality and of ways of dealing with the world that must be supplied in sequence in order to lay the ground for healthy, happy sexuality.

A delightful example of the developmental viewpoint and of the modern parent's perceptions of sexuality in the preschool years of any child, able or disabled, is the following observation shared by McBride (264):

At this age children want to know "how things work" and how their bodies function. They are fascinated by what seems to have a special relationship, as mothers and fathers have, with a beloved person. Naturally they envy their parents who sleep together, fighting off loneliness and bad dreams, side-by-side. . . . They are also eager to experiment with self-gratification. They already know what they like to eat, whether a blanket or thumb is more soothing, and what it is like to relax on someone's lap when they are tired. Of course some of this behavior may be criticized at this point as babyish, so they keep looking around to see how adults relax and enjoy themselves. As they look around, they usually wish (perhaps not out loud) that they had a husband or wife (if you cannot act like a baby, they figure, you might as well act like a grownup) and if the child is a girl she may resent her mother's good luck in having her father for a husband, just as a boy resents his father. Being angry does not seem to help, so the child usually resolves her/his feeling by trying to be more and more like the parent of the same sex, who seems to be getting all the attention the child wants. The little girl figures that if she can grow up like her mommy, she can get a husband like her daddy. And the boy imitates his father's behavior so he can be "man" enough for his mother to feel for him what she feels for her husband. . . . confidence is beauty . . . the self-confident person can convince us that what she/he has is beautiful. In effect every child should be encouraged to think, "Prove to me I am not special and beautiful," rather than to be shunted into a competitive world that emphasizes values that someone else is supposed to have. . . . When I watch my daughter stroke the silky binding of her blanket in a blandly erotic fashion, I cannot help wondering whether all the adults who have mastered the complexities of sexual intercourse, have forgotten to enjoy themselves as sensual creatures in the process of developing mechanical efficiency. We tend to equate the "Oedipal–Electra" period with the awakening of specific curiosity and behavior, but we forget that it is also the time for learning and that the *body is generally sensuous.* Eyes were made for looking at scarlet balloons; hands were made for fondling velvety fabrics; bodies were made for dressing up in exotic outfits and for covering with warm sand. . . . There is a reciprocal nature to the child's identification with the parents. The daughter wants to be like mommy because daddy obviously likes the way she looks and acts, but the mother may encourage the daughter to pun like the father because he has the more developed sense of humor. Parents should maximize the child's opportunities for learning about human values from both parents.

While it is true that adverse experiences or lack of experience during a critical stage of ego development make it harder for youngsters to handle the demands of succeeding growth stages, parents of those disabled youngsters who may have to accumulate life's building blocks slowly need not despair. Erikson (127) believes that personality development continues throughout life—both the good and bad effects of childhood can be reversed by future experiences. "The human personality has inherent strengths. . . . the kind of individual a child is and his ongoing interactions with society are going to influence him for better or worse in the future regardless of the kind of childhood he had." (116)

SCHOOL AGE: BOYS AND GIRLS GROW AND GROW

One of the traditional arguments against starting sex education in the years preceding puberty was a popular interpretation of Freud's concept of the "latency period." It was assumed by advocates of later sex education that during this phase of a child's psychosexual life, sexual interests and activities were well repressed. In contrast, current thinking and research now recognize that sexual interest and activity may be somewhat masked by the fact that the primary focus of a school child's attention turns from himself to the newness of the outside world (335, 362). At this period, curiosity about sex is present, but communication skills are immature. In the case of disabled youngsters, many adults—parents and professionals—do nothing to enhance communication since they are unable to contemplate the disabled as future adults with adult sexual desires (35). Then again, other adults complicate the communication gap by completely denying any handicapping features of a youngster's disability and projecting unrealistic goals. This places undue stress on reaching possibly unattainable future satisfactions. Fortunately, there is a growing recognition of the normal sexual interests of middle childhood and of constructive communication methods that relate to the capabilities and incapabilities of youngsters with physical or mental disability. Constructive communication will help to direct the disabled youngster's particular balance of capabilities toward developmentally related feelings about being male or female and will help them to trust, to love, and to understand interpersonal relationships.

BOY–GIRL DIFFERENCES

Until recent years, we have lived in a culture where a preteen boy or girl was encouraged to polarize companionship. Accordingly, the boys went off to Boys Club, Little League, or gangs. The girls were steered toward dancing classes, Girl Scouts, etc. However, even in the midst of this, some girls of overanxious mothers found themselves pushed into an opposite life-style of pseudosophistication. They were primed in the techniques of soap opera romantics before they could enjoy the type of boy–girl friendship that is preparatory to dating. More recently, the women's liberation movement has challenged sex polarization by introducing the concept of unisex roles. In view of these shifting sands in cultural and situational attitudes, it might be well to ask what is really known about the biologic, psychologic, and social factors of boy–girl differences? Only by being well grounded in what the normal youngster has to face upon entering society can we be wholesomely responsible toward the youngster who is different.

To begin at the very beginning, at conception the basic biologic difference of male (XY) and female (XX) is laid down by the sex chromosomes. As Beach points out, most of the basic sex differences between male and female develop between fertilization and birth. However, differences between masculinity and femininity (sexuality) do not begin to develop until the second or third year after birth; and their full maturation occupies a span of 15–20 years (25, 279). Table 1–1 compiles the results of studies which were directed at *HOW the sexes differ–not why* (148, 266, 422). The major findings of these studies indicate that, while slightly more boys are conceived than girls, they are more susceptible to infection and less responsive to antibiotics (148). Therefore, infant mortality is lower among girls (450). Until the age of 5 months, girls lead in ability to perform the movements that are prerequisites for creeping, sitting, they generally remain ahead in skills that require fine movements and motor coordination, such as tying bows and skipping (422). [During preschool years, parents usually provide sex typed clothes and toys, but there is little cultural difference made in early socialization (254).]

Some researchers consider agression one of the behaviors where a genuine difference exists between the sexes in all cultures. For example, Maccoby and Jacklin claim that aggressive differences are found in social play as early as age 2; and in childhood, boys are more agressive physically as well as verbally. This includes fantasies and mock fighting (254). Most studies confirm physical differences such as the fact that girls move toward maturity more rapidly than boys. X-rays of both hand and knee show that girls are on an average about 20% ahead of boys at any age up to physical maturity. [As far as mental skills are concerned, verbal skills develop earlier and more rapidly in girls while school-age boys are better in math, science and visual-spatial concepts (146, 254). While some investigators have found no evidence of brain differences between the sexes (422), Beach refutes this (25, 103) and Kimura claims that recent findings indicate that females have more mature neural develop-

TABLE 1–2. HOW THE SEXES ARE SAID TO DIFFER

	MALE (XY)	FEMALE (XX)
Conception Immunity	160/100 (148) More susceptible to infection; less responsive to antibiotics (450)	122/100 (148)
Biologic body structure	Testes, vas deferens, scrotum, penis Male hormones Pubic and facial hair	Ovaries, uterus, vagina, labia, clitoris Female hormones Breasts, pubic hair
Biologic brain structure	Possible effect of fetal male hormone on brain (103, 279) Greater development of parietal lobe (229)	Greater development of left temporal lobe of brain (229)
Constitutional strength	More prone to physical and psychosocial disorders (148) Crib deaths 55–83% male (45)	Lower mortality: (130 XY) to 100 (XX) deaths
Infantile activity	Correlated with amount and nature of maternal handling (148) Higher head raising in newborn (148)	Apparently independent of maternal handling Greater ability to perform movements that are prerequisite for locomotion and coordination (311)
Energy expenditure	Higher (148) More physical and verbal aggression (146)	More passive and dependent
Skills	Better in math (254) and science (103) Excellent with visual-spacial problems (146, 254) Impossible to dismiss biologic determinants (148)	More rapid and earlier development of verbal skills (254) Higher verbal ability as teenagers (146, 254)
Maturation sequence	Puberty reached by 65% between 14–16 years (103)	Puberty reached by 50% at 13; 80% by end of 13th year (103) Skeletal maturity 2 years ahead (103)
Rearing	Preschool: sex typed clothes and toys, but uniform in socialization (254) Influenced by interpersonal relationships (193, 266)	School age: less freedom after school hours; more household tasks (155) Influenced by interpersonal relationships (193, 266)
Socialization	Greater difficulty in school (103) Higher deliquency (103) Earlier use of contraception (103)	More active in student power movements in college (131)
Genito pelvic erotic arousal pattern	Initiator of petting Turned on by visual and narrative stimuli (148) Peak of sex powers reached earlier	Expected to set limits (103) Turned on by tactile stimuli (148)

ment of the left temporal lobe (language processing) and males more parietal lobe development (sensory processing) (229).] Ounstad and Taylor (311) have documented the myriad of basic constitutional sex differences of medical and developmental importance.

It is also a fact that today girls reach puberty earlier. Anytime between 9 and 17, a girl (normal, retarded, or physically disabled) can begin to menstruate. Anytime between the ages of 12 and 15, boys (normal, retarded, or physically disabled) can have spontaneous ejaculations (also called nocturnal emissions and wet dreams) while they are asleep (209). Although their sex interest and tensions will become stronger and more obvious as they reach adolescence, these tensions are formulated in preadolescence. It becomes increasingly important at each developmental stage for young people to reaffirm their identity as being either boys or girls and to have this identity accepted by their associates.

The emphasis on *how* the sexes differ is being augmented by new and needed research into *why* sex gender, sex roles, and sex identities interrelate differently: what impact do the biologic forces of hormones and brain structure have upon personality, family, and social forces that attempt to mold gender identity and gender roles? (278). Today, adult sex roles and sex responsibilities are under critical observation as a result of the impact of multicultures, as well as of women's liberation, economics, and new patterns of family life. However, most behavioral researchers believe that there will undoubtedly remain a transitional psychologic period when "boys learn how to be boys and girls learn how to be girls from absorbing information, skills, and acceptance from members of their sex" (92, 313). It behooves education to enhance this communication with useful information.

FACTS AND FEELINGS

Today, there are very few *un*informed teenagers, but there are a great many *mis*informed ones who liberally share their impressions with one another. So it is important that young people have adequate resources to check their knowledge and to clear up some of their confusions and incorrect impressions. Some parents feel equal to the threefold task of discussing the biologic facts related to hormonal changes, the potential reproductive capacity that these changes initiate, and the family's attitude toward sexuality. Other families (of both normal and disabled youngsters) find that they cannot or do not wish to discuss any or all of this triad. One must also realize that to some parents a child's developing sexuality is associated with his coming emancipation from the family, and there are parents who cannot face this next relationship. It is also understandable, from the viewpoint of a parent of a disabled youngster who has added financial and time-consuming burdens, that the question of whether this teenager will ever be independent takes priority over questions of sexuality. Some families have the feeling that, if sex is not discussed with their disabled youngster, it might never come up in his or her experience. Then again, as Diamond explains, other parents feel that knowledge about sex may raise false expectations and hopes (104). Lastly, it is difficult for a number of people to recognize that either their parents or their children can be sexual. Regardless of age, elderly parents are often considered "beyond it" and children "not yet ready."

There is, however, no sexual vacuum for even the most disabled child living on the fringe of our society in residential care. In addition to the variety of observable body changes and the variety of feeling tones experienced and confided by peers and attendants, the American diet of television and movies presents an array of body development in a variety of exciting coverings, accompanied by a variety of interpersonal techniques! Most cultures consider sex so basic to personality and to social interaction that some consensus is reached on approved group behavior. Eckert points out in his research review that every culture that has survived has found it necessary to control sex with elaborate social mores that are transmitted to children as guides to behavior. It is his contention that America has a great need for sound developmental sex education so that a young person may be helped to formulate his individual value system . . . to grow up with good feelings about being a boy or a girl . . . to have good feelings toward the other sex, to have boy friends and girl friends at all ages, to fall in and out of love a number of times before they grow to love a mature person with whom they desire to spend the rest of their lives in an intimate love–sex relationship involving children as well as each other. Eckert (113) concludes, "In American culture such a life seems likely to lead to the personal fulfillment of each person—to a mentally healthy existence."

Growth and Body Changes

All school-age boys and girls have sexual feelings which are *unrelated* to their intelligence or disability. Some may express little interest in sex, while others have a great deal of curiosity about it (349). Curiosity may not hover around intercourse, rape, or other genital gymnastics which some adults fear may become preadolescent concerns. It may relate to simple boy–girl realities, such as why the girls are so big—they're getting their braces lengthened one after the other while the boys stay the same size. Or, are the pimples that a blind girl now feels on the face of her friend catching? Or, why did the other kids laugh when Tom said the brace straps rubbed on his penis—what's a penis anyway? No child is so isolated that he does not recognize growth changes in others whom he sees during a clinic visit, a special class, or at camp. The blind boy may be quick to pick up voice changes—he, too, spots differences. This is the time for identifying patterns of growth and body changes that go on between the ages of 9 and 18, but how different individuals are in the pace of these changes! At a time when youngsters want to be "one of the boys" or "one of the girls," they may need assurance that their lag or their precocious curvatures are within the regular pattern. It is the time for learning more grownup names for body parts—inside and outside, primary and secondary sex characteristics. These names are important because they turn up in dictionaries, books, slides, and educational films that are now available to schools, camps, counseling groups, and churches (see Appendices A, B, and F).

Coming Events—Not Surprises

Uninformed youngsters often respond to body changes with alarm, and it is particularly important that retarded youngsters and children with physical disabilities be prepared for the onset of puberty. In addition to the changes in structure, new functions should be discussed in a matter-of-fact way. If parents or care personnel view the onset of menstruation in girls or the evidence of spontaneous ejaculations in boys as they should be viewed with normal youngsters—as indications of growing up—their attitudes will direct the handicapped child toward positive attitudes. There are many excellent approaches to teaching young girls about menstruation, such as those prepared by manufacturers of sanitary napkins. These are equally useful for youngsters who are disabled. However, the retarded girl may require a simple matter-of-fact statement that one of these days she will have some bleeding, just like another girl whom she knows. She should be assured that it will be "okay and it doesn't hurt you," and it will come back (209). It is not to be viewed as an illness or anything to restrict her activities—just part of growing up and having breasts like mother, a girl friend, or the nurses (335). Boys will need assurance that erections are an automatic bodily adjustment that occur periodically and that they are perfectly normal and natural. Under no circumstance should a youngster be teased or made to feel guilty for erections. The same holds for nocturnal emissions or wet dreams. These spontaneous ejaculations should be expected in disabled as well as normal boys between the ages of 12 and 15.

A child should not only be helped to anticipate the physical changes of puberty and adolescence, but given an assurance that associated feelings will be respected (163). The first or last youngster in a group to reach puberty may need emotional support to see this difference in its proper perspective. Boys and girls at the stage of development when puberty is imminent may be able to sit together and accept the facts of life as outlined in a biology class. In fact, boys should be well informed about changes in girls and vice versa. However, when it comes to feelings, their stumbling efforts at communication may be more successful in same sex groupings or in individual counseling sessions.

Masturbation—A Present Reality

There is, however, an area wherein some grownups still become stutterers and fumblers: masturbation. This is a unisex activity, as innocently acquired by boys as by girls and as frequent among the disabled as in the general population (22, 205, 349). It is encountered by parents, clinicians, contact care personnel, all members of the helping professions and educators. Some old-fashioned people call it self-abuse; advocates call it self-pleasuring. Most educated people refer to it as autoeroticism or masturbation. In itself, it is one aspect of general sexual development. Treating it with hysteria or punitively can create a problem where none need exist. After all, just as a baby explores and plays with his fingers and toes, he eventually discovers the pleasurable excitement of coming upon his genitals and finding a new way of experiencing his body—one that satisfies and soothes. A recent English study of 700 4-year-olds found that some 17% of these children engaged in genital play quite casually, while a Kinsey study reports that nearly 80% of boys 10–13 years of age are able to reach climax (230). Some authorities estimate that the prevalence of masturbation in general society is above 90% for males and above 60% for females. While many boys and girls discover orgasm long before puberty, masturbation is considered a particular aspect of adolescence. It is also common in adult years—in and out of marriage—and not uncommon in advanced years. In summary, masturbation has increasingly been accepted as part of the normal process of sexual maturation.

However, in our Western society there are adults, including parents, who have been taught to frown upon this behavior. They hold onto false folklores which threaten dire consequences, instead of considering masturbation a harmless, soothing activity that society restricts to privacy. If a child is capable of distinguishing between privately acceptable versus publicly acceptable behavior, Gordon, one of the leading consultants to programs for disabled youngsters, suggests that the child should be taught to confine such activities "to places and times when they will not be disturbing to other people, just as one learns that urinating is done in the bathroom" (157).

Same Activity—Different Reasons. While this is an excellent rule of thumb, one must take into consideration that there are disabled youngsters who require specific training to enable them to distinguish between public and private situations. The prepubertal youngster whose multiple impairment includes retardation or the one who is blind require special help. There are no cookbook answers. However, insight into the way the child experiences his world can suggest helpful solutions to empathetic staff. Childhood activities, such as skipping rope or using hands and fingers for fun activities, are more than diversions in these children's lives; they relate the child not only to his capacities but also to his environment.

The blind youngster is frequently placed in new environments—new classroom, new bathroom, new bus route, etc. These novelties that mean added excitements and wider horizons for a normal child, initially may mean new hazards to the visually impaired—new unknown spaces. To explore them the blind child has to lower his level of activity. Since he cannot see, he must proceed cautiously. This further increases his tensions, and there may be lapses in a youngster's capacity to distinguish between privately acceptable versus publicly acceptable behaviors. This is in no way meant to imply that masturbation is observed more frequently among blind children. Rather, the problem of the blind child is used as an example to demonstrate that there are different possible reasons for what is outwardly the same behavior. In one instance, a blind youngster may masturbate as a relief from tension; in another, he may masturbate as a pleasurable way of experiencing his body. In both instances, one can readily appreciate how difficult it is for someone who is sightless to recognize what is generally accepted as privacy in the seeing world. The writings of Scholl (378) and Torbett (428) are particularly helpful for gaining more insight into the effects of blindness on selected physical, mental, emotional, and social aspects of development.

Any careful observer in clinics or residences for physically disabled youngsters has also been witness to the variety of needs, other than sexual tensions, that give rise to masturbatory behavior: from tight panties or skin irritations, leather brace straps rubbing the genitals, deliberate attention seeking, to long periods of idleness and boredom. Masturbation is not really an unusual or abnormal response when multiply disabled youngsters are left in wheelchairs to stare emptily in dull halls while waiting for therapy or during unscheduled periods. Keeping a tray on the child's wheelchair where some toy, book, or game can be placed is far more effective in encouraging appropriate behavior than castigating looks or threatening remarks by contact care staff.

Excessive masturbation at any age is a clue that some needs of the individual are not being met through interpersonal relationships; moreover, these needs may be entirely unrelated to sexuality (54, 210). The impact of boredom and alienation on masturbation habits is illustrated by a case history of a 10-year-old boy with Down's syndrome who was referred to psychiatry for examination by a nurse because of a wide spectrum of self-stimulatory activity (masturbation, skin picking, head banging, etc.). The psychiatrist found during the interview that the youngster engaged in play transactions, showed good eye contact, and was eager to participate in active games. His daily schedule was drab, however, and his parents barely got there more than once a year. With the initiation of group recreational activity, a full day's school program, and contact with a foster grandparent (who visited the boy on an average of thrice weekly), the boy's self-stimulatory behavior (masturbation) disappeared completely within 2 weeks (268). This case illustrates how a so-called abnormal sexual activity frequently associated with mental retardation can be the result of the individual's hunger for meaningful personal relationships. In turn, this may be a result of how staff are trained (or not trained) in institutions that house many of our mentally retarded citizens. Poorly trained staff may actually program the retardate's behavioral repertoire in a negative manner.

During puberty and adolescence, masturbation may serve as more than a temporary physiologic relief of tension or a fleeting pleasurable body experience. It is also considered by researchers as a normal behavior pattern that can be a helpful preliminary in learning the individual patterning and timing of stimulus and response of the "lust dynamism" (320). In other words, it may help the developing youngster to achieve a sense of identity in relation to his or her sexual self-image and sexual responsiveness. At this developmental stage, masturbation is often accompanied by fantasies that may be heavily laden with remnants of childhood preoccupations. There may be alternate periods of asceticism until the youngster develops a capacity to substitute flexible internal controls for the external controls of childhood (349). There is nothing harmful about masturbation for normal or disabled youngsters, other than the shame and guilt which misunderstanding adults feel impelled to inflict. While some adults restrict their punitive attitudes to threats and predictions of doom, others invade the privacy of youngsters. For example, a well-adjusted young girl in a residence for the orthopedically disabled had a private room with a lock upon the door, but if she locked the door for a short period of privacy, a member of the staff invariably unlocked the door to see why (305).

Masturbation may play still another role for some youngsters who have been propelled into inappropriate sexual relationships. For them it was found to provide a more appropriate and acceptable behavior. Psychologists associated with one of the progressive institutions for mentally retarded found a surprising absence of masturbatory behavior among the boys whose sexual behaviors such as homosexual contacts, were considered deviant by the staff. Three out of four of these students eventually accepted the counselor's direct suggestion that masturbation is quite a prevalent and generally healthy behavior when no other outlet is available. The learning technique for this was novel. Students were provided with index cards on which to make daily records of the frequency of satisfying masturbation as against the number of sexually inappropriate responses, i.e., homosexual contacts. From these records the counselor drew weekly graphs from which the student could gauge his progress in the substitution of healthy masturbation for other inappropriate behaviors (357).

Sex Education Includes Masturbation. Since masturbation is now an acknowledged aspect of sexuality, educators have focused on masturbation as part of an education program for preadolescents in special classes or special institutions. There is general agreement that instructional groups should be small enough for participants to have eye contact with the leader and to ask questions directly—rather than being obliged to raise one's hand in a crowded classroom. Separate sessions for boys and girls at early teenage may prove helpful for more open discussion. A third useful teaching principle is never to show a relevant audiovisual aid unless there is time to discuss fully what the young people thought they heard and saw and how it can add to their general perspective of the physical, emotional, and social aspects of sexual behavior. The scope of the lesson should be broad enough to initiate discussion on masturbation so as a) to acknowledge the strong sexual feelings and tensions that come with puberty and b) to recognize that boys' wet dreams and masturbation by boys and girls are outlets for such feelings. Specific points to be learned during these group lessons are

1. What is masturbation and how can it be recognized under any other name? A teacher who talks about "manipulation of the genitals to achieve erotic arousal" or "rubbing your penis or vagina" may be met

with blank looks. The youngsters may be more familiar with "rubbing your privates," "playing with yourself," "jacking off," "beating your meat," etc., etc. Whatever terminology is used to make it clear what the discussion is all about should be respected, but it is necessary to get the point across that this is written about in books for young people and for adults under the name of masturbation (157).

2. How the students feel about masturbation and what others have said about it? This question may provide the opportunity to discuss old wives tales, rumors, any confrontations experienced, any unnecessary guilt feelings, any feelings of satisfaction, etc. It is here that it is possible to point out that most people masturbate at some time in their lives, but don't do it in the presence of other people or in public places. It's also the time to indicate that it's all right *not* to masturbate if for any reason one doesn't feel good about it, because nobody likes the feeling of guilt (34).

3. Why do people masturbate? Some people resort to it because of boredom, nervousness, or excitement, all of which could be better resolved by more meaningful activities. However, as a source of sexual gratification, it is used by almost all males and a great many females, reaching a peak at adolescence. It may not necessarily stop then, since some married men and women, as well as adults whose sexual activities have been curtailed by lack of a sexual partner, may find it a release of sex tensions. It may be helpful for youngsters to know that masturbation is part of the sexual expression of some adults throughout their entire life (164, 210, 230).

4. What approaches are taken to the subject by books and curricula written for boys and girls of their age? The fact that not only is masturbation not the hush–hush subject they have been led to believe it is but also that materials exist for them, for their parents, and for their teachers could be a welcome insight (36, 54, 125, 157, 164, 191, 199, 205, 223, 269, 279, 309, 317, 349, 372, 376, 377, 428, 435).

5. What questions do students have about any points raised in a book or a visual aid that may not have been covered already in the group discussion?

Disability—Facts With Feelings

The advent of formal schooling brings a major shift into every child's world. During this period a youngster must learn to channel his emotions, to develop some independence and autonomy, and to define his emerging sexuality in terms of culturally acceptable manners (68). Youngsters who have a disability are no exception. In fact, school-age youth who vary from the normal may be either smothered wholesale in special settings which harbor the nonsex attitudes of care personnel or suddenly faced with varied concepts of masculinity or femininity when they are integrated with normal youngsters.

Many educators forget that disabled children who enter community schools in special classes or as "mainstreamers" in regular classes confront an additional reality that no longer can be overcompensated for by home or by clinic (49) (Table 1–2). While examining the developmental processes of a group of disabled children through their initial elementary school years, observers have found that realization of the chronic aspects of their disability may come to some youngsters with traumatic impact. Theirs is not only the problem of what girls' clique or what boys' team leaves them out. Theirs is the sudden and major realization that they have a disability that will not disappear in a world where special consideration or privilege more often brings out prejudice than benign acceptance.

For years an orthopedically disabled youngster may have responded to encouragement to "walk better" and may have given up hours of free time to practice this, having "cure" in mind as the reward for this virtue. Now he finds that "better" is not good enough to go along with the school crowd. He cannot climb the stairs, and he self-consciously has to get into the faculty elevator with all the adults; his hopes for cure have to settle for more pragmatic solutions. For years the acceptance of being a child-leader among

TABLE 1–3 MAINSTREAMING DEFINED*

The concept of *mainstreaming* is often misunderstood or inappropriately defined. In an effort to resolve this dilemma and provide some direction the following definition is proposed:

Mainstreaming refers to the concept of providing appropriate educational service to handicapped children, regardless of the level of involvement in a setting as near to traditional educational practice as possible.

This definition does not—
    suggest a massive return to or placement of all children with learning problems in the regular grades
    refer to separate settings as equivalent placements
    mean the end of all self-contained special classes as a service vehicle for children
This definition does suggest—
    a continuum of service alternatives appropriate to allow placement of children as individuals not members of categories
    some system other than the present dichotomy of either placement in regular class or placement in special class
    that preventive service to children with potential learning problems is as important, if not more so, than interventive service to children who have already demonstrated their learning handicap
    a need to integrate all levels of handicapped children to the maximum extent possible.
    Integration may be only in nonacademic areas, play areas, lunch areas, or through flexible scheduling which allows peer interaction between handicapped and nonhandicapped children on a regular basis.
    a need for a greater understanding of handicapped children for all school personnel (preservice and/or in-service seems mandated)
    placement of handicapped children in their home district whenever possible to insure home and school common peer relationships
    new roles for educational personnel in providing service to handicapped individuals.

---

*Coons DE: IRUC Briefings Vol. 1, No. 3, May, 1976

other clinic and special nursery groups may have bolstered the ego of a diligent disabled child. But mainstreaming may require that he spend years in cooperative participation before any of his leadership qualities can reassert themselves among the wider range of talents of this larger group. Insight is painful. This insight has frequently led to a "severe depressive period—which can be followed by a gradual emotional readiness to see his condition as a part of himself and a hesitant beginning to incorporate it into his life" (272). It is here that a compassionate teacher, parent, or counselor may prove to be the good listener who can eventually help a child balance his capabilities against the awesome load to which he has suddenly awakened.

ROLE MODELS

Many socializing agents, in addition to the family, influence a school-age youngster's attitudes, sex perception, sex goals, and role models. School, peer groups, clubs, part-time activities, churches and synagogues, movies, television and magazines, as well as social class, bring a wide variety of information and *mis*information to the average preteen (426). Some of these influences may vary or be missing in the lives of very sheltered disabled youngsters. Their social experiences, on the other hand, may include residential schools, foster homes, clinic visits, or special classes. However, unlike the nonhandicapped, disabled children are minimally socialized (35). Strong efforts should be made in any setting to encourage the development of satisfying interpersonal relationships outside of the disabled youngster's immediate family.

At this time of life, friendships among one's peers provide youngsters—including disabled youngsters—with alternatives to the models previously stressed by parents. Friendships help a child to appreciate different temperaments, differing achievements, ways of peer leadership or cooperation. Participating in a friendly group of the same sex may give each child a chance to see the many varied responses among their same sex pals: do all the boys like baseball, or do some prefer music or chess?—do all the girls giggle and tease at this age, or are some considerate and thoughtful of one another? Participating in mixed groups gives each child some idea of how many and what type of agressiveness girls as well as boys exhibit and what type of things he wants to talk over with a girl friend or a boy friend. Friends at this age are special feedback instruments among a wide variety of new outside experiences.

Special grownups, such as a favorite teacher, therapist, or a camp counselor on whom one gets a "crush," show the child that there are adults other than one's parents for whom one can feel affection. Fortunately, more men are entering the helping and teaching professions. Thus, a male therapist, teacher, camp counselor, or proxy grandfather may become one of those significant others who adds dimension to the life of a disabled child. These men may show a child with no father or even a child with both parents that one can find love in more than one place.

Three distinct aspects of sex role differentiation and sex typing influence a youngster's sexuality: a) early identification of the individual as male or female (see Basic Sex Identity), b) sex role preference or the sex a child would like to be, and c) sex role standards or acquisition of behavior and attitudes which are culturally appropriate for the youngster's sex (19x). Although there is a present liberal movement for reinterpretation of specific tasks of sex role modeling, it is important not to involve the disabled preteen in the confusions of artificial unisex attitudes. The challenge of "anything you can do I can do better" is not rational if merely based on stereotyped sex competition. However, if the chosen activity is related to the individual's temperament, capabilities, and needs, it can be productive. For example, the disabled boy who learns to make his own breakfast so that his working parents can get to their offices on time is no sissy. In fact, he is preparing himself to enjoy his own future bachelor quarters. Similarly, the disabled girl who likes to tinker and fix things may use this as a prelude to more mechanical work tasks to be found in some of the modern sheltered workshops. He is not *less* a boy nor she *less* a girl for these. Adults should be careful not to sponsor *non*sex attitudes but to encourage each sex to respect itself for what it is and to expand into whatever activities are compatible to the individual's temperament, capability, and needs.

SPECIAL SEX EDUCATION

Sex mores in the last few decades have not invented new concepts, but the wide range of love–sex–marriage relationships in our society has found more outspoken defendants. True, there are still many strong advocates of traditionally accepted values who believe as McBride does, (264) "It makes sense for both sexes to have the same goal for the adult years, moving from healthy self-love to shared intimacy with a loved partner and on to helping the next generation do the same." On the other hand, other young adults have goals which see value in other kinds of interpersonal relationships, such as sex without marriage, marriage without children, adoption of children by single women and men, homosexual marriages, etc. All of these alternatives to human relationships are now openly discussed and reach the papers, movies, and television—coming into homes, coming into institutions.

It is little wonder that parents of both able and disabled youth experience confusion in such a multiculture. It is also not surprising that, although many parents feel inadequate themselves, they are skeptical about delegating sex education. Particularly irritating to concerned parents are some educators or members of the helping professions who feel that their personal experience is a guide for the young. All of us who have attended sex education seminars have heard some colleagues assert with conviction that, when they ask, youngsters should be told details of a specific adult's sex life. "I'm honest with them—when they ask what I did, I tell them with no frills attached." This so-called honesty is actually a self-centered confessional. It sets up this adult's personal beliefs as moral law and is a poor substitute for a careful explanation of the horizon of attitudes in our society, for the responsibilities associated with any type of behavior, and for the probable social consequences within our seemingly carefree society of different forms of behavior.

Fortunately, with the increasing responsibility of sex education leadership, and with training courses and materials geared to developmental levels (see Appendix A), the titillating individualized approaches are disappearing. Today, there is opportunity to learn from others' planning and the techniques they used to reduce opposition to sex education (415). Today, there are competent instructors among parents, church educators, physical education and health educators, as well as counselors in the various helping professions. However, since classroom teachers are in such steady contact with young people, they should be aware of those biologic and psychologic aspects of sex which relate to the developmental level of their students—or to know of qualified resources. Since children of different cultural backgrounds and religious faiths make up the classrooms of the United States—in regular or special classes—a wise teacher does not promote conflict among value systems differing from her own but respects the background and religious resources of each child. Developmental psychologists who have access to a national perspective report the following trends:

In a few schools the first instruction in human reproduction is given in the first grade, to be repeated at regular intervals throughout the rest of the child's precollege education. The instructional materials, for the most part, emphasize the biologic aspects of conception and birth; more delicate questions, involving both moral and social aspects of sexuality, are typically left to the teacher to handle. It is the latter aspect of sex education that disturbs some parents who insist that the teacher may instill too liberal or too immoral a viewpoint toward sexuality in their children. Such parents, like those who blame television for their child's delinquency, tend to overlook the fact that the influence of the teacher is very small in comparison to the influence the parents themselves exert on their child's morality. Although critics of sex education in the schools have been successful in having programs removed from some schools, it seems that these critics constitute a minority. In several recent surveys made in northern and eastern states, more than 70% of the parents polled voted in favor of continuing—and strengthening—programs already in existence. (103)

Parent–School Cooperation

Parents of disabled youngsters ask many of the same questions asked by parents of the fit. One of the most frequent parental concerns is whether sex education in school encourages sexual intimacy. Research disproves this. For example, experimental programs in Oregon and Wisconsin schools convinced many educators and public health workers that intensive sex education programs in those states have led to a significant reduction in illegitimate births, veneral disease, and juvenile crimes. In fact, the continuation of the comprehensive program in San Diego schools for more than a decade shows that when a sound program is developed, it can enlist long-term public support (113, 415).

Since parents delegate to schools the teaching of many forms of communication skills, it is reasonable to hold that the teaching profession will increase its competency in sex education sufficiently to carry out this charge responsibly for both able and disabled youngsters. Actually, as a study (224) carried out by Planned Parenthood of Southern Pennsylvania concludes, "Parents and teachers have separate but complementary roles in helping to make the exceptional child's sexuality a positive part of his identity, and by working closely together, agreeing on expectations, limitations and goals, a great deal can be accomplished (224, 225). This merits serious consideration. In fact, Balester puts it even more emphatically when he charges the advocates of sex education in special education with the responsibility of "clearly stating what are the valid expectations and limitations of their procedures" (18). Blom would add to this the option of alternatives for children who do not wish to participate in sex education programs because of parental objections or other reasons (40).

When this option was first offered to parents of brain-injured teenagers in the high-school classes of ICD Rehabilitation and Research Center, a few took advantage of having their youngsters attend other programs. However, the number of students excluded was usually reduced by midsemester as parents went to counseling sessions or conferred with other parents whose youngsters were in both the biology and sex education seminars. In other words, it is not enough to inform parents that a course in sex education will include information about a) body parts and functions, including reproduction, b) feelings and reactions, c) satisfactory relationships with oneself and others, plus d) values and responsibilities. It is necessary not only to share the curriculum and its correlary resources for parents, but also to orient parents as to how teachers plan to respond to the needs of youngsters in special education.

Bass has written very meaningfully in this area (22). She states that the basic principles which apply to sound sex education for normal youngsters also apply to the impaired. However, with less information and few opportunities to check what they may know, the disabled have more misinformation. In addition, isolation and over protection have resulted in poorer judgment and fewer social skills, so much training must be directed toward acceptable social behavior (268). They must be helped to understand that, while some people opt for marriage and parenthood, others find that marriage and children are not necessity's for happiness. Many people choose not to marry or not to take on the added responsibility of parenthood. Bass is among those observant counselors who have discovered how little exceptional children know about the basic make-up of a family and the various roles played by parents, peers, and relatives. She finds it useful to break down the responsible ties of these family roles into tasks that youngsters can understand and in this way illustrate substitutes for parenthood. In fact, sex education as a part of a broader course of family life education should include differences between boys and girls, heredity and the chances of passing on an impairment, the changes at puberty, dating, choosing or not choosing a marriage partner, sex and birth control.

Special schools for disabled youngsters, especially residential schools where parents are not available on a day-to-day basis, have a very direct responsibility for sex education. This responsibility includes sex education for the professional staff and for attendants, as well as for the student body. While officials at many residences still try to avoid this subject—and perhaps it is better to do so than to offer a poorly organized, misleading hodgepodge that is lacking in developmental goals—others have helpful experience to share. For example, an excellent study on "Sex Education Programs for Visually Handicapped" gives several useful cues about the state of the art in 1971, both in and out of institutions (36). Of 273 institutions and organizations contacted, 118 (43.2%) replied to a questionnaire about the type of sex education provided and the materials used. Among the respondents were 44 public schools, 32 residential schools, and 42 agencies from 39 states and the District of Columbia. The six-page summary of this report is well worth reading since it covers many aspects of sex education relevant to programs for other disability groups. In essence, 16 public school systems had sex education curricula from kindergarten through 12th grade, and 9 had programs only at junior and senior high. Residential schools were restrictive: 3 offered sex education only at upper elementary and 12th grade, while 7 only presented it at senior high level. The material was covered in a variety of classes with health, biology, home economics, and physical education taking the lead. Several residential schools used out-of-class time, providing sex education in a cottage or dorm setting, in on-campus religious groups, and in special workshops. One agency used the local chapter of Planned Parenthood; others offered programs to parent groups and participated in work–study programs and summer programs for teens and adults. Most of the respondents indicated that their programs were intended to teach image, hygiene, and the elements of reproductive biology. A few public schools included the intent to "develop a positive and wholesome attitude toward sex" (36) and to "teach the physical, psychology and social aspects of relationships" (36).

Sensory Loss and Special Sex Education Needs

A wide variety of teaching aids, including commercially produced audiotapes and records and locally produced braille and large type print books, must be used in sex education for the blind child. Many visually handicapped youngsters have a difficult time understanding basic concepts and learning details because so many sex education materials are heavily visually oriented (36). This can be better appreciated by the sighted reader who only has to think of some everyday experiences to realize what the blind miss: seeing other girls develop different size and shape bosoms, miniskirts, see-through blouses, the gaps between halters and jeans, the hairy chests that stick out of open shirts, how different people look even more different when walking around in underwear at home or at the residence, etc., etc. Among the misconceptions picked up by blind youngsters, Perkins Institute has found many referring to the dimension, texture, and location of the genitals (125).

Torbett is among many educators who feel strongly that "sex education for the blind must take into account the sexual negativism of American culture and work to overcome resistance to the use of touch so necessary to learning by blind children" (428). Bass has found some clever approaches to this problem in schools that use "French" dolls with genitals in teaching young children and rubber models originally produced for teaching medical students in teaching teenagers. Some Planned Parenthood clinics have copies of the Dickenson–Belski models of the birth of a baby and some useful books in braille are Duval's *Facts of Life and Love for Teenagers* and Johnson's *Love and Sex in Plain Language* (22).

Several residences for the blind have had long-term experience with curriculum development, as well as with the use of sex education materials, and may prove useful resources for the novice instructor (378). The Illinois Braille and Sight Saving School in Jacksonville, Illinois, has had a program since 1965 (199), and the Oregon School for the Blind has developed a curriculum guide which includes its experiences with program and materials (309). The program developed at Clovernook Home and School for the Blind includes a 4-week summer workshop for visually impaired youngsters which covers physical, emotional, and social aspects of sexual maturation, grooming, hygiene, and cosmetics as well as drug use and abuse. It aims for the development of personal growth in awareness, self-expression, and individual responsibility (223).

Some 80 per 100,000 youngsters are totally deaf, requiring special education. As staff of the school at Lauridale, California, point out, one step which parents can take in sex education is to be familiar with stages of development of sexual feeling in children. An outline of these, from infancy to age 6, is provided to help parents develop a vocabulary for communication about sex, as well as to provide early nonlanguage cues which lay the bases for later concepts that a child will need when learning about reproduction (191). Most deaf children have hearing parents, a statistic which has not changed since 1910 (377). As a result, most of these parents are unprepared for a deaf child, and his interpersonal relations and the means of communication which are so important in the sexuality of an individual thus get off to a difficult start.

In general, the early entry of deaf children into formal schooling was not encouraged until 1960 when federally supported programs for the preschool education of handicapped children were developed. Even in these programs a large share of deaf students attend residential schools where they are closely supervised in their heterosexual development. If specialized sex education curricula for staff or students are part of general education in residential schools for the deaf, few of them reach print. The curriculum of the Illinois School for the Deaf in Jacksonville is a notable exception to this. Its content in general is similar to that of curricula for normal youngsters, including units on physical growth, social hygiene, marriage, childbirth, and family living (205). The family living unit discusses family planning and birth control, as well as the chances of the students' having a deaf child themselves. Even where sex education programs following developmental interpersonal relationships are available, counselors of deaf youngsters have found them experientially naive, needing concrete examples in order to make abstract concepts meaningful. While interest in sexual behavior was high, knowledge of reproductive functions and responsibilities and of the reasons for rules governing sexual behavior was limited. A great deal of work and repetition were required to increase the depth of awareness among the deaf students from rules memorized by rote to a more mature grasp of concepts (372).

Individualized Developmental Approaches

Sex education for the disabled is beginning to rest upon a sound personal and social developmental schema which has evolved from constructive experience in our normal multicultural society. Teaching sex education to physically disabled, retarded, blind, deaf, or brain-damaged children is essentially similar to teaching it to the normal youngster—if one meets the young person at his developmental level and selects instructional materials, as well as methods of communication, which ensure two-way understanding. How each disabled person reacts to physical and emotional espects of sexuality depends on his experience, his learned patterns of behavior, and the guidance that he has received up to that time. Actually, there is no sex stereotype that can be associated with any one disability. For example, observant members of the helping professions point out that all retarded children and youth have sexual feelings and drives which are unrelated to mental ability. Some boys and girls with low IQs have little interest in sex and low or weak sex drives, while others have a great deal of curiosity about sex and strong sex drives. Every individual is unique in terms of personality, physiology of sex, and his perception of it. The way the retarded express their sexuality will depend greatly upon the attitudes of those who care for them (349).

Those who care for the retarded have put a great deal of thought into bridging the communications gap as well as into meeting specific growing-up needs. Most of the curricula devised for trainable and educable retarded recognize their limitations in understanding concepts of sex and provide methods of communication which include visual and tactile cues. Such curricula also help adults to recognize whether they are making contact with a student and, if not, what other routes to take. Appendix B lists several well-tried curricula for young people in special classes and special schools, as well as for those being prepared to leave a residential setting for life in the community. A good example of the thought that has gone into curriculum development is Iowa's in-service training program for teachers, "A Social Attitude Approach to Sex Education for the Educable Mentally Retarded" (269). These lesson units on social attitudes include sex education within a broader development of relevant social skills. The *preliminary* lessons for ages 4–7 refer to a healthy body image, proper toilet habits, male and female roles, growth patterns, respect for others, and a good self-image. Ages approximately 7–9 (the next developmental level) at the *primary* level are taught social development, growth, differences in people, understanding negative feelings, and human reproduction. *Intermediates,* ages 9–13, learn about embryo and fetal development, social and physical development, emotional and physical aspects of sexual maturation. *Advanced* students, at 14 years and older, have units on personality, heredity, environment, basic needs and emotions, adult attitudes, authority, their peer group, dating, premarital sex relations, veneral diseases, smoking, alcohol, drugs, marriage, and family living.

There are many other good curriculum concepts which tend to calm the titillation and raw emotions that naive parents and professionals bring to their first contacts with the question of sex education for youngsters whose disability forces them to lead more sheltered lives. For example, the basic thoughts behind *A Resource Guide in Sex Education for the Mentally Retarded* are a) Awareness of Self—becoming a boy, becoming a girl; b) Physical Changes and Understanding Self—becoming a man, becoming a woman; c) Peer Relations—boy friends, girl friends, boy and girl friends; and d) Responsibilities to Society as Men and Women (349). Another concept which is particularly important in these days when large institutions are being closed and residents are being placed in communities is community preparedness for retardates. Austin State School has developed such a curriculum for mentally impaired adolescent males (205). A counterpart for females, *Puberty in the Girl Who Is Retarded* by the National Association for Retarded Citizens, is designed to help matters for youngsters who must adjust to mainstreaming—living in the community (435). (see Appendix B).

With the present legalized trend away from institutionalization sex education becomes even more important (22). Poorly planned propulsive mainstreaming leaves the almost-normal youngster in a "noman's land" where lack of acceptance leaves him wondering with whom to identify. There is an almost universal need for socialization training to accompany specific sex education in order to afford the "special" preteen appropriate techniques for establishing developmentally related relationships(435). Having fewer opportunities for socializing, these children find it difficult to make friends with a wide enough group to establish comparisons and recognize likenesses in attitudes. For example, unless opportunity is provided, they are likely to be less sophisticated and less acquainted with the general jargon known to the average teenager (157). The handicapped preteen youngsters should be able to recognize and verbalize the physical differences between boys and girls and the bodily changes which occur during puberty—which are likely to occur to them and which have occurred to some of their friends. They should be able to use words which indicate clearly their ability to label body parts and body changes. For those youngsters (normal and disabled) who are accustomed to "street" language or colloquialisms, educators advise a compromise communication (157). Instead of discussing or deploring these expressions, help the youngster to learn the grownup synonym (*i.e.,* "The curse is what grownups call menstruating," or "wet dreams" are what professionals call "nocturnal emissions."). Never cut off discussion by criticizing a popularization; keep the communication channels open by adding synonyms, including those socially acceptable to grownups or those found in a dictionary or book.

IMPORTANCE OF EARLY FORMATIVE YEARS

The psychosexual development of youngsters with mental or physical disabilities parallels that of the normal child in sequence and trend, if not in age. Therefore, it is important for many adults who do not think of sexuality as a form of learning before adolescence to become aware of normal developmental sexual interests and goals. There are some pioneer curricula for children in special classes and special schools which can serve as beginning cues to the thinking of parents and professionals who endeavor to deal constructively with children who have special needs.

One of the real challenges in dealing with this "age group," on the threshold of puberty or at the developmental period of entering society, is not with the children. It is with the *competence* of their contact care personnel, be they parents, teachers, helping professionals, aides, camp counselors, or anyone else. Are these potential guides acquainted with the developmental facts of this stage of growth and with the peculiar needs of their disabled students? Moreover, can the adults handle their own feelings sufficiently to handle daily incidents with proper emotional weight? And most important, can they recognize when they don't know how to handle a situation regarding sexual curiosity or behavior? Do they then know to whom to go or to whom to refer this child, this parent, this colleague?

2 ADOLESCENCE AND YOUTH: Marking Time on Society's Threshold

The adolescent mind is essentially a mind of the moratorium, a psychosocial stage between childhood and adulthood, and between the morality learned by the child and the ethics developed by the

The adolescent mind is essentially a mind of the moratorium, a psychosocial stage between childhood and adulthood, and between the morality learned by the child and the ethics developed by the adult. It is an ideological mind—and indeed it is the ideological outlook of a society that speaks most clearly to the adolescent who is eager to be confirmed by his peers, and is ready to be confirmed by the rituals, creeds and programs which at the same time define what is evil, uncanny and inimical.—Erik Erikson

Childhood Society

TODAY'S SOCIOSEXUAL OUTLOOK

QUANTITIES

Never before have so many people lived in the United States and occupied so much space "from sea to shining sea." We have a population of some 204 million people, and the number of births was 3,141,000 or thereabouts in 1973. There are 40 million single people, 60% of whom are 18–29 years of age—the decision-making years (353). Approximately 25 million people of all ages, or 10% of the entire population, have physical impairments with some activity limitation. Some 3.5 million are men aged 17–44 years, while 3 million are women aged 17–44—the decision-taking years (408). With the advent of antibiotics and modern rehabilitation care, life expectancy of the average person with a disability is not very different from his normal counterpart. Studies on this topic are fragmented into selected special disabilities or special populations of institutional persons, but the trend is quantitatively in favor of the longer life, even for individuals with some activity limitation.

QUALITIES

The quality of life for the disabled, as well as the able, will depend upon the degree of freedom experienced and savored in a variable environment. Within the sociosexual climate, Fairservis has a well-taken point that

Too many in the West regard the genitalia, rather than the men or women who possess them, as the symbols of sex. . . . The difference between the sexes is not simply a matter of planning, but in its ideal sense, a matter that may complement or supplement the opposite sex. It is a mutuality that transcends biologic identity, and yet in its fullest expression emphatically identifies the individual as a woman or a man (132).

Coming from this ideal to the everydayness of life, as it is lived, Erikson's neat phrase that "in the past anatomy has been destiny" describes thousands of years of human life, from prehistory until recent times (128). Actually, it describes the individual in terms of his or her role, and refers to couples in terms of fecundity. Figure 2–1 illustrates this destiny wherein sex was linked to reproduction as a responsibility of marriage.

In the 1920s, there was a radical change which brought sexual expression to the foreground, and to this the 1970s added a wider horizon of sexual exploration (Fig. 2–2). Now sexuality and sex are consciously divorced from reproduction. They are conceived as a mutual pact between two persons, of opposite (or even the same) sex, who seek genital satisfaction, emotional satisfaction, or love—or all three—according to the needs and demands of this relationship. It is an attempt to make a logical self-contained package of sexual satisfactions without the boundaries of marital commitments or socially defined responsibilities. There is nothing re-

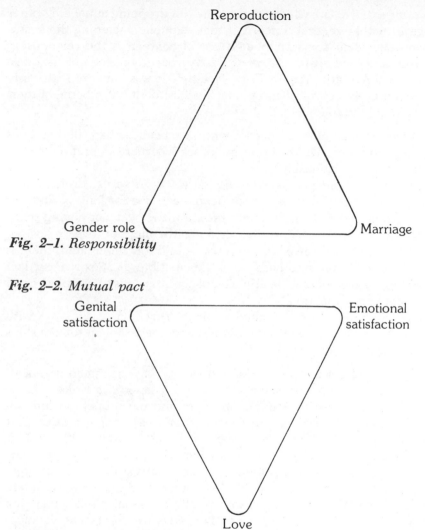

Reproduction

Gender role

Fig. 2–1. Responsibility

Marriage

Fig. 2–2. Mutual pact

Genital
satisfaction

Emotional
satisfaction

Love

ally *new* about these mutual pact relationships, but in recent years there have been more of them, and more are openly contracted. However, just as liberation from biologic destiny was needed in one era, so do some of today's young people need freedom from being pressured into mutual pact relationships.

Unfortunately, too many relationships are founded only on flight *from* boredom, *from* responsibility, or *from* the peer ostracism of being thought "square." The pendulum has swung from the Puritan ethic which distorted normal healthy feelings, thereby forcing sex into merely a procreative duty, an unwholesome preoccupation with the *techniques* of the sex act as the be-all and end-all of sexuality. In this latter day perception, the failure to develop a big sexual "relationship" is often erroneously equated with total personality failure; in contrast, the "love act" or "being sent" may be considered by some as the opiate which compensates for dropping out of life's other challenges. Another general concern of today's public, including the avant-garde who take their sex straight and out of context, is the relationship between sex and good health. *Harper's Bazaar* recently tossed out the question, "Is Sexual Activity Vital To Good Health?" It was answered variously by several authorities of social and personal adjustment (207). Some of their replies included the following:

—Obviously no. There are people who have been celibate all their lives who are in good health. On the other hand, sex is certainly a part of healthy living and healthy relationships.

—There are some people who are very low in sexual drive, sexual interests, sexual responsiveness. These people can live for long periods, or perhaps for their entire lives, without getting upset over not having sex."

—It's not sex that remains vital for a healthy life, but love.

—Sex has to be expressed in some way and if it is sublimated, there is no harm done to the physical body or to the emotions. . . . Sex a must? Is it part of having good emotional health? Yes, of course. . . . it's a natural physical and emotional body function.

—Sex will have all sorts of salutary effects, particularly if it is sex with someone you care about—that is the highest and deepest of all relationships —so it isn't vital, but it's wonderful!

Obviously, destiny is no longer chained to anatomy, nor need it repeatedly ride into life's shore on a surface wave of passion. As Erikson again cues us in, personal destiny today rests more and more upon an individual's developmental potential in collaboration with opportunities that may be offered by a partner or by society. If responsibility (Fig. 2–1) is included in a mutual pact (Fig. 2–2), the sequence of human experience will result (Fig. 2–3). An integration of those relationships between people that foster mutual growth and development offers those ultimate fulfillments spoken of as "generativity" by Erikson, "self-actualizing creativity" by Maslow, or "love" by May. However, personal development and societal opportunities for fulfillment do not offer such ultimates to all who might wish them. Therefore, a mutual responsibility pact (Fig. 2–4) may set the course and the price for one or more of six peak experiences desired: expression of gender role, genital satisfaction, emotional satisfaction, love, marriage, and reproduction.

In 1952, in one of the few studies that compared opinions about the developmental tasks of early adulthood, Havinghurst found that disabled and multiply impaired young people agreed closely with normal young adults in giving high rank to preparing for marriage and family life within the following tasks: home, taking on civil responsibility, selecting a mate, learning to live with a marriage partner, starting a family, and rearing children (188). At that time, little consideration was given to the preparation for these goals or the actual developmental levels of those disabled individuals who intellectu-

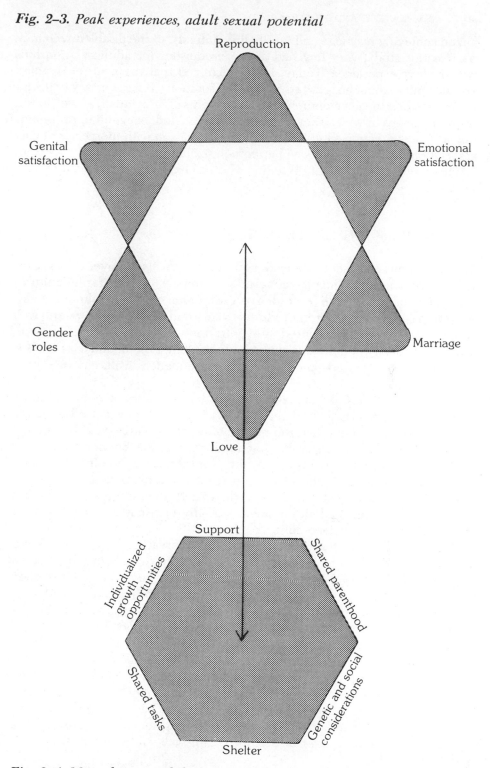

Fig. 2–3. Peak experiences, adult sexual potential

Reproduction

Genital
satisfaction

Emotional
satisfaction

Gender
roles

Marriage

Love

Support

Individualized
growth
opportunities

Shared parenthood

Shared tasks

Genetic and social
considerations

Shelter

Fig. 2–4. Mutual responsibility pact

alized achieving marriage and family life. Actually, of the disabled who took part in this study, very few had any prerequisites for adult relationships within their experience. Today, it is recognized that the goals of disabled young adults cannot be realized by blanket solutions. It is necessary to distinguish between the developmental achievements of individuals, as well as the different stages in which they have become disabled: congenital, prepubertal, adolescent, young adult, etc. Obviously, a person with memories of past associations and lost abilities will approach sexuality in a different way from a person with a congenital disability who has had no or few social experiences.

THE ADOLESCENT CHALLENGE

Cultural habits represent a delicate equilibrium developed over the ages for mutual interpersonal and intergenerational support (342). Different cultures have allowed for diverse sex role expression and sex act fulfillment under accepted conditions. The required repressions and inhibitions were also well defined, and generally accepted. Religious tracts, operas, and novels abound with the audacity of individuals who have stretched the boundaries of their own society's tolerance—and taken the consequences, willingly or unwittingly.

Until recent times, the average man on the street was so geographically restricted and so class bound that he was fairly well acquainted with the extent of permissiveness and the nature of reprisals which would meet any actions unacceptable to society. But modern man has not stayed put; his travels or migrations have brought him face to face with cultural choices. Furthermore, this generation has been bombarded by messages via television, radio, printed matter, and a wide variety of interpersonal contacts which have transgressed all boundaries of any previous class or any prior geographically determined culture.

Some young people have interpreted their observations to mean "no holds barred," while others have been swamped by confusion. Some self-elected advisors of the young have encouraged reckless satiation of immediate desires, quoting "rights" without responsibilities and quoting precedences among varied cultures, *but not* necessarily those cultures with which the youngsters have any lasting contact. Other adult advisors have threatened doom under all circumstances without recognizing that there are cultural alternatives open to all youth, able and disabled, depending upon their varying capacities to cope with and to learn from experience. Gordon's common sense approaches seem to weather both extremes. While it is necessary to refer to sex education curricula (see Appendix B) to back up Gordon's direct and chatty style, his approach to the disabled youngster and his parents is one of well-intentioned interest in getting at the facts and feelings of obscure issues (161).

In an evolving multicultural society, such as the United States now represents, there are ethnic and interethnic ties, religious factions and interfaith alliances, racial and interracial forces. In every cultural group there are disabled youth who grow up in protected isolation, as well as a minority among them who struggle to join the mainstream (365). Therefore, it is relevant to determine what the actual tasks of adolescence are and what the able and disabled hope to accomplish during this developmental phase known as adolescence. Understandably, the actual chronologic age range of the disabled will vary according to any social lag which may be due to mental or emotional retardation, lack of opportunity for experience, overprotection from experience, etc. Nevertheless, during this time of explosive change, there are specific developmental tasks involving sexuality, *i.e.*, objectives to be reached:

1. Movement toward peers . . . toward independence
2. Establishment of intimacy or the capacity for friendship
3. Ability to make commitments and recognize intentions related to them
4. Control over sex and agressive drives
5. Synthesis of ideas about self and authority into a value system relating to the sexual area
6. Testing youth-specific identities in sexuality (masculinity, femininity) in heterosexual relationships within personal and social roles—toward an integration of personality

Sexual behavior at this time of life is experimental and sporadic both on the physical level and on the social level as the youngster tries out social roles and develops a value concept of what is acceptable to peers, parents, and ethnic groups. Finding someone who cares serves some needs for dependency, and this reaction to caring persons lays the basis for later love relationships.

Puberty is a physical entity within adolescence and is reached by the disabled in much the same time frame as that of the able. Like normal youngsters, the majority of girls with disabilities menstruate between the ages of 10 and 13, while boys with mental, physical, or emotional disabilities start ejaculating semen or have wet dreams usually between the ages of 13 and 15. The impact of our "sexploiting media, pornography, myths from 'gutter' discussions, graffiti in our public school bathrooms, and premature and sometimes involuntary sexual experiments" reaches all of them daily (157). Any counterimpact based on satisfying developmental needs will have to keep in mind the intense self-scrutiny of the age range: "The Me Other People See," "Will Anyone Love Me?", "Everybody's Doing It—Doing What?", and "What's My Thing?"

THE ME OTHER PEOPLE SEE

Unfortunately, it is a human social tendency to reach toward the expectations of others, rather than to seek our own potential. In this respect, disabled adolescents and youth are in particularly vulnerable situations (416b). The emphasis placed on visibly dramatic success in our culture masks the daily courage and integrity by which the disabled forge their lives. [A typical cultural veneer is public overrating of the few disabled who were accidentally favored by life—"the polio victim who broke track records, the one-legged pitcher who made the major leagues, the great composer who was deaf. . . ." (456)] Research evidence clearly supports the conclusion that public *verbalized* attitudes toward the disabled are generally not *un*favorable, but the deeper lying and unconscious attitudes of those who have no interpersonal contact with them are often hostile—a hostility arising out of fear of the different, the unknown. A disabled youth can be the object of such extreme attitudes as someone rushing to be helpful in seating him, but then ignoring him during the group discussion since basically he is not thought of as one of the group. In the terms of one sensitive young person, "That is being included out."

Social distance in more personal areas is equally great. In one study of unimpaired college students, 65% said they would not marry and 50% would not even date a person who had an amputated leg. In the same group, 85% would not marry and 72% would not date a deaf person (293). There is a stigma on the lives of most young people growing up with a disability. Generally, it represents the most salient and frustrating problem to be overcome in their rehabilitation, because it restricts their life space and interpersonal relationships (123). Concurrently, research also indicates that the stigma is reduced when non disabled persons *work closely* with disabled persons *over a long time period.* Realistically, since youth is a volatile period in the lives of the able as well as the disabled, "work," "closeness," and "long time" do not fit into general patterns of present day youthful behavior. However, recent legislation initiating the integration of those disabled students who can profit from regular classwork (mainstreaming) into classrooms with normal students may eventually provide an environment in which "the me people see" is more than the superficial labels of some medical diagnosis (365).

Stigma may be camouflaged as protectiveness, an overprotectiveness which infantilizes its recipients. For instance, teenage retardates are often referred to by teachers and ward attendants as "children." This is a comfortable attitude for those adults who do not know, or do not wish to know, how to educate the youth to recognize and to handle sexual impulses in a manner that is both socially acceptable and legally permissible (268). Parents of youngsters with any type of disability find it hard to believe that their son or daughter is old enough, is interested in, would not be confused by, would not be stirred by, etc., sex education. However, Gordon (160) quotes a father with a better memory: "In remembering what an emotional time adoles- cence was, I recalled how troubled and guilty I was at times at the nature of some of my thoughts. Now, both my wife and I are concerned that our handicapped son will be additionally incapable of understanding what these thoughts mean." As Gordon indicates in his reply to this father, the best approach to adolescent turmoil may be simply to explain to a youngster that anyone is likely to have suicidal, aggressive, or sexual thoughts. Furthermore, everyone has them at some time—all thoughts, wishes, dreams, and fantasies are part of normal growing up. An adolescent should be helped to realize that there is no need to feel guilty about any thoughts. Both older and younger people should try to understand that behavior may be "wrong," but not thoughts (160, 163).

Finally, we come to the self-protective voluntary infantilism which may develop as a youngster's response to society's demands. An excellent illustra- tion of this is given by Hathaway in the following excerpt from the youthful memories of a most perceptive young woman who had a disability:

When I found that the only social success I could possibly hope for among the girls and boys of my own age consisted in my being thought cute and funny and childish, in my thirst and hunger to mix with them and to be accepted, I began to cultivate in myself for these social needs the character of the appealing little clown. I slipped into the ancient role that is always expected, it seems, of the im- perfect ones of the world. I was Punch, the queer little human toy, the jester at court, respected and beloved in a way in which no other kind of person is re- spected and beloved (187).

Difficult as adjustment is for those who have grown up in the shadow of society's attitudes toward their disability, it is even harder for those who become disabled as teenagers or young adults.

They experience the acceptance and sexual expression of their humanity, but having internalized society's concept of the handicapped as asexual and something less than human, they apply it to themselves in their new state. Their concepts of self-worth and self-dignity are lessened or overturned, their sexual self-images distorted, and they become embittered, more emotionally and psychologically handicapped than they are physically (35).

WILL ANYONE LOVE ME?

As Riesman indicates, the responsibility for character formation in our soci- ety has shifted from the family to the peer group and to the mass media, peergroup surrogates (352). The effect of the peer group is further compli- cated by variations in the teenage code which are influenced by residential area, socioeconomic status, religious or goal perceptions, and other determi- nants of group segregation and identity. Individual personality differences greatly influence these variations, as can be seen in a single locality or school where teenagers subdivide into groups with different patterns of relationship (boy–girl, boy–boys, girl–girls) and different sexual morality. As Money points out, there are the "rock-n-roll" set, and the hot rodders, some of whom are prone to delinquency and sexual promiscuity, versus the squares and the creeps, some of whom are academically serious and ambitious and more reserved in their dating and going steady. Usually, there is no special name for the in-betweens, and sometimes no in-between group. It is a tough dilemma that some teenagers are thrown into, to have to make a decision about group loyalty and identity. (274)

If it is a tough dilemma for normal teenagers, the mentally and physically disabled youngsters' problems are compounded. Although they have access to the same mass media, they find few models therein, especially if they are isolated from society at large within an institution or a special school, or homebound with a visiting teacher as their only link to the community.

Communication is the largest single factor determining what kinds of relationships an individual establishes with others and what happens to him in the world about him (373). It is the very stepping stone of sexuality. In fact, the aspect of sexuality in which emotional fulfillment is gained through companionship depends upon the subtleties of communication. Unfortunately, the disabled youngster's opportunities for broadening communication are limited (98). This throws an extra challenge to such a youngster's primary contacts: family, therapists, teachers, camp counselors, etc. Too often, these primary contacts tend to build up an unrealistically rosy atmosphere in an effort to make up for the rest of the rejecting world. Parents may insist on favored treatment for this one family member; teachers or therapists may overpraise some rather average attainments, hoping to maintain morale or to hold an idolized position in the affection of these disabled youngsters; and siblings may hide their jealousy and frustration, giving in graciously as one does to a much younger child. These artificial attitudes, with outward masks of affection which frequently accompany them, are poor guides to the growing youngster on "how to win friends and influence people." As Gordon so aptly cautions, it is not fair to make a young person so dependent on this type of affection that he expects and demands it of everyone as a valid expression of approval, trust, love, and friendship.

She or he must learn early that strangers in our society do not hug and kiss one another. If she doesn't, it will be difficult to tell her when she is older that often she must not show affection this way. You may ask, how can she learn this? By telling or showing your child how, when or why you demonstrate affection to others. For example, if an old friend walks into the house and you give her a hug and a kiss, turn to your child and say, "I'm so glad to see Mary again, I want to kiss her." And after the traveling salesman leaves, point out that you *didn't* touch him in any way because you never saw him before and it wouldn't be right to do so. In other words, keep explaining behavior and very firmly correct behavior when it is inappropriate. (160)

For the retarded, explanations should be given at the time or immediately after the specific behavior occurs; for the intelligent, emotionally or physically disabled young person, the proper time is as soon after the behavior as privacy and constructive choice of words or meaningful reference to the topic can be found.

The cultural tendency to infantilize youth who are different is not warranted, even in institutions for the severely handicapped (98). Secker, an

English director of a special school, indicates that students in schools for the severely handicapped should spend their last years at school in a mixed group so that the first sexual interest that they display may be handled with care by a trained staff. She understands that 15 and 16-year-olds certainly want a boy or girl friend and that boys admire the attractive visitors and young teachers. In fact, institutionalized youth show many familiar signs of adolescence whether it be their spotty faces, swings of mood, laziness or unwillingness to conform, or the readiness of boys and girls to giggle and blush. Trained to be sensitive to this stage of development so as not to complicate difficulties but to guide pupils through them (381), the staff at this school are asked to teach the rules and conventions that are acceptable in our society.

Studies of young people who are not institutionalized also point up the developmental lags brought about by social isolation (290). For example, although retarded adolescents and youth who were living at home claimed to have friends of both sexes, further questioning by Morgenstern revealed that heterosexual contacts occurred primarily in the classroom or on the job. This lack of informal peer contacts or interpersonal experiences was felt to be one of the factors contributing to the lack of sex information among these youngsters, since sex is a topic usually discussed among normal adolescents. Morgenstern also found students of special classes unfamiliar with conventional sex terminology, often displaying vague understanding or misinformation about marital relationships, reproduction, and birth. The responses they gave to questions about sexuality were the kinds of answers usually given to very young children: for example, babies were said to come from hospitals, and male–female differences were described in terms of clothes, hair, or personality traits. Few students mentioned anatomic differences. Upon questioning, it was found that interest in marriage and in having children was high. Brighter subjects tended to emphasize abilities and personality factors as desirable characteristics in a mate while the younger and more retarded spoke of looks and clothes (285).

Unrealistic approaches to dating, courtship, and marriage may be found in many studies of the reactions of mildly or moderately physically handicapped youth. The results of an Ohio community study of adolescents with cerebral palsy substantiates research along these lines. It revealed that, even among those students who were of normal or superior intelligence and in the sexually conscious age range of 16–20, fewer than 40% had any dating experience—either alone or chaperoned. Despite this, over 80% of this cerebral palsy group anticipated marriage. At the same time, half of the older members of this group were described by psychologists as frustrated, disturbed, or having such unrealistic concepts of their abilities that counseling was indicated (315).

In widening their social horizons beyond the immediate family circle, most young people first join one or more peer groups. After this, dating becomes the second big step in establishing wider interpersonal relationships. Readiness for dating is stimulated by mutual confidences, teasing and bantering, as well as by sexual discussions among pals. As Rebuck observes,

Dating is a personal and at times intimate relationship. It means to play, frolic and sport with one another. It implies the exchange of kisses and caresses. It is toying with temptation. And for the handicapped it can mean frustration. To begin with, for the handicapped to even date, he must have someone to date, and generally speaking must require transportation to-and-from his activity. This means that his parents must furnish transportation, be available if anything goes wrong. . . . Another problem for the handicapped person when dating is where they can go or what is available to them to do. (339)

While observations of concerned adults and studies of disabled youth are important to put our knowledge of the needs and problems of this age group into perspective, true insight comes out of the mouths of the involved. The following letter of an 18-year-old boy with cerebral palsy, written to a national organization for the disabled, brings us closest to an adolescent central question: Will anyone love me? It was handwritten, in a laborious but clear penmanship (324):

Dear Sir,
I would like to know if there is anything wrong about form a get-together organization in my own.
I am getting sick and tired of waiting so long to some way.
I want action now before it another delay go on and on again. I try either way to bring handicapped together.
I need only how to bring a social gether club in the hope that I find a better way to run an organization. I have all the money to run a program, but I need a boy friend who can belong to a club. I don't have any friend at all.
I do not have a girl friend who I can get marry. I don't need someone who is normal then who is a C.P. I am born with it. But I cannot go out look for someone who don't know about. Please tell me how I am going to get a girl who are C.P. and religion is ——.

Sincerely yours,
P.S. Please send me a copy of the book which I can find out how I can get some social activities in my state, and find a girl friend here.

For those who confuse sex (genital satisfaction) with sexuality, this letter provides a moving illustration of the difference in very simple adolescent terms. It reveals the writer's feelings about maleness and femaleness, his desire to trust and to love, his attitudes toward interpersonal relationships, and his search toward understanding of relationships among living things (in this case, personal effort and social organization) (163).

EVERYBODY'S DOING IT

In the great American tradition of exaggeration, everyone who isn't *we* (our inner circle) is *they*. It is not unusual to hear that *they* wouldn't work if work were available, *they* don't know how to live in a decent neighborhood, you wouldn't want your daughter to marry one of *them*, would you? In a country of 200 million people, the *theys* are those people who seem a threat to the individual adult speaker and his property or to his hard-earned and sacred status quo. Adolescents and youth, whose developing sexuality includes making new relationships outside the family, have not yet solidified their own inner circle. However, they also have their *everybodys*. What parent has not lived through such cries of horror as: *"Everybody* is going but me" . . . or *"Everyone* knows that" . . . or "Gee Whiz, you never let me do anything, *everyone* is doing it." If *everybody* seems omnipresent, is in possession of all admirable attributes, and is normal youth's amorphous model, what impact does this *everybody* have for the young person whose differences of body or mind have isolated him from peer gossip, peer critiques, or peer and model resources?

Naturally, the impact of values of the *everybodys,* or of the people in the immediate circle of both able-bodied and disabled youth, will vary with the decision-making capabilities and the emotional stability of individual youth. How young people arrive at these decision-making capabilities is a fairly neglected aspect of present day education. One useful clue to understanding the patterns of all children's value development comes through the studies of a Harvard psychologist. Kohlberg's research defines a definite unvarying sequence of "thought stages" in the evolution of moral reasoning (232). The sequence is not much affected by a child's social, religious, or cultural environment. However, these factors do affect the *rate* at which a youngster progresses to sequentially higher stages of thinking about good and bad, about human rights, and about human responsibilities.

This sequence begins when a child determines the right or wrong of an act by whether it has been rewarded or punished. At that point, he unquestionably accepts the adult's edict. This is followed by a "conventional" or "Golden Rule" level of moral thought where the youngster understands that, in order to get along with other people, he must treat them as he wishes to be treated. Next, he arrives at a "law and order" mindset wherein he respects authority and is willing to do his duty and set a good example. (Some educators believe that children can be helped to reach this stage of moral reasoning by the sixth grade and that only about 25% of adults in Western societies go on from there.) Higher levels of moral reasoning imply the ability to remove oneself and one's own interests from the weighting factors and to decide the values in a situation purely on the basis of principle that is motivated by a concern for justice. To the parents, educators, and other contacts of disabled children and teens (at all physical, mental, and emotional levels) value education is a highly confused area in our multiculture. However, it is one that requires empathetic research to determine the level at which each youngster stands and to provide a cooperative moral climate where all are learning to respect the dignity, rights, liberty, and individuality of other human beings.

Street Language

Since parents and members of the helping professions are not always clear about what youth (able or disabled) know about sex, what they want to know or how to get the information across, accidental learning is still the major route to sex education. As a result, a hodge-podge of sex is learned from friends through the medium of cuss words or dirty jokes and from the frank sexual themes of television, movies, and news media. Translation is a two-way road through the language barrier. As far as disabled youth are concerned, some counselors believe that it is very important for them to understand the language associated with sex, including the so-called dirty words. Without this, the (physically) disabled may find themselves being teased, used, and *above all,* not accepted by less naive peer groups. This non acceptance or rejection by one's peer groups "can lead to excessive masturbation, perversion, or homosexuality" (339). Irrespective of whether one perceives these particular dire consequences of a language barrier, it is irrefutable that information can only be built on a basis of mutual understanding. Therefore, it is up to adults who are in contact with disabled youth to learn, acknowledge, and make constructive use of varieties of dirty words, cultural slang, and everyday misinterpretations. These street words can become passports to individual and group discussions, leading students toward wholesome literature on sex education (367, 431). While glossaries of slang or street terms are a useful part of every adult leader's kit (47), the "translations" referred to here can best be illustrated by a paragraph from *A Resource Guide in Sex Education for the Mentally Retarded* (349):

INSTRUCTIONAL OBJECTIVE: To Be Able to Discuss Verbally The Meaning of Masturbation—Teaching Tips

It is important that the teacher determine what pupils know about masturbation. You might begin by making a comment such as "There are things we do which feel good but which we worry about because other people say its bad. This makes us uncomfortable. We don't know if other people are right, or if because it feels good, it is good. We may not know why we do it." The kids might mention nail-biting, daydreaming, thumb-sucking, etc. Pursue these briefly. Encourage self-expression. In focusing on masturbation, ask the group if they have heard of "jacking off" or "masturbation." Observe their response. Some will likely laugh, others may appear embarrassed. If you encourage discussion, you might evoke such responses, "It *means playing with yourself, pulling it, beating your meat, jerking off,*" etc. Street terms should be acknowledged, but take advantage of these candid terms to offer a definition of masturbation such as "It means rubbing your penis, or vagina."

In this example, the objective of the teacher was to introduce both the idea and the terminology of masturbation as well as to make it acceptable as a topic for discussion. This topic is particularly relevant to adolescent boys and girls since it is one of their early concerns. Boys almost universally engage in some masturbation during their teens; girls to a lesser extent. It is important to make adolescents understand that masturbation is essentially a normal response to increased sexual development. Through it the adolescent learns that

sexual excitement and engorgement and erection of the penis or the clitoris can be initiated at will and that orgastic climax with ensuing predictable subsidence of tension can be quickly brought about or repeatedly differed by the manner of masturbation. This contributes to a developing sense of mastery over sexual impulses and the new sexual capacities, and helps the adolescent to prepare for heterosexual relationships. (167)

Obviously the language of the Committee on Adolescence of the Group for the Advancement of Psychiatry, as quoted here, will not get the message over to teenagers.It is likely that some members of a student group may be unfamiliar with even the basic terms penis, clitoris, vagina, etc. The teacher should find out what words they are using for their "privates" and help them to become familiar with those that can be found in dictionaries and other books. For instance, some students may refer to a penis as a "ding-dong" as a hangover from childhood, a "prick," or a "stick." A vagina may be known to some as a "pussy," a "cunt," a "box," or a "slit." It may be helpful to point out that these alternative ways of labeling body parts are not "wrong," but they will not be as useful in the future as the dictionary words will. Actually, in a country with as many subcultures and economic strata as the United States, "translations" will be necessary for many generations. They are particularly pertinent at this time, now that mainstreaming the disabled is an educational priority of national scope (365). Therefore, parents, counselors, and teachers must make every effort during conversation with exceptional children not to express themselves in words that are above or below the youngsters' capacity. Discussions about sex must start with the words and ideas at the youngsters' level of comprehension and lead them toward wider horizons.

Playing the Field or Going Steady

Erikson reminds us that a young person's identity is not modeled simply on a parent, but on the parent's superego (127). In other words, in seeking his or her own identity, a boy and a girl go beyond patterning themselves after their parent of the same sex and actually choose the parent's ideal image for a boy or girl as a model. Today, with the wane of parental influence in many circles and the barrage of media influences, sex models spring from the movies, television, center pages, and peer braggadocios. As Cox states so well:

Playboy and Miss America represent The Boy and The Girl . . . Playboy merely continues the comic-book tactic for the next age group . . . [it] speaks to those who desperately want to know what it means to be a man and more, specifically, a *male* in today's world . . . the skilled consumer is cool, unruffled . . . sex becomes one of the items of leisure activity that the knowledgeable consumer of leisure handles with his characteristic skill and detachment . . . sex must be contained, at all costs, within the entertainment–recreation area. Don't let her get "serious" . . . when playtime is over, the playmate's function ceases, so she must be made to understand the rules of the game . . . departmentalized sex (91).

Our culture publicizes extremes. It flirts with those young people who do not have the temperament for normal relationships or the opportunity to "play the field" by setting up the sex and romantic love temptation. Going steady, or "premature monogamy" as May calls it, is a feature of our time:

our insecure age when all values are in flux, at least the *steady* is steady. Always having a date with the same fellow or girl on Saturday night . . . always knowing this one is available, allays anxiety of being lonely. But it also gets boring. This leads naturally enough to early sexuality: sex is at least something we can do when we run out of conversation—which happens often when the partners have not developed enough in their own right to be interesting very long to each other as persons . . . substituting premature sexuality for meaningful intimate relationships relieves the young person's anxiety at the price of by-passing opportunity for further development. It seems going steady is related to promiscuity. I define *promiscuity* with Webster as the *indiscriminate practice of sexuality whether with one person or a number:* sex is indiscriminate when used in the service of security or to fill up an emotional vacuum. But promiscuity is a lonely and alienating business. (262)

In the midst of flaunted extremes of going steady or playing the field, normal wholesome youth struggle to make friends, join clubs or gangs, participate in Scouts, 4-H, hobby groups, social action and political demonstrations, and takes any excess energy out in sports. Youngsters with disabilities must be helped toward such activities even though it is sometimes difficult to discover activities within the capabilities of an impaired youth. Gordon's books stress that disabled young people should be permitted to experiment with virtually anything acceptable that interests them, unless it is clearly impossible because of a particular incapacity. Further, if a person displays no interest in something (or anything) at the start, parents and helping adults should take the initiative and try to stimulate interest. Since so many disabled teenagers have trouble making and keeping friends, parents should seek to "team" them with other impaired adolescents and introduce them to varieties of organized social experiences (305). Such experiences as summer camp, clubs, or play groups are nonthreatening and provide relief from isolation. They also provide opportunities for body-building and isometric exercise and for *noncompetitive* sports. Spectator sports are entertaining, can be a topic of conversation, and may be a good way to generate interest in participant activities. Social experiences with handicapped peers are a rehearsal for other relationships, since a youngster who has already acquired a minimum of social skills with his own peers may function more adequately in the more competitive society of the nonhandicapped. As Gordon (160) said, "We have to stop thinking in terms of all-or-none projects and learn to appreciate the partial, nearly imperceptible growth accruing daily that makes entrance into the nonhandicapped world possible."

Parents, disabled youth, and members of the helping professions often are so overzealous in efforts to promote physical restoration and intellectual accomplishments that they may overlook some existing constructive efforts in socialization. If disabled adolescents are to adjust to other people and develop sexually, two primary requirements must be met: these youngsters must be given the opportunity to make and learn to maintain contacts with others (305). Associations for the Retarded, the United Cerebral Palsy Associations (UCPA), and the Easter Seal Society, among other agencies for the disabled, have recognized these needs and provided resources for companionship through sports, summer camp experiences, and group activities which include counseling for self-actualization and interpersonal relationships. In addition, there are journals with excellent cues for creative living, such as *Rehabilitation Gazette* and *Accent on Living*, which are written by and for the handicapped (5, 341). These can be read with profit by anyone who admires initiative and wholesome approaches to life and to one's fellow man, which are essentially the bases for satisfying sexuality and good sexual relationships.

Homosexual Behavior: Phases and Facts

Homosexual behavior is sexual activity between two persons of the same sex. It may take such forms as simple touching, kissing, petting, friction, stroking the genitalia, mouth–genital contact, and anal intercourse (for the male) (438). It has been recorded as a minority group phenomenon throughout the ages and is regarded at present in different ways by different societies (140). In many of these, homosexuality is an acceptable substitute when there is no opportunity heterosexual behavior. More often, it is regarded as an alternate form of sexuality that is transitory in character or as a normal healthy form of sexual interaction for those who are potentially bisexual. There is cultural and clinical evidence that homosexuality and heterosexuality are not mutually exclusive forms of behavior. Hoffman points out that homosexual behavior penetrates every socioeconomic, religious, professional, and geographic group and is not restricted to any particular range of intelligence or "looks" —today, one is dealing with "a phenomenon that involves literally millions of Americans." (26)

With respect to civil issues, homosexual conduct between consenting adults is not illegal in most of Western Europe and Canada (414). However, legislation in the United States varies because many politically active people have differing opinions in regard to homosexual behavior: some see it as immoral, abnormal, or indicative of mental illness; others see it as undesirable. Among these are supporters of the 1976 ruling of the U. S. Supreme Court that gives to state legislatures the total responsibility for the legality of consenting private sexual activity between adults. At present, many states have laws still on their books that were based on English common law which at one time decreed homosexual behavior to be a felony. However, in 1968, England changed its stand on the subject and homosexual behavior between consenting adults is no longer against English law (438). The tedious effort required in the United States to repeal old laws state by state, especially in view of charged emotions that are based on ignorance and fear, produces additional problems for homosexuals as well as for administrators, therapists, or researchers in areas related to the study of sexuality. Furthermore, many people who are not interested in homosexuality are concerned about the potential infringement of personal privacy in the Supreme Court ruling. Since the Supreme Court gives to state legislatures the full responsibility for the legality of consenting private sexual activity between adults, there is always the possibility that any of the 50 states could pass laws that are critical of selected aspects of heterosexual, as well as homosexual, alliances. This would violate American concepts of freedom and of privacy rights and could lead to years of confrontation within state courts and confusion around the country. Needless to say, the Gay Liberation group and the National Organization for Women (NOW) Lesbians have opted to challenge this Supreme Court decision. They continue to press for the rights of all *consenting adults* to choose their sexual partners, in their case—homosexual partners. Be that as it may, homosexuality is not a serious threat to our society, even if the warnings of its enemies were accepted at face value. Only about 5% of American males and an even lower percentage of American females are exclusively homosexual throughout their lifetimes. The majority of youth and adults in our society continue to prefer heterosexuality or celibacy.

Research into this complex and controversial area of sexual preference is ongoing but inconclusive (414). Members of the scientific community believe that few homosexuals are so inclined by constitutional forces. However, the etiology of homosexuality in any one person and whether that person should be treated to help him adjust to his homosexuality or readjust to heterosexuality remain serious questions to be decided on an individual basis (276, 414). Even the Commission on Sexuality of the American Medical Association (AMA) could not decide what attitude to take toward this highly complex factor of human behavior. Although the AMA monograph on Human Sexuality exposes and dispels the usual myths and sterotypes about homosexuality by detailing their inaccuracies, it takes no definitive stand on whether or not homosexuality is an alternate sexual behavior or an illness (86). According to Gebhard, the collective opinion of members of the Institute for Sex Research, based on extensive interviewing and other data is that "homosexuality is not a pathology in itself nor necessarily a symptom of some other pathology" (151). Hooker of UCLA states in this same article that homosexuality "as a clinical entity does not exist. Its forms are as varied as are those of heterosexuality." (151) Elsewhere she identifies it as a variation in the sexual pattern that is in the normal range—a minority group phenomenon (26). Both the American Law Institute and the Group for Advancement of Psychiatry have urged that the legal system concern itself with sexual behavior only when it involves a threat of force, activities with a child, invasions of privacy or when it constitutes a public nuisance (380). The American Psychological Association took a similar stand (9).

While parents of able and disabled youngsters who lead sheltered lives tend to feel that homosexuality is far removed from their life-style this is not necessarily so. In the first place, some homosexual behavior exists in many societies, being more common in adolescence than in adulthood. Many youngsters in our society are said to "go through a homosexual phase" (choosing a person of the same sex for one's closest relationships and erotic play). For most people this is not a fixed choice, and the transition to heterosexuality is usually made when opportunity affords it (212). The labeling of what might appear to be "homosexual activity" in childhood and youth is being questioned. Around puberty, the natural curiosity of many youngsters may lead to genital manipulation and exploration. This may occur in same sex or opposite sex company. Actually, the shocked reaction and responses of any adults who come upon it may be the most traumatic part of the experience for the children involved. This so-called sexual play (homo-or hetero-) is devoid of any emotional love commitment. Therefore, it is more an aspect of growing curiosity than sexual orientation per se. It is unlikely that disabled youngsters would not notice their own body changes and wonder about how their friends are also changing. So it is important for parents, rehabilitation staff, and teachers to avoid sensational reactions to instances of exploratory behavior or youthful erotic play.

Emotional reactions of "hating girls" or "hating boys" at adolescence may be more a sign of consolidating masculinity or femininity than of any homosexual trend. Conversely, having a best friend or a bosom pal at this stage of development is a very usual and happy first emancipation from the primary family ties and dependencies. Disabled as well as able-bodied adolescents have such friends. In fact, one of the most beautiful illustrations of this is given in the NOVA film called *Joey*. The blossoming of two severely handicapped, cerebral-palsied, institutionalized boys through their empathetic understanding of one another's needs and abilities is eventually translated to the outside world. Joey's pal, who can barely type, puts down Joey's laboriously dictated thoughts, freeing Joey's mind although his athetoid body remains bound and contorted in his wheelchair (99). The willingness of a pal to see the real person behind the grotesqueness of disability and to find a means of communication is what every youngster needs in his adolescent struggle for identity. This capacity for close friendship must not get lost among the many confusions about relationships that abound today. In fact, it is particularly important to respect and encourage teenage questions such as whether close friendships between people of the same sex will lead to homosexuality. One example of how this question might be handled is taken from *What's Happening*, a magazine put out at Emory University School of Medicine: "It is perfectly natural for friends to spend time together and to show affection for each other, males and females. There is no need to question good warm feelings. And if the subject of sex comes up, remember you are the one who can choose to say no or yes to a male friend as well as to a female friend" (452).

There are situations where a disabled youngster's opportunity for choice is extremely limited however (48). Large, isolated institutions have traditionally maintained same sex enrollment, and too often have same sex staffing. In this setting there is little opportunity to learn appropriate sexual responses or to observe the normal variety of heterosexual relationships. In order to promote natural relationships between the sexes, if students of both sexes are not enrolled, at least some semblance of the cottage system should be attempted. This type of organization assigns a small group of youngsters to a residence that is headed by a couple. While it is no substitute for healthy family life, it does give those youngsters who may be leaving the institution at some time in their lives some exposure to adult roles. As for mixed sex student populations, one can anticipate the many problems this may bring to large, impersonal residences. But the one irrefutable argument that cuts across the many realistic hesitancies is Gordon's priceless quip that "The only way to discourage homosexuality is to risk heterosexuality" (158). Until more realistic settings are provided for institutionalized persons, any homosexuality among these populations has to be viewed with compassionate understanding of the personal search for relationships and love in a restricted environment.

An unrestricted environment may inadvertently direct some disabled youngsters away from heterosexual responses, which is another reason for caution against massive, uncontrolled mainstreaming of impaired youth into unprepared environments. As long ago as 1956, in discussing brain-injured youngsters and their related behavior problems, Anderson wrote:

Several of my male homosexual patients have given histories which were quite similar, namely, that they were inept or clumsy and that they had trouble catching on, and in the area of sports, particularly baseball, they were a total loss. This caused them to be left out of the gang, to be considered "sissies" and therefore unwanted by either girls or boys. The result was involvement in fringe sexual activities, which then became a life pattern. (12)

To conclude this still controversial subject, there are a few "facts" which can be shared with today's youth:

1. Homosexuality is a minority choice; only about 4–10% of adults prefer sex relations with someone of the same sex.
2. Some adults who prefer homosexuality call themselves *gay*. Women are known as *Lesbians*—a term derived from the reputed sensuality of people living in ancient times on the Greek island of Lesbos.
3. There are places where homosexuals are welcome, and there are places where they are not welcome and are in fact, ostracized.
4. Some homosexual behavior exists in many societies, but in 1976, the U.S. Supreme Court gave each of the 50 state legislatures the responsibility for deciding on the legality of homosexuality in its own state. Many citizens agree with Gay Liberationists and NOW Lesbians that whatever any *adults consent* to do *in private* should be legal.
5. Some young people may have one or more homosexual experience, but this rarely inhibits their adult choice of an opposite sex partner when opportunity affords it.
6. The law protects young people against adults who try to force homosexuality (or heterosexuality) on them. Parents and school, institution, or camp authorities should support such laws.
7. Young people have the option to say NO to a peer or to an adult who offers them unwanted sex relations—whether homosexual or heterosexual.

Is Contraception Just a Trip to the Drugstore?

Teenage sexual activity is a growing entity. Between 1971 and 1976, premarital intercourse among young women aged 15–19 increased by 30% (460). This is also documented by the increasing number of pregnancies in this age group (332). More than 200,000 teenagers (85,000 whites and 121,000 blacks) gave birth to out-of-wedlock children in 1974 (447). If the present rates of illegitimacy continue during the next ten years, some 1,500,000 unwed girls will give birth to about 2,000,000 babies by 1984. Unfortunately, morbidity and mortality rates are so high for pregnant teenagers and so many of their infants are developmentally at risk that mere statistics underestimate the problem (327, 457). Add to this the rising incidence of venereal disease among sexually active youngsters who are successfully using contraception or resorting to abortion, and the need for helpful social concern becomes apparent. Educators who promote mainstreaming of the disabled are concerned since they appreciate the impact that new freedoms and problems can have on socially and sexually naive disabled youngsters.

State laws, the policies of professional societies, attitudes of the public, and the behavior of individuals are all changing, but at different speeds in different locations (211, 296). Consider these, plus the many and complex emotional needs which drive the average youth toward increasing sexual activity (327). Then consider irrespective of value judgments, what is the present status of the *technology* on which young people depend for contraception (457). On the one hand are the regulations of the Social Security Amendments of 1967, whereby state agencies must make contraceptive information available to any person of *childbearing* age who asks for it. We also learn from public health studies that 1) condoms are acceptable to adolescents, 2) adolescent males will accept a sizable share of the burden in pregnancy prevention if given the opportunity, and 3) small neighborhood commercial outlets have a potentially important role in nonclinical contraceptive distribution programs (7). On the other hand, we learn from careful studies reviewed by the Child Study Association of America that many sexually active youngsters are seriously misinformed about birth control methods—some believe that pregnancy cannot result from the first sexual experience or cannot happen unless one is married. Others espouse the use of Saran Wrap as a condom or of carbonated beverages as contraceptive douches (whereas they are perfect cultures for bacteria!) Still others risk pregnancy believing that they can rely upon the boy's withdrawal or the girl's capacity to guess her safe period (72)! Even among those who are knowledgeable, one of the most serious barriers to contraceptive use among youth (able or disabled) is the feeling that being prepared is "unromantic." In fact, the counselor who talks to youth about contraception had better keep in mind some of the complex psychological reasons why high schoolers and college students who have free access to protection do not use it. Among discovered reasons are:

1. Unwillingness to acknowledge reality ("He insisted" . . . "She led me on")
2. Caution exceeded by pleasure when there is an opportunity for sex
3. Stereotype of femininity (as pregnable) and masculinity (as virility)
4. Belief that the cloak of motherhood exceeds the social stigma of being unmarried
5. Unconsciously delaying entering the competitive world

6. "Love" between partners (trying to be chosen)
7. Guilt caused by contraceptive readiness because it is misinterpreted as "prostitution"
8. Unconscious desire for pregnancy as the price to be paid for sex play
9. Shame if ignorance of contraceptive techniques is revealed
10. Hopelessness, fatalism, and feelings of nihilism among some poor and disadvantaged

Even though effective contraception is made readily available and proper use is explained carefully, youth will want to know, honestly, how really dependable is it? At Princeton University, a sociologist Ryder, interviewed 6752 women and found that only 4% of pill users and 5% of those using intrauterine devices failed to prevent unwanted pregnancy in the first year. But, 40% of those who douched, 22% who used foam, 21% who used the rhythm method, 17% who used diaphragms, and 10% of those for whom condoms were the birth control device became pregnant within the year (363, 364). These are results for *couples* who use contraception because they want to control the number of children conceived within 5 years. Such couples put forth far more planning and use more caution than may be expected of teenagers. Therefore, those who advocate access to birth control for teenagers and youth must also accept the existing technologic risks accompanied by emotional and intellectual hazards. Some eligibility standards may have to be considered or some backup for contraceptive failure may have to enter original planning unless society is ready to assume responsibility for the children of children.

While dependability, convenience, comfort, availability, and expenses involved in contraception may be general concerns of all groups, a specific that is too often forgotten is that *disability*, like personality, is not a single category. As one wit mentioned to a group of professionals who were sincerely concerned about the contraceptive needs of a variety of physically disabled, mentally retarded, and emotionally labile youth, "Abstinence from sexual intercourse is the no-fail, all-disability solution!"

Under proficient leadership, emotionally disturbed adolescents of high school age can profit from sex education which includes specifics of contraception. Presenting factual material to small groups of disturbed students, followed by open discussion of any question, has been found to provide a milieu in which anxiety is minimized so that learning can occur and feelings be expressed (216). However, it takes more than an adapted sex education group approach with an overview of contraception to deal with youngsters having pathologic distortions of motivation. Close collaboration with the youngsters' psychologists or psychiatrists may be necessary to decide upon a course of action for individuals whose heterosexual interests may be superficial masks for unconscious homosexual urges, desires to dominate rather than to share an interpersonal relationship, or an attempt to use sexual activity at this time to run away from depression, anxiety, dependency, or alienation (344).

Among the physically disabled a contraceptive problem that is at present universally neglected by researchers is the questionable interaction of chemical agents. To date, few studies have been made to identify the interaction of chemical birth control agents (such as the pill, the injectables, or the shots) and the medication taken by some disabled persons for seizures, neuromotor relaxation, hyperactivity of brain damage, diabetes, etc. Also, very little discussion can be found on the feasibility of mechanical contraceptives such as diaphragms and IUDs for girls and condoms for boys when there is a loss of genital sensation as found in spina bifida or when motor dysfunctions such as paralysis, spasticity, and athetosis intervene against convenient and effective use. Poor arm and hand functions make it difficult or impossible for a boy to put on or remove condoms and for a girl to handle a diaphragm. Although many casual sex educators speak with seeming authority about IUDs, one rarely hears the important claim of Scandinavian workers that women who have not been pregnant, given birth, or undergone a recent miscarriage may suffer side-effects with the use of IUDs such as chafing of the uterine mucous membrane which may cause long menstrual periods and spotting between periods (303). While a physically disabled girl who wishes to be sexually active may have no physiologic problems with the pill, how many are emotionally mature enough to plan intercourse or delay desire until it can be fitted into the time that the pill *starts to be effective?* How many really know that it is necessary to refrain from intercourse, or use another means of contraception, during the first 7 days of pill taking during the first cycle— or that girls having 21-day menstrual cycles should avoid intercourse unless other contraceptives are used until they have come to the second cycle of pill use? (231). How many self-elected sex consultants are ready for the counseling and education needed during these emotionally fragile times? It is obvious that much more study must go into these facts and feelings.

With all the talk in America about rights, mainstreaming, or normalization, one has to scrape the literature with a fine tooth comb to come up with any practical pointers on contraceptives that are gleaned from the experiences of young individuals with different disabilities. However, more has been written about the use of contraceptives among the retarded. There are those who believe that basically this population may use the same contraceptives as the nonretarded. They suggest that the simplicity of the IUD for women and the condom for men makes them most appropriate. Because none of the existing methods of contraception are 100% satisfactory, improvements are being sought in the direction of subcutaneous and subdermal progestin implants, progestin-releasing IUDs, prostaglandins, hormonal control of ovulation, postcoital estrogens, and reversible sterilization (240).

Not everyone in the field is willing to make a blanket statement that the retarded can use anything that the nonretarded use. Much depends on the method, the level of the user's intelligence, *and* the supportive guidance of a responsible adult (23, 58, 226). Some capable and reliable retarded girls remember to take the pill, and some boys do learn to use condoms. Although the IUD is popular among family planners who work with the retarded, it can be expelled or pulled out (48, 136). Many planners are in favor of the progestogen Depo-Provera as the contraceptive of choice for retarded youth and adults. It is injectable and remains effective for 90 days. However, the FDA, concerned about side effects, has withheld approval of this drug as a contraceptive. There is no perfect drug; each has to be weighed in terms of lesser alternatives. Many protagonists, including Brenton, of Depo-Provera believe that it holds fewer hazards than other contraceptives—and than hysterectomies which have been resorted to (48).

Family planning for the retarded may also include a clear understanding of the state welfare department's responsibility for providing contraceptive service to all, plus the cooperation of trained personnel, parents, and physicians (156). A specialized family clinic has been set up by the Planned Parenthood of Metropolitan Washington, D. C. to explore the methods of family planning most useful to the mentally retarded. Staff of this special clinic leaned heavily on 1) training suggestions from Kempton, Consultant to Planned Parenthood of Southeastern Pennsylvania, 2) illustrative drawings prepared by Planned Parenthood of Seattle, and 3) a flip chart explaining contraceptives from Planned Parenthood of Northern New York (97). As for the cooperating physicians, a 1970 city-wide study revealed that the education of the medical students, interns, and residents about indications and contraindications and techniques of contraceptive control is "on the basis of our experience, in need of great improvement" (94). If the education of these potential health leaders is questionable when related to the contraceptive needs of the normal population, it may be inferred that applied research and wider training is needed for those who will counsel the disabled.

Doubts and questions related to contraception need not detract from their inestimable value and general usefulness for pregnancy prevention, but more research is essential. Present contraceptive technology must be put in its place, that of a good—but not a "fail-safe"—resource, as it is too often recommended to teenagers by lucky peers or by overindulgent advisers who stop short of including abortion as a backup or sterilization as a responsible alternative.

Sterilization: The Fail-Safe Option?

If intercourse is elected, the only existing 100% fail-safe alternative to contraceptives is sterilization. Voluntary sterilization is increasingly sought in the normal population among adults who feel that they now have all the children that they wish to bear themselves, who are concerned about possible side-effects of the pill, or who object to other methods of contraception. As a result of technologically well-advanced procedures, about 3 million Americans have been voluntarily sterilized (448).

For the male, vasectomies can be done on an outpatient basis, usually in a physician's office under local anesthesia. A cut is made on one side of the scrotum to locate the tube (vas deferens) that transports sperm cells from the testes to the outside. About ½ in. of this tube is removed, the remaining cut ends are tied with silk thread and turned away from each other, and the incision closed. This procedure is repeated on the other side of the scrotum and completed in less than an hour. No gland or organ is removed so the sex hormone continues to be produced and penile erections continue. After a short time, semen without sperm is ejaculated. Pleasure during intercourse is not affected by sterilization.

Women having tubal ligation, laparotomy, laparoscopy, or culdoscopy require only short hospital stays (226). Female sterilization leaves the ovaries intact and does not interfere with menstruation, with the production of those hormones that ensure secondary sex characteristics associated with femininity and sexual response, or with pleasure during intercourse. Modern techniques may be performed under general or local anesthesia.

In tubal ligation an incision is made just below the navel. After locating the fallopian tubes (which carry an egg cell from the ovary to the uterus), the surgeon removes the middle section of each. The separated ends are tied, the incision closed and 3–5 days later the woman goes home. The "Band-Aid-Operation" or laparoscopy can be done on an outpatient basis in less than 30 min. by a qualified physician. A cut is made in the abdomen, only large enough for the surgeon to insert a cylindrical instrument containing a light, a small scissors, and a source of heat. He locates the fallopian tubes, cuts them, seals them with the heat source, and covers the abdominal incision with a Band-Aid so it heals without scarring (38).

These procedures are generally irreversible (446, 448). Although fertility has occasionally been restored to both men and women after complex and expensive surgery, no guarantee is ever given. In spite of this, the popularity for these procedures increases. It is estimated that more than 8 million Americans have chosen sterilization as a means of birth control. However, only 2000–3000 operations a year are performed on persons under 21 and fewer than 300 on persons under 18 (59). The reasons offered for choosing sterilization over other methods of birth control include

1. medically confirmed genetic reasons for not having a child
2. inability to assume responsibility for a child
3. a couple's desire not to produce any more children than they have
4. contraindications to health or capacity to utilize other forms of birth control

The disabled group for which the most data on sterilization exists is that of the mentally retarded. Some reasons for parents favoring this approach for their retarded youngsters are compassionately pointed out by Morgenstern. He cites actual situations, such as that of a mother who sponsored the sterilization operation for her daughter but suffered anxiety since the girl did not know what had been done. Other parents felt such an operation necessary for responsible living in a difficult society, but were also not comfortable with the idea. Another mother felt comfortable about discussing it with her daughter and generally favored the operation. Parents of retarded boys were afraid their sons might be named in a paternity suit by an unscrupulous woman or that they themselves would be responsible for support and care of a baby—so sterilization seemed to them the logical solution to these concerns (285). A recent study of family planning for persons handicapped by mental retardation finds that parents' attitudes to sterilization are influenced by 1) fear of their son getting a girl pregnant or their daughter becoming pregnant out of wedlock, 2) the extent to which the son or daughter may be living or may look forward to living without supervision in the community, 3) participation of their child in community life or opportunity to live in a group home—at which time sterilization would be favored, and 4) the worry of parents with retarded sons living at home that members of the community might overinterpret the boy's erotically suggestive behavior as evidence of possible intent to rape or to employ sexual violence. Parents also fear that their retarded boys may be the first to be viewed with suspicion, even when innocent, in a community where rape or molesting occurs. With antisocial behavior on the increase (or more specifically reported in the media), such anxiety is not without foundation (97).

Although studies of attitudes help to give a wider understanding of any problem, there is no substitute for real life situations to help us focus on potential problems and their possible range of solution. For example, four courts in the United States recently held that the retarded person's rights would be violated by allowing sterilization in the following instances (198):

1. (Texas) A retarded woman had two retarded children and all three were living with her mother, who petitioned for sterilization for the daughter.
2. (Kentucky) The mother of a retarded 35-year-old woman, who had her daughter and the daughter's two children living with her, petitioned for sterilization for her daughter.
3. (California) The father of a retarded adult woman who had no children but who was sexually active petitioned for her sterilization since she had an adverse reaction to contraceptive pills and an IUD was medically contraindicated.
4. (Indiana) The mother of a teenage boy who was permanently brain damaged as the result of a car accident petitioned for an order allowing a vasectomy.

Strong controversy has been stirred up 1) by these decisions, 2) by counter requests for federal regulations that would allow the use of federal funds which "would permit sterilization of incompetent individuals over the age of 18" *only if* "the individual has requested sterilization and has given . . . informed consent," and 3) by a suit filed in New York in January 1976 in which a group of physicians challenged the constitutionality of any federal, state, and local sterilization regulations (106, 109, 198).

In spite of all these legal complications, which eventually may have to be untangled by the Supreme Court, voluntary sterilization—at the request of the individual who will be sterilized and who can pay for it—is legal and available in all states without restrictions, except in Utah where its use is limited to medical necessity. Some physicians may not care to be involved in these procedures, however (38, 226, 448). Information about specific needs or sources of help can be found at local Planned Parenthood groups or by contacting the Association for Voluntary Sterilization (see Appendix D). Involuntary sterilization, on the other hand, has some vociferous opponents, many of whom wish to challenge the 23 states having provisions for compulsory sterilization for mental retardates living in state residences or in sheltered homes supported by public funds. This emotionally laden question has many realistic legal and living complexities which are influenced by the capability and responsibility of the individual in question and the supportive features of the community in which he may live as deinstitutionalization is implemented (59). There is no single solution for all needs, and one of the truly complicating factors is the inability of some professional personnel, as well as laymen, to consider each case on its own merits rather than on generalized emotion or blanket legal solution. For example, most people talk about "the retarded" as if they were a single entity. In the first place, there are several categories of retardation; in the second place, there are physically disabled individuals who fit into each of these categories. The population in question is larger than pure statistics may indicate. Table 2–1 gives the four accepted levels of mental retardation with corresponding IQ ranges for two commonly used intelligence tests (6). Although even people with normal intelligence do not necessarily make wise decisions in matters concerning personal and social action, study is still needed to assess at what level of retardation a decision can be made and responsibly carried out.

According to a survey on "Capacity, Competence, Consent" that was reported in the *Columbia Human Rights Law Review,* it is common law that parental consent suffices to authorize medical treatment for a minor child on the assumption that the treatment is potentially beneficial. The dual incompetence of retarded children complicates the problem of establishing "benefit." An unusually thoughtful overview of these complications is presented in the April 1976 issue of the Hastings Center Report (443). Walters, Director of the Center of Bioethics of the Kennedy Institute at Georgetown University. who is against sterilization, raises the questions of irreversibility of the procedure, dubious benefits, uncertainty of intellectual development of the retarded, etc. However, Gaylin, President of the Institute of Society Ethics and the Life Sciences, and Professor of Psychiatry and Law at Columbia Law School, questions the long-run advisability of transfer of the power of decision from the family to the state. In reviewing the legal dilemmas posed by sterilization when consent is tenuous, he turns to the benefits of social living that it could allow to those retarded who are usually denied

TABLE 2–1. LEVELS OF MENTAL RETARDATION*

LEVEL	IQ STANFORD BINET	IQ WECHSLER SCALES
Mild	68–52	69–55
Moderate	51–36	54–40
Severe	35–20	39–25
Profound	19 and below	24 and below

*Abstracted from AAMD: Manual on Terminology and Classification, 1973

the pleasure of affection, tenderness, and sexual contact for which they may indeed have capacity.

Money, concurs with this concept of benefits of social living. He believes that the beneficial effects of the retardates' capacity for affection, tenderness, and solicitous care of a sexual partner could be encouraged by introducing morally approved sterilization at puberty. Heterosexual love affairs and partnerships might then replace the illicit homosexuality which is the only resource for loving in today's sex segregated residences. He points out how impressed he was by the joy made possible in a Singapore leper colony some years ago when common law marriages were permitted among the residents, provided they did not have children. "We could release the same joy," comments Money, "in our austere mental deficiency institutions which are at present often little better than stock yards" (275).

Is Abortion Out of the Taxicab?

Only in recent years has abortion for the poor and needy left the horrors of self-induced or taxi–coat-hanger butchery for the haven of sterilized clinics and hospitals. However, opinions about its use differ in our multicultural society. Not that the safety is debated. No, indeed, the risk to life and health from early legal abortion by trained practioners in the first trimester of pregnancy has been sharply reduced. Statistics indicate that the risk to life is now far less than that of carrying a pregnancy to term (96). But, what is debated are attitudes toward abortion. Some individuals, and some churches, oppose abortion on what they consider to be moral issues. Other individuals and other churches, as well as the forefront of women's liberation movements, consider it every woman's ethical right to make any decision concerning her own body. They say she should have a *choice* for or against abortion (73). Many individuals in both groups are against transfer of human and family rights to the legislature (3).

One of the great questions of all ages for all groups has been when to look upon embryos and fetuses as "babies." Only as recently as 1975 did experts at the World Health Organization finally reach agreement on 28 weeks' gestation as the time at which a fetus can be regarded as a potential human survivor—"can be considered to have reached a stage of development where it has a reasonable expectation of survival." According to statistics, fewer than 10% of babies delivered at 28 weeks live, even when cared for in the most advanced hospitals. Since brain activity is the critical factor in determining the ability to live, some neurologists suggest that the period between the 28th and 32nd weeks of pregnancy, when human "brain life" begins, should be established as the time that the fetus can be considered to maintain an independent existence (453).

Over the years, society's increasing acceptance of abortion has significantly changed legislation and medical practice regarding legal abortion. By 1970, some states in the U.S. had repealed all abortion laws, while a great many others had either revised their laws drastically or were in the process of doing so (325). Meanwhile, medical complications from illegal abortions in New York dropped from 6524 in 1969 to 3253 in 1973—a 50% drop due to availability of hygienic legalized abortion! Similar experience in municipalities across the nation influenced the Supreme Court decision of January 22, 1973, which declared the abortion laws of two states to be unconstitutional invasions of the right of privacy. Thus, the right to free choice was restored, and a new set of considerations evolved from this decision: the question of a husband's consent and of parents' consent relevant to minors or incompetents (16, 448).

To understand whether abortion is available to or prohibited for disabled youth who are sexually active, it is necessary to keep abreast of legal trends (319, 319a). By the end of 1975, an 18-year-old unmarried woman could legally consent for all aspects of her medical care, including contraception, in 46 states and the District of Columbia; she could consent to an abortion in 49 states and the District (319). However, in only 25 states and the District may girls under 18 obtain abortions without parental consent. A recent study in New York City revealed that the average single person who had an abortion was in the 18–24 year age range, was white, had finished high school, and had taken some undergraduate courses. Upon further inquiry, it was discovered that these girls used either no contraceptive method or a less effective one (333, 437). Interestingly enough, this is paralleled by a report on young women 13–28 who were admitted to two state psychiatric hospitals. Of 41 sexually active, 17 of them had 26 pregnancies as a result of laxity or ineptitude with contraceptives. Of these 26 pregnancies, 11 were aborted and 15 resulted in live births; 7 babies were kept by the mothers. These histories of girls in both normal and emotionally labile populations suggest a high incidence of unprotected intercourse, unwanted pregnancy and unwanted birth (1). An additional complication of the psychiatric group was that the children born to those girls were rejected and then became wards of the state. Obviously, sex education and meaningful counseling are inadequate at present.

A survey of the literature related to abortion for physically disabled or retarded youth shows no specific studies on this topic. Actually, this decision for or against abortion is not made on the basis of any one or another disability. Rather, it is related to the *nurturing capacity* and the *responsibility for family life* of the pregnant girl and her mate—be they able or disabled. Therefore, most references in articles or books on individuals with handicaps will be equivalent to, "For specific information about abortion, consult your physician, your local Planned Parenthood Association or your City and County Health Department" (448).

Although abortion is a topic that evokes strong feelings pro and con, many people are unfamiliar with present day medical technology for abortion. The most effective modern technique is vacuum aspiration without anesthesia and with, or without, paracervical block. This outpatient technique has been used up to the 12th week of pregnancy without any deaths in 22,000 cases, ranging in age from 13–56 years, studied in Yugoslavia and 26,000 cases from

July 1970 to August 1971 studied at the Center for Reproductive and Sexual Health, Inc. in New York City (31, 295). English experience with outpatient abortions suggests that the patient should return for consultation at 48 hours and 7 days after termination of pregnancy—and possibly 4–6 weeks later— and modern clinics observe this (2). At present world-wide research indicates that there does not appear to be more satisfactory methods of terminating a *second*-trimester pregnancy than the saline procedure or hysterotomy, but techniques will improve with research (16). Also, the need for later abortion will diminish with improvement in contraceptives, improved pregnancy detection tests, and greater acceptance of legalized early abortion for adults and minors. Current pregnancy detection methods do not work until 8–15 days after a missed menstrual period and are sufficiently inaccurate to lead to abortion for false pregnancies in 20–40% of cases. However, a new 1-hour test for detecting pregnancy as early as one week after fertilization, has been reported by endrocrinologist–biochemist Saxona of New York–Cornell Medical Center. This test, which requires only a few drops of blood, has been evaluated by Landesman on more than 500 patients with 100% accuracy (235).

The influence of abortion on the mental health of girls and women who elect it is stated in one careful study as "without any ill effect and no guilt feelings or psychological illnesses" (218). A recent report of the World Health Organization indicates that in spite of cultural differences, where pre- and postassessments have been made of women electing abortion, psychologic benefit commonly results. An often forgotten item that this report includes is that adverse reactions have been observed in women who have been *refused* this option (204). Other studies show that evidence of conflict at the time of the decision is not an indication of future psychologic problems. In fact, sexually active teenage girls do not see abortion as a single panacea, but can accept it without guilt if *unwanted* pregnancy occurs as a result of contraceptive failure or failure to use contraceptives (7).

Abortion counseling at ethical social agencies or clinics is not "for abortion" as its enemies claim. It aims to assist the pregnant woman to come to a decision about an unwanted pregnancy, to implement the decision, and to control future fertility. Most professionals agree that counseling "should be supportive, nonjudgmental and educational" (15). To ensure this, the American Public Health Association recommends the following four standards:

1. Counseling should serve, when appropriate, to simplify and expedite the provision of abortion services. It should not impose unnecessary medical risk by delaying the obtaining of these services.
2. Psychiatric consultation should be available, but not mandatory. As in the case of other specialized medical services, psychiatric consultation should be sought for definite indications and not on a routine basis.
3. Abortion counselors may be drawn from the ranks of highly skilled physicians as well as trained, sympathetic individuals working under appropriate supervision.
4. Preventive measures, including contraception and/or sterilization, with

specific plans for follow-up should be discussed with each abortion patient (15).

VD: How Unromantic Can You Get?

A survey of 30 major cities in the U.S. reported by the *New York Times* stated that gonorrhea is rampaging throughout the country. Venereal disease (VD) was reported as "now the nation's most common communicable disease, except for the common cold. Teenagers in the 15–19 year bracket may be the second largest group of VD sufferers" (369). Among the factors responsible for this situation, public health officials list: increased promiscuity, especially among youngsters, including those from the middle classes; general ignorance; and "ostrich-like behavior on the part of victims who refuse to name their contacts, as well as educational institutions that oppose teaching of VD prevention in schools" (34, 159, 369).

Actually, no fewer than 13 diseases are known to be transmitted sexually, including syphilis and gonorrhea. Most of them can be easily cured or prevented, but if left untreated, they can have serious consequences. If parents, educators, and the young people themselves fail to heed warnings, millions of youngsters will run the risk of blindness, arthritis, sterility, and pain from gonorrhea or insanity, paralysis, heart disease, disfiguration, and death from syphilis (388).

VD is a problem which must be faced by the mentally and physically disabled as well as by the general population—now more than ever, since mainstreaming brings the groups into frequent contact with each other at socially vulnerable stages of development (365). The concurrent advantages of integration should be demanded, that is, disabled youth should have the opportunity to use educational resources for teenagers who are already functioning among the general population. Three basic elements responding to youth's need for awareness about VD are 1) crisis resources or information channels such as the "hot lines" that youngsters can dial for facts, for information about resources, for panic relief; 2) diagnostic and free treatment facilities at accessible community locations; 3) preventive education—for parents and for youngsters via the media, the libraries, the schools, etc (74).

While many parents and educators of the disabled are willing to include this topic among their responsibilities, they often have difficulty in knowing where to start. The truism that you start with what the student already knows is quite applicable. In a discussion with a group of multiply handicapped youth, a male nurse asked the blunt question: "VD, or venereal diseases— do you know what they are, how to identify them, and what has to be done to prevent or to treat them?" In reply, he found much misinformation as well as sheer ignorance, even among high schoolers (339). At the level of teenage educable mental retardates, a study revealed that this group "lacks knowledge in conception, contraception and venereal disease—a need for education in these areas for both parent and the adolescent is stressed" (175). The experience of a nurse–educator with a group of hospitalized disturbed adolescents was similar. Student reactions, documented in daily progress notes, included anxiety, anger, empathy, openness, and rejection. There was noticeable reluctance on the part of some members of the group to discuss venereal disease or to take free materials about it, although they helped themselves liberally to materials on other aspects of sex education seminars. In the long run, this nurse–educator found that, when classes were organized around factual material, in a tolerant milieu, open discussion of frightening feelings and learning can occur (216).

Some parents and educators find local Health Department materials useful; others are more comfortable with such materials as those of Planned Parenthood or Child Study Associations. As a starter for parents, teachers, and youth, the common sense book, *Facts about VD for Today's Youth,* is written in down-to-earth, considerate fashion by Gordon (159), an educator who has had many years of contact with exceptional youth. This topic is also covered within the curricula of agencies listed in Appendix D. For example, the Special Education Curriculum Development Center of Iowa University has a section on venereal disease in *A Social Attitude Approach to Sex Education for the Educable Mentally Retarded* (269).

WHAT'S MY THING?

The disabled teenager with a healthy curiosity about sex is bound to look around for "authorities" as well as for opportunities to get feedback on his feelings and opinions. En route to becoming a decision-making individual, he'll be tapping different resources; so it behooves us to look at the state of the art of today's *people* resources (452).

Sex Education: Who Needs It?

Historically, parents were the original objectors to any sex education outside the home. They had very definite ideas and felt in control of their life situation and that of their youngsters. However, the freedom of the media, the exposure to varied cultures and the recent trends toward keeping disabled individuals in the community (mainstreaming) have raised parental anxieties. Parents are not always clear regarding what their youngsters know, or should know, about sex (164). In fact, many cannot bring themselves to discuss topics like masturbation, homosexuality, or sexual intercourse with their children. Many parents feel that knowing too much too early may lead to sexual misbehavior, but most experts have an opposite view. They find that sexual behavior comes from experimenting with the unknown out of curiosity (339). As a result, many parents are now the first to agree that they are the ones who should be having sex education, and some of the best programs keep parents abreast of topics and materials covered in school classes.

Historically, it was also believed that a good higher education presented factual, sensible, ethical knowledge about sex. However, this area of biologic facts, psychologic impacts, ethical variations, and social consequences is too complex to leave to what is called the "liberal arts." In a handbook for teachers and counselors, Foote (50) presents a thought-provoking essay wherein he states, "In terms of the ultimate effect, it may be far more important to introduce sex education into the training of teachers than into the curricula of students."

Furthermore, it came as a jolt to some people that, when Yale turned coed in 1969 (600 women to 4200 men), not only was it necessary for the health staff to meet female needs, but also students needed help, advice, and services relating to sexual problems (402). In fact, when the report *Sex and the College Student* was completed (173), one reviewer suggested that it should be given the widest possible circulation—among teachers, students, parents, alumni, and the general public as well as among the deans and other college officers to whom it was primarily addressed—"the report's developmental perspective and respect for the individual, if more widely shared, could create a revolution of honesty and understanding far more important than any 'sexual revolution' that has so far occurred" (228).

Although a physician used to be considered the family's healer, moral crutch, and revered advisor, the increased demands for health care and the political failure to support the education of sufficient physicians to meet this demand leave the physician little time for the listening ear and compassion that once marked the family doctor. Therefore, it should come as no surprise to see a comment such as: "The education of medical students, interns and residents as to *indications, contraindications* and *techniques* of contraception control is, on the basis of our experience, in need of great improvement (94, 436). To this, it should be added that young physicians need to learn how to work with other professionals and delegate responsibility appropriately in the psychologic areas. Individuals who seek counsel may be helped by the physician, parent, educator, counselor, etc. to develop decision-making skills for the alternatives available to them in their particular life-styles and their particular developmental attainments.

Unfortunately, too many adults of all professions are jumping on the "sex bandwagon" as if they were out to sell the disabled a product. For example, a sincerely worried remedial teacher cried out at a recent rehabilitation staff conference, "How can I push sexuality without frustrating those who can't use it?" This person, obviously, confused sex with sexuality; sex is only the genital part of sexuality, although there *are* aspects of genital sex which do not involve intercourse which are relevant to adolescents. This person also confused his role. Neither sex nor sexuality need to be "pushed."

The educator in all disciplines needs to learn 1) how to assess the developmental level of the adolescent he is addressing, 2) what materials are available for himself and the student at that level, 3) what interpretations (to and from street language, audiovisuals, tactile aids, etc.) may be necessary, 4) what legal rights or responsibilities are involved, 5) to whom to go or to whom to refer the adolescent when the contact person's information or capacity to counsel has reached its limit, and finally, 6) how to direct information toward the nonintercourse and nongenital aspects of a young person's personality and growth which lay the foundations of sexuality when parental or agency permission is not granted for specific discussion of intercourse. Sexual behavior is a function of the total personality within a multicultural society. Correspondingly, sex education must be broadly conceived and should incorporate biology, psychology, and special factors affecting the student's personal, interpersonal, and social relationships. Furthermore, it should be reality-oriented, recognizing not only personal fantasies or ideal norms but also possible sexual options at the decision-making level of the inquirer (157, 232, 438). Today, another reality-orientation required of sex education is awareness, not only of teenagers' options for sexual behavior but also of the varied legal impact on specific actions and needs (193a). Legislated confirmation of minors' rights has moved during the 1970s into the areas of health care and sexual matters. All states now have laws permitting minors to consent to venereal disease treatments on their own. Many have similar provisions relative to contraception and pregnancy, but the variations in legislation and its interpretation from state to state must be considered. The ramifications of this may be seen in Appendix L. The appendix presents the age of majority and the ages at which state legislation, court action, or attorneys' general opinions have specifically affirmed the legal right of individuals to consent for medical care in general, for contraceptive services, for examination and treatment of pregnancy and venereal disease, and for abortion. It illustrates the varied legal stance of the 50 states and the District of Columbia, as of December 31, 1975. On July 1, 1976, the United States Supreme Court decided two cases that substantially expanded—yet qualified—the right of access of adolescents to safe, effective sex-related health services. As summarized by Paul, these two decisions (Danforth and Bellotti) mark a major step in eliminating parental consent requirements which have prevented young people from obtaining such needed sex-related health services as contraception and abortion (319a). Specifically, parents can no longer arbitrarily veto a younster's request for abortion and the constitutionality is doubtful of common law parental consent requirements for all sex-related medical services, including contraception. However—a very important "however" in the case of many developmentally disabled youth—a minor's right to consent for any medical service depends on the minor's ability to demonstrate sufficient intelligence and maturity to establish that he or she is capable of giving "informed consent." In this regard, the minor must understand the nature of the proposed medical procedure, the risks involved and the available alternatives and must have the capacity to make an intelligent and informed choice. In assisting minors to understand the "nature of proposed medical procedures, risks, alternatives," etc., the sex educator now has the additional responsibility of supplementing his compassion with knowledge of legislative realities.

Unfortunately, many are hawking the same wares to developmentally disabled individuals as they are to others who may have experienced some actual dysfunction of sex organs as a result of accident or disease processes. The educator must learn a *range* of options and learn how to offer them to those who are guardians of the adolescent or to those adolescents who have decision-making capabilities and the permission to use them. The sexuality specialists and sex educators cannot sluff off their responsibilities by citing predominantly biologic stresses. As Wolfe has mentioned in a related context, "We have a species-specific capacity to be not only human but humane" (454). To be humane recognizes not only personal desires but also personal responsibilities toward other people, be they sexuality relationships, sex partners, potential offspring for which care is questionable, etc.

There *are* parents, educators, health professionals, members of the legal profession, and contact care personnel who recognize the gaps in their own learnings, who are sharing their experience and studies, who are open to the very real issues in the life of each young person with a disability, and who are willing to search compassionately as each young person in this multiculture asks, "What's my thing?" Others must join them on behalf of the disabled adolescent (163).

The Search: Where Is My Model? What to Believe?

The search for identity is the "American condition" (85) and the sex search refers to the genitalization of one's personal identity (255). This poses problems for American youth who live in a many-rooted society where too often people feel rootless, uprooted, or confused. These feelings complicate sexual goals and subsequent sexual behavior. Some professionals gloss over or avoid the critical decisions that have to be made by adolescents and youth. They hide behind a cloak of words wherein sexuality is discussed with seeming expertise, but too often it is equated with popular fetishes such as stroking seminars, primal screaming, automobiles for sensuality, or health foods for abstinences. The true search, as identified by Maddock, is the very realistic compound question: *"At what ages, under what circumstances, with whom and in what forms is genital activity to take place in a person's life—and with what results, both for the individual and society?"* (255).

Youth, as well as their advisors, must face the many components that require consideration if sex is not to be divorced from responsibility and if a romantic unreality is not to substitute for those interpersonal relationships to which the sexual act brings mutual growth. For the adolescent, able or disabled, premarital sexual conduct (homosexual or heterosexual) has many possibilities: 1) abstinence, 2) continence, 3) masturbation, 4) chastity, 5) necking, 6) petting to orgasm—experimental or romantic, 7) "going all the way"—experimental or only if attracted to someone, if engaged, or if some interpersonal contract of fidelity has been reached, 8) with or without planned protection (contraception, sterilization, or abortion (112, 177). The decision an individual makes should help to develop a social life, including relationships with the opposite sex, that is physically and emotionally satisfying as well as personally and socially responsible.

It is important that the young person, as well as his would-be advisors, realize that even in the event of complete protection from procreation there will still be developmental struggles depending upon the individual's capacities and goals, and the complementary capacities and goals of any partner in exploration. Adolescents and adults advising them must face realistic questions about their sexuality; and society, itself, must face some of the searching questions posed by Sorensen (401):

1. Must sexual intercourse remain a key expression of independence among so many young people?
2. Is permission for sexual infidelity to be an important dimension of love in many people's lives?
3. Will sexual satisfaction in its deepest physical sense be increasingly ignored by adolescents in favor of the hurried desire for nonvirgin status?
4. Is sex to become for some adolescents a tool for regarding and punishing one's self and others?
5. Can more adolescents consider sexual intercourse a loving act when taking precautions against VD and unwanted pregnancies? How can they be persuaded to feel so?

Where Is Society At? When we ask anyone to face up to these questions, it is only fair to start by finding out, "where is society at?" Now that communication makes the average person, able or disabled, part of a world culture, such casual items of world-wide opinions as published in TIME recently are in the public domain:

These days nobody expects Miss World to be a blue-eyed virgin," said Julia Morley of the British organization, Mecca Ltd., that runs the annual contest. She should know. Last year's Miss World, Marjorie Wallace of Indiana, was dethroned by Mecca after 14 weeks because her busy love life was grabbing headlines. This year the judges went out of their way to avoid looking so stuffy. They chose Unmarried Mother Helen Morgan, 22, of Wales. But no sooner had Helen picked up her $7,000 cash prize than she had a fit of conscience. Three years ago, she had a fling with a former Cardiff nightclub manager named Raymond Lovegrove ("She always insisted on going home to her boy friend every night," said Lovegrove and now his wife Linda is threatening to sue him for divorce, naming Helen as correspondent). Reluctant to hurt her 18-month-old son Richard (the child of former boy friend Boutique Owner Christopher Clode) by more publicity, Helen abdicated. It was back to virgins for Mecca. The new Miss World, Runner-Up Anneline Kriel, 19, of South Africa, whose boy friend is a theological student, says: "I will ward off the wolves. In South Africa, it is important for a girl to be a virgin when she marries" (141).

The national U.S. scene is no less varied in its printed confidences. One need not have read the article which prompted these responses* to get the messages (142):

To The Editors:
    During the past year I have not read a single article on present day sex mores in America that does not leave out some vital question germane to the subject under discussion. This is glaringly evident in the article "Kids, Sex and Doctors" (Nov. 25). What is left out is *responsibility*. If Leah Newman, 16, is living away from home and supporting herself, then her statements hold good. But if she lives at home, supported

by her parents, then she has a responsibility to them and they have a responsibility to her—a responsibility larger than just supplying food, clothing and lodging. There must be some moral guidance and some rules of conduct. She is asking for license, not freedom. If there is to be any moral integrity in America, we must recognize that every "right" has a corresponding responsibility, and when we demand our rights without accepting our responsibilities, our moral sensibilities are lopsided.

W. W.
North Ferrisburg, Vt.

May I ask Leah Newman, the doctors, civil liberties groups, and all who advocate medical services for teenagers where "sex is concerned without involving the parents," if they will keep the parents uninvolved when it comes to billing for these services and paying for contraceptives? Will they care for these kids in their homes while the kid is getting over VD, the abortion and/or related trauma?

S. B.
Woodside, N.Y.

Society exhibits even more ambiguous values toward individuals with disability—irrespective of their developmental capacities. The enormity of the problem may be glimpsed by looking at a few illustrations from real life. For example, there is earnest study and general acceptance of sex education and family life responsibilities for the blind. Society gives its stamp of approval to verbal descriptions or to plastic models devised to help blind adolescents learn about the physical aspects of sexuality and sex. However, verbal descriptions or hard plastic models can innocently convey many possible misconceptions to a youngster who has never seen the opposite sex or felt another's body—especially true of only children in single parent families. On the other hand, the concept of allowing a blind person to touch a member of the same sex at different growth stages or of the opposite sex at any stage is not totally socially acceptable as yet, nor have any general seminars questioned whether it should or should not be an accepted value (386).

Turning to other inequities, the retarded are incorrectly lumped as a social and legislative unity in spite of wide differences in capacity for responsibility (215) or even moral judgment. While assessment of moral judgment is in its early stages in our culture, Kohlberg's developmental sequence indicates one possible direction for future research related to individuals with developmental lag. Very briefly, Kohlberg postulates that there are six stages of moral growth within three major levels which apply to people in general. At the Preconventional Level, children in Stage 1 recognize whether something is good or bad by whether they are punished or rewarded. In Stage 2, right action is considered whatever satisfies the individual's needs. At the Conventional Level, children in Stage 3 try to maintain the expectations of their family group, or nation, for these are perceived as valuable in their own right. In Stage 4, right behavior consists of doing one's duty, showing respect for authority, and maintaining the given social order for its own sake. At the Post-Conventional or Autonomous Level, those in Stage 5 define right action in terms of general individual rights and standards that have been critically examined and agreed upon by a whole society. Finally, in Stage 6, right is defined in accord with self-chosen ethical principles having a universality beyond the group, the country, etc. (232). A certain level of mental maturity is necessary for a given level of moral judgment; this is where more research relevant to the retarded is indicated. However, cognitive maturity in itself does not assure moral judgment. While all morally advanced children are bright, not all bright children are morally advanced since other aspects of the personality and its environment are strong contributing factors (103). It is possible also to conceive of positive personality and environmental factors which may enable some mentally retarded individuals with less limited cognitive abilities to maintain a moral stage of development that is compatible to specific responsibilities and privileges of sexual and social life. More study is needed in this area. (232).

Many states arbitrarily make it a crime for a man to have intercourse with a mentally deficient woman. In other states compulsory sterilization and voluntary sterilization laws name broad categories of disabilities, but often fail to differentiate between those in these categories (mentally ill, epileptic, etc.) who are capable of responsibility and those who are not. The problem is compounded by the rights of the disabled to give voluntary consent, the rights of children to a good home and competent, responsible parents, the problems of the helping professions to act responsibly in a confrontation atmosphere, etc. (318). In other words, decisions on social values for different levels of individuals who have disabilities and for those who would hope to act responsibly on their behalf need to be shifted from legal confrontation to cooperation in our multicultural society.

Disabled Adolescents: Options and Values. Where is the disabled adolescent in this social environment which seems to have many options but simultaneously lags in laying the preparatory groundwork? Havighurst, believing that the period from ages 12–18 is primarily one for social and emotional learning, has prepared a list of developmental tasks for adolescence. When this list was presented to disabled as well as normal young people, essentially the same rank order was given to these ten developmental tasks by both groups (188):

1. Achieving new and more mature relations with age mates of both sexes
2. Achieving a masculine or feminine social role
3. Accepting one's physique and using the body effectively
4. Achieving emotional independence of parents and other adults
5. Achieving assurance of economic independence
6. Selecting and preparing for an occupation
7. Preparing for marriage and family life
8. Developing intellectual skills and concepts necessary for civic competence
9. Desiring and achieving socially responsible behavior
10. Acquiring a set of values and an ethical system as a guide to behavior

Since sexuality is an evolving, dynamic force that can only be understood in relation to the rest of development at any particular phase, it is impossible to generalize about individual sexual behavior. Among members of the normal population similar actions may have totally different meanings, depending upon the individual and the context. For example, premarital intercourse may be a consequence of maturation for one college student, but a symptom of deep-seated feelings of inadequacy for another; homosexual behavior may be a transitional experiment for one adolescent, but a token of serious psychopathology for another. Premature labeling, like automatic and inflexible discipline, fails to recognize that sex is only one aspect (albeit a crucial aspect) of the student's overall development (173). Therefore, in considering guiding values for exceptional persons, Maddock (255) asks us to understand their sexuality

in relation to his or her physical, mental, emotional and social development so that appropriate channels of sexual expression can be discovered . . . to provide accurate information and sound guidance with the goal of enabling the exceptional person to become sexually active as his or her capacities, his or her physical and emotional health, and the welfare of other persons of society will allow.

It is important for professional workers to keep in mind the two levels of present day approaches to sexuality: first, the general goals and, second, the highly individualized needs of the disabled person within the context of his particular life-style. Since sexuality of the retarded is gaining increased attention, these two levels may be clarified by illustrations from that area. General goals may have group considerations as well as individual considerations. A recent group action by the new California Department of Health mandates that *provisions shall be made toward heterosexual interaction appropriate to the residents' "developmental level" in state facilities for the mentally retarded.* Speaking at a 2-day meeting on Human Sexuality and the Mentally Retarded sponsored by the California State Departments of Mental Hygiene and Public Health, held in July 1973 at Sonoma (California) State Hospital, McKean discussed the implications of this mandate for professional and nonprofessional staffs of the institutions, parents of the retarded, and other members of the general public. He indicated that this mandate will have a number of controversial aspects, as well as conflicts between various rights and sets of mores. The conference, attended by key staff members in state hospitals, regional centers, and community programs for the retarded, dealt in large part with the development of sex education programs for the retarded. Referring particularly to this new mandate, Sandtner, who developed the Sonoma State Hospital's sex education program for the retarded, warned that the needs and fears of parents, professional and nonprofessional staff, and others dealing with the retarded in the community must be considered along with the needs of the retarded themselves (64).

Another statement of general goals of sexuality, which grew out of years of experience with retarded populations in institutions and the community, is Gordon's *Sex Rights for People Who Happen To Be Handicapped.* This booklet should be read to fully appreciate the following list in its humane context (161):

1. People with special needs, as all people, should have free access to information on sexuality and birth control.
2. Masturbation is a normal expression of sex no matter how frequently it is done

and at what age. It becomes a compulsive, punitive, self-destructive behavior largely as a result of guilt, suppression and punishment.

3. All direct sexual behavior should be in privacy. Recognizing that institutions and hospitals for the retarded, mentally ill and delinquent are not built or developed to ensure privacy, the definition of what constitutes privacy in an institution must be very liberal—bathrooms, one's own bed, the bushes, basements are private domains.

4. Anytime a physically mature girl and boy have sexual relations, they risk pregnancy.

5. Unless they are clear about wanting to have a baby and the responsibility that goes with childbearing, both male and female should use birth controls. (Staff should not condition girls of any age to believe that every woman wants and must have babies in order to be "normal.") Birth control services and genetic counseling should be available to all disabled adults.

6. Until you are, say 18, society feels you should not have intercourse. After this, you decide for yourself—providing you use birth control.

7. Adults should not be permitted to use children sexually.

8. In the final analysis, sexual behavior between consenting adults (regardless of mental age) and whether it is homo or hetero, should be no one else's business —providing there is little risk of bringing an unwanted child into this world.

The following additional factors need to be considered:
1. We need greater acceptance of abortion as a safe, legal alternative to bringing an unwanted child into this world.
2. Voluntary sterilization can be desirable protection for some individuals who can function perfectly well in a marriage if there are no children.

While these general goals and "rights" are increasingly useful for enhancing communication in heretofore hush-hush areas, there is no substitute for examining the specific merits of individual situations (416a). For example, there are three retarded youngsters: Girl A, Girl B, and Girl C. Many people think of them in terms of stereotypes, i.e., what to do about these retarded girls. True, the three are amiable, trusting all grownups almost to a fault; they all try hard and succeed at simple tasks assigned to them. Does society hold the same sexual options for them—should it? Actually, Girl A is a ward of the state which has the authority to see that she continues an asexual childlike existence in a sex segregated institution. However, the state does not have the authority to offer birth control, sterilization, or abortion (if indicated) nor does it wish to be confronted with the legal responsibility for any child which might be the issue of a more liberal policy. Girl B has been released from an institutional setting by authorities who believe in blanket integration of the handicapped into their communities. Unhappily, funds were not available to help the community build the necessary supportive resources. Furthermore, the parents of Girl B are both employed and of a religious faith which does not accept contraception or abortion, and they have no consultation available for guidance on the one hand or consideration of sterilization on the other. This premature ejection into an unprepared community and parental policy leaves a young girl alone at home for many hours without protection in a permissive environment. Actually, Girl B is part of a large family clan of boy and girl cousins where peer activities are carefully kept from adult scrutiny by the more alert youngsters. As a result, she lives a hazardous existence, at least sexually. On the other hand, Girl C whose capacities are identical to A and B, has parents who supply permissive support—they can afford a trade school geared to her work potential, they have collaborated with her counselor on sex education, on the use of contraceptives with consideration for abortion—if necessary and if needed, and on consideration of sterilization since Girl C will never be able to assume responsibility for child rearing. Blanket decisions about sexual options are also made for disabled youth and are equally questionable as those generalizations for "the" retarded. For example, we find two young men, D and E, who are alike in most characteristics and could easily be taken for one another in group situations or even by some professional generalizations. Both have had moderate physical disabilities since birth, but having above-average intelligence and being industrious by habit they have reached high school and have professional potential which will render their disabilities no vocational handicap. However, Youth D has accepted his visible disability and made friends at camps for the handicapped as well as at high school with normal peers. He has no compunctions about dating normal or handicapped girls, as long as they are fun to be with and find him so. On the other hand, Youth E has never accepted his disability and has gone to all measures to avoid other people with disabilities. He has always striven to substitute study and work for recreation and friendships. His scholarship overnormal integration goal may bring him in contact in the future with a partner who takes joy in fulfilling this desire, or it may leave him in a no man's land of unattainable hopes. As a counselor for the multihandicapped explains so tenderly,

Handicapped teenagers and young adults are subject to the same cultural influences that we are. For the most part, they expect, and desire, to meet and fall in love with beautiful girls or handsome men, not handicapped, who fit their image of the idealized sex object. Some achieve this dream. Others are faced with the agonies of "settling for" something less ideal, perhaps another mildly handicapped person (299).

As Freeman points out,

with the onset of adolescence, multiple changes occur which makes the previous adaptation (of a handicapped individual) less successful (145):
1. There may be actual deterioration in physical condition, either permanent or transient.
2. The adolescent (and his parents) must gradually give up the fantasy of being cured "some day."
3. Peers may become acutely aware of differences, so that the patient may feel even more left out than before.
4. The handicap may preclude certain activities which provide social status and feelings of competence as driving, dancing and athletics. Physical attractiveness, particularly for girls, is of great importance.
5. Sexual maturation brings with it problems of impulse expression and great parental and neighborhood concern—for example, a boy whose indiscriminately affectionate behavior was formerly "cute" may be arrested when he snuggles up to strange girls after adolescence.
6. Leaving school may be a shock, since realistic preparation for vacation may have

been inadequate or the staff at work may be much less tolerant than special educators were.
7. There may be a changeover of professional staff dealing with the child and his family at this crucial time and it may be difficult for adult services to "pick up the pieces."

These sobering pointers from a thoughtful psychiatrist who has counseled the disabled and their parents for many years are cited to help us all to remember the individual consideration which each individual needs as his search for personal identity widens to include his sexual freedom. Sexual freedom (one aspect of human freedom discussed by Bandura [19] is defined here

in terms of the number of options available to people and their right to exercise them. The more behavioral alternatives and social prerogatives people have, the greater is their freedom of action . . . Behavioral deficits restrict possible choices and otherwise curtail opportunities to realize one's preferences. Freedom can therefore be expanded by cultivating competencies . . . in maximizing freedom, a society must place some limits on conduct because complete license for any individual is likely to encroach on the freedom of others.

For the able, as well as the disabled, sexual freedom is a learning process: learning to choose among alternatives where one tries to understand the duties and responsibilities inherent in the selection, as well as its rights and privileges. After all, no individual can exist outside of some supportive social net—each must find his personal oasis.

DISABLED YOUTH'S DILEMMA

In our highly technical and increasingly specialized way of modern life, adolescents and youth are forced to mark time before the economic world can absorb them. Today's economic unreadiness to accept youth distorts centuries of cultural practice wherein a transition was made during this stage of life from a state of total socioeconomic dependence to one of relative independence. We live in times when this transition is continually pushed ahead: after high school . . . after college . . . after graduate work . . . etc. Disability only serves to aggravate the delay.

Both the physical transition, from the initial appearance of secondary sex characteristics to sexual maturity, and the psychologic processes of identification that develop from those of a child to those of an adult are ignored in our overbusy world, unless they happen to turn up as a delinquency. In cases of disability society has concentrated on what is not working, physically or mentally, and thereby has avoided the many wholesome possibilities that could contribute to a meaningful way of life for the disabled. However, a new trend is on the horizon. Nordquist is in the forefront of this trend when she observes that the sexual problems of disabled youth would be less acute if more harmonious attitudes existed in the environment—parents, relatives, staff at organizations, and the average person with whom the disabled come in contact. All these people need good, practical sex education, combined with some knowledge of the sexual limitations and possibilities in disability and tempered with wholesome good will (305).

Every person, and especially the disabled adolescent, needs a support system that will augment his or her strengths and facilitate mastery of the environment. In this case, *mastery* implies being a part of an interacting world and *support system* implies the "enduring pattern of continuous or intermittent ties that play a significant part in maintaining the psychological and physical integrity of the individual over time" (66). Without such support systems, young people are left in confusion, their identity development may be arrested. Sexually this can lead either to concentration on early genital activity without intimacy, or conversely, on ignoring the genital element and becoming blindly absorbed in social, artistic, or intellectual fads which could lead to permanent weakness of genital polarization with the other sex (127, 128):

If individuals who comprise the support system were knowledgeable in the wholesome aspects of sexuality, sex education could begin at the beginning, subtly developing concepts and attitudes toward masculinity and feminity from infancy (391). Then adolescents, including the disabled adolescent, would be ready for sex instruction, having responsibilities as well as privileges, and would be better prepared to deal with the titillating impact of modern audiovisual media and with the bravura of their contemporaries.

There have been earnest, studious efforts made by the Child Study Association and by Planned Parenthood to include problems of disabled youth in their educational materials. In recent years momentum has increased. The Institute for Family Research and Education has sponsored a National Family Sex Education Week. It is their contention that since parents are the one continuous contact from infancy, they are the main sex educators of their children. Cooperation among religious, educational, health and government organizations is urged in order to give parents positive reinforcement in this very dynamic area (205a). This spirit of cooperation is an innovative step that will help parents of disabled youngsters and could be useful to the "proxy parents" who comprise the helping professions. The recent thrust to acquaint disabled adolescents with their sexuality is not enough. They must be helped to handle their sexuality responsibly.

3 DATING, COURTSHIP, AND MARRIAGE: Relationships and Options

Man is his own Pygmalion and in fashioning himself, he fashions mankind!—Irving Stone

Washington Weekly Reader

GOALS AND GRATIFICATION

In the 1930s, much psychologic emphasis was given to the neurologic basis of sex in animals, and man was included in his merited place among the animal kingdom. At that time, sex was often listed among the four primary drives (thirst, hunger, avoidance of pain, and sex) with the notation that it was the only one that could be denied or for which substitutes could be found without actually endangering the life of the individual. As studies on motivation were pursued, it was postulated that all other motives, including love or affection, were derived or secondary drives. During the ensuing years, some students of man continued to see him as a complicated bundle of drives. But others finally came to the conclusion that he was more than just a bigger rat (experimental animal—not a character reference!). One of the latest and most provocative hypotheses is presented by Harlow, who sees the basic drive for sustenance as consisting of two fundamental components. The first, called love or tender loving care, can be equated with the need to be touched, fondled, communicated with, and accepted. The second component is food; vital as it is for survival, it may be neglected in the absence of love. In this context even the reproductive drive is seen as related to the fulfillment of this basic bipolar drive for sustenance (183).

DESIRE

If one takes these historical cues and considers sexual desire a complex combination of the physiologic sex drive and those attitudes toward interpersonal intimacy that are accumulated throughout an individual's lifetime, many possibilities for encouraging (or aggravating) this desire exist. Attitudes toward sex, these complex distillates of cognitive concepts and related emotions, may support or suffocate the sex drive, which in turn denies or encourages desire (95). This is experienced by the unimpaired individual as well as the disabled (391).

Singh takes this a step further in his claim that the sex act for men consists of three major occurrences: desire, erection, and ejaculation. He suggests that desire can be built up in a number of ways. One useful route is through fantasy; the disabled male may also have dreams in which he is fully functioning sexually. To many, this will give sexual desire. Another factor building up desire may be the individual's need to prove himself to himself or his mate.

Hohmann finds increasingly more individuals disabled by injury are raising many questions early in their recovery regarding their potentiality for sex (195). The variety of expressed desires do not differ from those among the general population. Essentially, everyone's sexuality is seen by Hohmann as possible combinations of one or more of the following desires: a) a massive build-up of autonomic and striated activity culminating in orgasm; b) a biologic process for procreation of the race; c) a means of bolstering the faltering ego and attendant self-esteem of the participant; d) a means of manipulating and controlling another individual who is important to the patient's life; and/or e) a means of expression of two individuals' personalities and of merging them in symbolic and physical feelings of tenderness, respect, and concern for each other and their pleasure. Hohmann indicates that no matter how seriously a person's spinal cord is injured, the last three options are available (195).

Although several studies consider the matter of libido, Griffith reports that specific statistical data were limited. For example, defining libido as interest in sexual intercourse, Jocheim and Wahle found that during the early months following cord injury, 7% of their spastic patients but none of their flaccid patients reported sexual desire. Eventually, 26% of the spastic and 6% of the flaccid patients affirmed interest (all lesions in this study were complete). Tsuji and associates claimed that libido was present in more than half of their population, while Talbot, Boss, and Comarr considered libido in a broader psychosexual sense and maintain that it is undiminished in spinal cord patients. Talbot amplified this concept of psychosexuality, asserting that it is expressed in a variety of forms, other than biologic activity. Its psychic and hormonal components are usually undisturbed in those patients who, thus, continue to think, feel, appear and sound like the men or women they were before injury (171).

On the other hand, Singh observes that, although 70% of patients whom he sees may be capable of sex to some extent, many "actually have a poor attitude toward the whole idea of a person with this type of injury engaging in sex." Singh sees many substantial reasons for this negative attitude, which he feels goes back to the patient's self-concept. He believes that how the patient perceives himself physically, esthetically, and socially provides a clue as to how he sees himself in relation to his world and hence reflects his life-style, including sexuality (395).

Lovitt is another more wary observer (252). He feels that the patient who focuses most of his energies and thought on sexual functioning is making an overinvestment in this area and may disregard or play down other crucial and more fundamental aspects of the total rehabilitation program. In Lovitt's experience, such a patient may become depressed, withdrawn, and refuse to take part in treatment activities. The patient seems to lose faith that these activities will enable him to gain back the self-respect which has been impaired by his other losses, primarily his sexual loss. Lovitt points out that additional research is needed "regarding the psychological aspects of sexual loss so that each patient may be most effectively counseled at the appropriate stage of his disability" (252). Some 5 years later, Teal reviewed 33 articles dealing with psychosocial aspects of sexual loss and found many concepts inadequately specified and validated (424). He, too, calls for more research on those perspectives which recognize that sexuality "involves living roles of a boy or girl, man or woman, husband or wife . . . it covers a whole spectrum of attitudes and is reflected in all aspects of the individual, his relationships and his activities."

Kaplan (220) points out that a person who feels ill and debilitated or is in pain is not usually interested in pursuing erotic matters. She indicates that hepatic and renal disorders are especially likely to be accompanied by diminished sexual interest, and diabetes is notorious for affecting the erective response of men very early. While impotence or ejaculatory problems may be the presenting syndrome of multiple sclerosis, Kaplan notes that in contrast, the granulomatous infections, especially leprosy and tuberculosis, have "gained literary fame by virtue of the fact that patients afflicted with these disorders may retain their sexual interest and capacity until the illness nears its terminal phase."

Although many observers have referred to the stage of depression that accompanies most patients' realization that theirs is a chronic problem with no quick cure, more investigation is needed in this area. Some additional cues may come from Kaplan's insights:

The mechanism by which such severe emotional states (depression, stress and fatigue) impair sexuality is not clearly understood. Some experts believe the phenomenon to be purely psychogenic. The person in a crisis is after all intensely engaged in mastering his difficulties and it is adaptive for him to concentrate all his energies on resolving these, to the exclusion of all diversions. On the other hand, it is also possible that the profound physiologic and endocrine changes which accompany severe depression and stress and fatigue states contribute to the loss of sexual motivation by affecting the central nervous system and the neurotransmitters and also by lowering the available androgen supply (220).

Until research contributes more resource personnel and some practical guides to these more complex approaches, we would do well to try to improve the quality of general counseling that reaches the disabled population (124). Berkman, who considers sexual desire a potent force for a person who is disabled, suggests using an educational approach. He points out that

When sexual development is viewed as a learning process, its mystical powers are dispelled and counseling techniques can be applied. The goals of sex counseling . . . are . . . to enable those who are counselled to grow in their capacity to manage sex creatively; to communicate effectively with their sex partners; to improve their sexual function so that their lives may be enriched (32).

GRATIFICATION

At a recent seminar, a young man having a developmental disability was brave enough to ask the whole audience, "Is an orgasm for everyone?" As if in direct response, Hohmann's writings contain some very pertinent points. He decries the inordinate emphasis that our society places on the notion of mature sexuality as *orgastic potency*. He postulates that this may have occurred as an outgrowth of the emphasis placed by psychoanalytic theory on orgastic potency as a requirement for psychosexual activity. This theory holds broadly that orgastic potency between a couple indicates a healthy and binding relationship. Hohmann sees this in different perspective.

In an oversimplified way, it is an assumption that if a relationship is satisfactory in the bedroom, life in the living room will be serene. Our experience shows that this assumption is untrue. If a couple can establish a warm, understanding, empathetic relationship in their day-to-day functioning, expression of sexual feelings between them will tend to be rewarding, regardless of the nature of that expression, so long as it is mutually gratifying and acceptable to both (195).

Granted that orgasm isn't for everyone but is important to some, what is the nature of the "normal" experience and is there a difference in the nature of experiences reported by the disabled? As Trieschmann points out, even among normal men and women, differences exist in the timing, intensity, and duration of excitement. Communication is the key to mutual satisfaction (430).

Most men in the prime of life can reach a plateau phase and orgasm fairly rapidly. After the orgasm, however, a man is incapable of further sexual reaction until a period of time has elapsed, the time varying according to the individual and his age. A woman's sexual response, on the other hand, is more complex, less predictable, and more susceptible to interruption. Some women experience a gradual progression from excitement and plateau phases to a series of orgasms. Other women may progress to the plateau stage and hover at that level. While still others progress rapidly, attain an orgasm and rapidly lose interest. During the excitement and plateau phases, communication becomes critical because interruptions or other changes can alter the level of sexual excitement of either partner and interfere with satisfaction. A comfortable couple, sensitive to one another, will coordinate those response cycles for their mutual enjoyment (172).

Researchers in sexuality among the handicapped report a wide variety of experiences as orgasm (171). For example, some spinal cord injured may equate the sudden increase of spasticity followed by prolonged generalized muscular relaxation with orgasm. At times, patients with incomplete upper motor neuron lesions reported painful orgasms, while individuals with complete lower motor neuron injuries occasionally reported pleasurable sensations in the lower abdomen, pelvis, or thighs. Comarr believes that the acuity of the orgasm in men seems to be mainly dependent upon the intactness of sensation associated with muscle contractions of ejaculation, while women with complete spinal cord lesions were anorgasmic but could be sexually aroused by tactile stimuli above the level of the lesion. Such is the power of mind that totally paraplegic women, without somatic sensation or any voluntary movement of the genitopelvic area, have reported experiencing vivid orgasm imagery in their dreams! (171).

This aspect of fulfilling sexual drive through fantasy and dreams is corroborated by several investigators. Singh points out that the dream or fantasy is usually on a par with the type of sex life before trauma (395). He finds that if an individual had an extremely active, fulfilling sex life before trauma, his dreams tend to follow that trend. In fact, in an overall study reported by Singh, 46% of paraplegic males had some type of sexual dream "and in none of them did the paraplegic see himself as disabled in any way." Teal observes that some paralyzed men and women are able to experience a highly pleasurable fantasized orgasm "by mentally intensifying an existing sensation from some neurologically intact portion of their body and reassigning the sensation to their genitals . . ." (424).

Hohmann observes yet another aspect of empathetic gratification. He claims that, at the time the partner achieves orgasm, paraplegics often report a sort of *paraorgasm.* If strong empathy is felt with the partner, Hohmann notes that the cord injured person "may show many psychological and physiological changes associated with the build-up of sexual tension to orgasm and the changes associated with detumescence such as profound muscular relaxation, decreasing respiration, slow heart rate, drowsiness" (195).

Gratifying as physical or fantasied orgasm may be, it is not the only fulfilling part of sex. "What is important is that two people give to each other what they have to give and take what is given. If the result is physical orgasm—fine. If the result is psychological satisfaction—fine. Either result is beautiful when both people are satisfied." This quote from *Sex and the Single Ostomate* reflects what Calderone told United Ostomy conferences: "There are many ways of making love without orgasm and achieving satisfaction" (37, 63, 385).

In the search for satisfaction, Hohmann (195) cautions men about being too inclined "to attribute to women precisely their own kind of sexual drives, attitudes and needs for orgastic potency, with relative disregard of the importance of the interpersonal relationship to a successful sexual experience." Many other counselors emphasize relations and place high value on interpersonal communication (282). In his dialogue with patient groups Diamond (104) brings out most poignantly that satisfaction is quite different from orgasm. He points out that sex itself is usually used as a means to communicate deep feelings.

These feelings can be provided with simple touches, glances, and personal interchanges which don't require elaborate gymnastics or idealized anatomy. Satisfaction is most often a result of good sexual communication and shared intimacy, and is independent of orgasm. Satisfaction and orgasm may be simultaneously sought after, but separately achieved.

In summary, "It is time," as Cole states, "to consider sexuality as a legitimate part of the rehabilitation process" (79). This is within the reach of all, according to Hohmann, "If the patient and his mate can understand that the expression of tenderness and intimacy between them is an integral part of the sexual relationship. They are then in a position to be realistic in their expectations of fulfillment from each other" (195).

SPECIAL NEEDS AND SPECIAL CONCERNS

The able-bodied, even professionals, tend to lump the disabled into a single category. However, many of the needs and concerns of individuals who have become disabled after having known a life free from impairment differ considerably from the needs and concerns of individuals who have been disabled from birth or childhood.

SUDDEN DISABILITY AND INTERPERSONAL FEARS

It is a common fallacy that a disabled person is automatically rendered physically inadequate or incompetent sexually as a result of his or her general injury or resultant impairment. As it becomes clear that the person will survive the physical insults of accidents or disease, treatment shifts from saving life and stopping the disease progress, if possible, to helping that person determine how to live in a society that knows very little about the sexuality and sexual needs of severely disabled persons (170, 379). Some people react to initial rehabilitation by claiming that they would rather be dead than helpless. It is Schontz's experience that, to many patients, especially young men with spinal cord injury, "helpless" may mean sexually incompetent. If normal sexual behavior is possible for this individual, he may reduce resistance to medical care as soon as made aware of the fact. If socially sanctioned or former sexual practices are not available to the patient, results can still be expected if the rehabilitant can be helped to discover new or less conventional means of sexual gratification or if he can be convinced that satisfying human physical and psychologic intimacy is possible without (or at least without orgastic) sexual contact (194, 379).

Professionals must stop looking at the individual as a "patient" and start regarding him as a "rehabilitation client" with whom one makes plans cooperatively. In the transition the suddenly disabled individual must slowly shift from the mourning for "what was" into the reality of sharing his fears and disappointments; this is the first step toward some new way of life. The contact care person, whether professional counselor or any other member of the rehabilitation team, must exercise great sensitivity at this stage (282). This is no time for Pollyanna glibness or false hopes cheerily enumerated. When asked what can you do for a grieving client, Stewart empathetically replied, "Sit with him and listen to him" (412). The client has every good reason initially to grieve over what he or she can no longer do or what he believes he or she can no longer be (provider, initiator or recipient, collaborator, etc.). This listener, at best, can help the grieving person to find expression to frustration. Only then will affirmation of remaining potentialities and alternatives have meaning.

Accompanying posttraumatic depression, many individuals experience a dramatic loss of sexual identity. Actually, there is often a wide discrepancy between the sexual function of a patient and his sexual identity. For example, Hopkins found among the spinal cord injured that there were all levels of remaining functional ability with regard to sex, but all experienced some change in sexual identity. This involved changes in their self-esteem with regard to many different factors: actual sexual function, society's imposed roles of masculinity and femininity, others' preconceived ideas about the disabled person's sexual role, etc. (200). Whether a man has actually been denied any of the pleasurable aspects of sexuality, many a disabled male feels a humiliating sense of inadequacy. Many fear initially that they may have to, or may wish to, relinquish all other aspects of manly behavior—independence, authority, and responsibility (418). For women, sexuality includes a range of behaviors from smiling through orgasm. For some disabled women, "not valuing themselves enough to allow themselves to accept the sexual part of themselves can be the first problem preventing adequate sexual function" (354).

Fears run rampant among the newly disabled and their families long before they are expressed. Among the many concerns that have to surface are several that Stewart has found to be fairly regular problems (412). For example, counselors often talk of *loss of self-esteem,* but it is necessary to find out in what specific way the client conceives the injury as a blow to being lovable or being a loving person. Since sex involves a shared *vulnerability* when clothes are shed, to what extent does the client fear not only facing his deformity and its related problems but having to reveal them to his partner? Relationships between the disabled and the *significant other person* have many tenuous aspects which include problems of role change and role conflict (as when able-bodied father has to be provider, governess to the children, and supervisor of the household as well as Daddy). Often both partners are concerned that their intimacies will cause a reinjury or, conversely, may fear that they are growing apart because the injured member is so wrapped up in his needs, losses, and frustrations as to change from his accustomed normal behavior. What many a counselor may also overlook is the guilt with which the healthy partner needs help. Stewart has a very good example of this in citing the wife who, at the same time that she's mourning her husband's losses, is mad at him because he was stupid enough to dive into shallow water and injure his spine permanently. She, too, has suffered a loss by his actions and this is not to be passed over lightly (412).

Some studies have stressed the realistic psychosocial strains which have led to marriage separations and divorces among paraplegic persons. However, Griffith et al. have challenged the inevitability of these results, stating

The dual assumption that, as a reflection of sexual dysfunction, divorce rates among these subjects are greater than among the nondisabled, may be erroneous. Conversely, coitus almost certainly is not the only factor in preservation of marriages involving a disabled partner, since many couples remaining together reported no continuing sexual intercourse. Comarr identified educational and income level, and service versus nonservice connected disability as significant factors in marriage–divorce and adoption statistics. More recently, Talbot and Hohmann have emphasized the recognition of human sexuality as a total spectrum of attitudes and behaviors. The forms of interpersonal relationships are manifold, as are the varieties of its behavioral expression. Undoubtedly, a fuller appreciation of these relationships and their expressions (including their fears) will be provided by the routine evaluation of both sexual partners, as advocated by Masters and Johnson. The inadequacies of limiting studies to the disabled partner have been recognized by those who have used that method (171).

Fears run rampant *even among individuals whose disabilities bear no particular relation to the sexual act itself.* Fear of a present or future partner's reaction to an amputation or fear of an esthetic backlash against an ostomy have been expressed by most individuals with these conditions. Even though there may be no visible impairment, individuals disabled by conditions such as cardiovascular problems also experience fear. Care recommendations issued to these people by their physicians would include reducing or stopping smoking, weight and cholesterol intake reduction, and regular physical exercise of a mild nature. However, as pointed out by Wagner, such discussions include

Not much about sexual matters. Consequently, the patient acts according to his limited knowledge, fears, opinions or superstitutions. He may make unwarranted reductions in his sexual activity, even to the point of abstinence. This begins a cycle of behavior that may hamper his full rehabilitation. The reduced sexual activity can lead to frustration and marital conflicts, factors guaranteed to impede recovery and often associated with increased cardiac symptomatology (440).

Suffice it to say here, individuals who experience recent impairment may also experience intense sexual anxieties which may have far-reaching effects upon their overall personality adjustment.

Lovitt has written a very perceptive article, "Sexual Adjustment of Spinal Cord Injury Patients," in which he proposes guidelines in an effort to orient rehabilitation personnel to aspects of sexual disability that are not always recognized by those who claim to treat the whole person. Excerpts from five of his main points are (252):

1. The *psychological adequacy* of the sexual behavior and adjustment in the physically disabled can be properly evaluated *only* in terms of its relationship to total personality functioning. . . .
2. The disruption of sexual functioning will symbolize or represent different types of trauma to a patient, depending upon his personality type and his psychologic reaction to disability. . . .
3. Sexual functioning of the physically disabled individual should be considered a mechanism for furthering one's personal adjustment and not as an end in itself. . . .
4. The most adequate psychosexual adjustment usually cannot be made until more basic problems that the . . . patient faces are reconciled.
5. It is at the later stages of the successful rehabilitation process that a reciprocal relationship exists between adequate sexual functioning and psychosocial and vocational stability.

Hohmann points out that in the past there has been a general feeling among some professionals that the less said to cord injured patients regarding sexual functioning, the better; and that "repressive mechanisms" should be allowed to take their course in stifling thoughts and preoccupations with sexuality (195). However, he cautions that while this attitude seems to have been fairly effective when dealing with a generation whose repressiveness of sexuality was a part of the general mores and a way of life, the *now* generation appears to have been raised with fewer inhibitions and less emphasis on repression of sexual thoughts and feelings. "Even so," Hohmann cautions, "for those people whose integrity of sexual functions has been altered, it is a topic which must be handled with great gentleness and consideration" (195). A great deal of research remains to be done regarding the psychologic aspects of fears associated with threats to an individual's sexuality and sexual functioning when the individual is faced with physical impairment which may change his established life, ways, and goals (404).

Lest we make the mistake of waiting for research while life itself may have something useful to say, valuable survival tips may be found through shared experiences (253). Happily, there are those "survivors" among individuals with disabilities who not only pioneer in human relationships, but have a gift for communicating their experiences. For example, when Service wrote her delightful account of "Glamour on Wheels," she swept her readers into her own believability as she argued, "Just because you live in a wheelchair doesn't mean you can't look pretty and attractive . . . Don't be afraid to treat yourself to a bit of glamour—it can take you out of the doldrums and make you feel attractive and feminine" (383). Another indomitable damsel, Zlotnick, gives cues to rolling sex appeal in a witty article called "Chrome-Plated Femininity" which appeared in *Accent on Living*. The following excerpts will undoubtedly provoke readers to go back to the original for her full gamut of cleverly worded common sense (461):

—So, wheelchair girl, you want to be attractive to the opposite sex (there, you said it, SEX, you're already on the right track). Where and how do you start this massive overhaul?
—You must emphasize to yourself that you are *female* first and disabled *second*—I am a *woman* with a disability.
—No matter how disabled you are you can still have a sense of humor, and you can flirt. Men are equally attracted to these qualities as well as to a good conversationalist.
—Now that you've made yourself into the most luscious and desirable person on your block, you can start thinking about other things and acquire new worries. For instance, who are these men who are suddenly falling at your feet and what are their motives? Why are they attracted to someone with a disability? Are they masochists or martyrs? Are they sincere or curious? Are they just acting brotherly until the *real* thing comes along? All that may depend on the image you put forth. If you are judging your self-worth by your desirability, then you must be attractive inside and out, to yourself and to the other person.

In the next issue of *Accent*, Rathbun wrote a follow-up to this article in her letter to the editor (338):

Chrome-Plated Femininity (Winter 1974) is a delightful. . . . Three years ago I wheeled myself into group therapy, a Re-evaluation Counseling class. At first, I suffered pangs of jealousy every time able-bodied John asked able-bodied Mary to co-counsel or put his arm around her in class. But gradually I learned that we women in wheelchairs can get good vibes from men. I began to see our dating–mating problem not as a question of attractiveness but rather in these terms:
If my hunch is right, what men fear most is that we will have expectations and be disappointed, making them feel like heels. Society is partly to blame, with its be-kind-to-the-handicapped propaganda. Disappointing a crippled woman in love is considered on a par with taking pennies from a blind man. "Ask for a date and you're

committed to take her to the altar," some men may reason. "It's safer not to ask her in the first place."
Let's face it, we handicapped women are vulnerable. If we're easily hurt, no wonder men sense this. I believe it's up to us to reassure them. First we need to change ourselves. Such feelings as "I don't have sex appeal" or "I'll never have another chance at love," must go. It's time we realized that, whether going out on dates or getting married, we needn't apologize for the extra trouble because we're worth it! Once we know this, the man in the office or social club will begin to see us in a new light. Let's remind him, though, "This is just a date. Maybe I won't want to be committed!" Now that we've checked out the able-bodied male, he can very well turn out to be dullsville or perhaps "just not my type." Mr. Right may be a handicapped man. Here's to chrome-plated masculinity!

It is possible to read the above quotes as simply good journalism by two Pollyannas. However, they do reflect an attitude that is increasingly found among alert disabled coeds at colleges such as the University of Illinois or Kent State, where social as well as architectural barriers have been considerately removed by the administration and student body. These oases where disabled students live active social lives and receive a college education illustrate a potential for integration that society would do well to emulate (206).

DEVELOPMENTAL DISABILITY AND INTERPERSONAL CAPABILITIES

Individuals who have been disabled from birth or childhood have no "normal" period of life to mourn or remember. Many have lived a cure-oriented childhood, fostered by clinically oriented professionals and care-bound families. Many have attended segregated schools, although they were capable of regular classwork, merely because of architectural barriers and lack of transportation—yes, in a country that can send men to the moon! Not many got to camps for the handicapped, those adolescent breaths of fresh air for stretching beyond family sights and for swapping peer fears and hopes. Very few move out of the family home for higher education, and even fewer share apartments with roommates when they go to work. So it is not surprising to find immaturity a characteristic that pervades all aspects of the personality of a disabled individual who chronologically reaches young adult years. In a study by Landis and Bolles (236) of young women between the ages of 17–30 years, there were widely different responses on matters of psychosexual development between chronically handicapped and normal groups, which reflected limitations of activity and social behavior among the former group (Table 3–1). The authors conclude that, in comparison with normal women, the physically handicapped are less autoerotic, are more emotionally dependent on their families, are less homoerotic, have fewer heterosexual contacts, give less evidence of masculine protest, have equal narcissism, and are less emotional about sex in general.

The experience of rehabilitation personnel who are in contact with lifelong handicapped people corroborates this study. Examples can be cited from

TABLE 3–1. PSYCHOSEXUAL DEVELOPMENT OF HANDICAPPED WOMEN COMPARED WITH NORMAL WOMEN

CHARACTERISTIC	HANDICAPPED (%)	NORMAL (%)
First knowledge of sex differences before age 6	11	33
Complete sex information before age 15	11	26
Little or no preparation for menstruation	78	55
No history of masturbation	74	50
Extremely close to family	23	3
No evidence of homoerotic behavior	23	8
Never been in love	30	3
Never had dates with boys	28	1
First date before age 16	18	52
No evidence of masculine protest	43	26
Recalled a desire to be a boy in childhood	43	69
Attitude of disgust toward sex	7	21

dwellers in a large urban city or a small rural town to illustrate what little opportunity the long-disabled person has for warm, close, personal relationships with other people. Instead, he often lives a life of distorted interpersonal feedback, since the give and take experiences that develop perspective are lacking. At an international meeting in England, Branch brought this out quite poignantly:

A handicapped person has a very limited area of friendships—he misses out on adequate boy/girl relationships during his teens and late teens. You know teenagers today, they have got a different boy or girl friend every week, and good luck to them! This sort of thing is quite normal and quite natural and is part of the normal development of a young person. So if you have gone through your teenagehood without having too many boy–girl relationships, or without having any at all, naturally at the age of twenty-five to twenty-seven to feel you have fallen in love with somebody is quite a big shock, because you have also to get over the emotional barriers. You have to gain confidence in talking and mixing with the girl, and all this sort of thing, so it is naturally probably more emotionally difficult to look at your relationships with your fiancee from a mature point of view (46).

This intelligent and articulate speaker helps us to see behind the surface of counseling experiences with less sophisticated people.

In contrast, Cook's report on a group of men and women in a midwestern sheltered workshop illustrates the average awareness of multiply handicapped young adults who came to sheltered work after sheltered living (88). Three years ago, two young women came into her office saying that everyone in the workshop was "up tight" about boy–girl relationships. They felt that a meeting with all 16 women from the workshop to discuss their concerns would be helpful. Cook agreed and at the first meeting they aired such concerns as their belief that the men were purposely dropping fish hooks off the assembly line worktable onto the floor so they could bend over and look up the women's skirts. They also claimed that some men were making advances and petting the women, and they didn't know how to react to this. It turned out that simply discussing these matters in an open and adult manner proved very beneficial, and it was unanimously agreed that such meetings should continue on a weekly basis. As time went on, the discussions moved to include topics such as conception, pregnancy, and childbirth. Cook then took the initiative of inviting a Family Planning Specialist from a local hospital to the meetings. The women were asked to come to the group sessions prepared with questions. Some of the questions brought to subsequent meetings were

1. What is sterilization, cesarean section, abortion?
2. Explain birth, the process.
3. What can you do if you can't have a baby, physically?
4. Are birth defects noticed at birth?
5. How do you know if you are pregnant?
6. How do you tell your boyfriend you are having a baby out of wedlock?
7. Is it okay if a girl does not have a period?
8. When a boy meets a girl, should the girl kiss the boy for the first time?

Naturally enough, the men from the workshop became curious about the meetings the women had been having. They also wanted meetings. Since no volunteers emerged to meet with them, Cook found herself "in the uncompetitive position of meeting with our 30 workshop men who ranged in age from 16 to 38 years." The following quotes directly from her report will illustrate some of the realistic aspects of meeting a group at the level of its needs:

Before meeting with them I did some soul searching of my own thoughts and feelings. It was important that I be comfortable, honest, direct and unembarrassed. Not all would know such terms as *sexual intercourse* or *masturbation*. I needed to use slang comfortably, as well as trying to get across socially acceptable terminology. Before I met with the group, I actually practiced using some slang terms aloud before a mirror! The person conducting the meeting must set the tone. I found eye contact with the group to be important and used humor to allay nervousness and make everyone more relaxed. In the three group meetings with the men, we were all quite comfortable, everyone was attentive, and no one got off the subject. We covered basic sexual terminology such as wet dreams, conception, masturbation, etc. Some of their questions were

Is there any such thing as a stork?
How many eggs does a woman have?
Does a baby always go 9 months?
When a man and woman get together, how long does it take?
When you nurse a baby, is that spelled the same way as our nurse at school?

Two big problems with these meetings were that the group was far too large, thereby limiting discussion and the adults were not grouped according to their level of social and intellectual functioning (88).

Although all individuals with developmental disabilities become adults chronologically, the capabilities of many of them to meet life at an adult level are as limited as those of this group in the sheltered shop. There is, however, a very active minority of individuals among the developmentally disabled whose combination of intelligence, character, personality, and sheer guts mark them as "overcomers." Unfortunately, one only hears of the outstanding talents, such as Sandy Brown who overcame a communication gap resulting from his incoherent speech by writing the delightful book, *My Left Foot*, which gained international recognition (55). Professionals are also aware of Earl Carlson who fought against the odds of athetosis to become a physician and who made a very real contribution to the early medical and care approaches for cerebral palsy (67). Too often, only the "stars" are brought to the public's general attention in this success-hungry era. But there are numerous less distinguished achievers who go unsung because finding a way to another's heart is not always newsworthy, nor is it done with the pomp and ceremony of academic degrees. It takes a lot of growing up through progressive interpersonal relationships, plus "a little bit of luck." Bobby and June Arts are one such couple whose 20 years of companionship have included world-wide travel. He has been crippled by cerebral palsy from birth, while she has had polio since the age of 12. They met at a camp for the handicapped at Hunter, New York. As Bobby humorously puts it, "That was when they still put mentally retarded people in with the physically handicapped. June came up to the first person she saw reading *The New York Times*—she figured he wasn't mentally retarded—and that was me!" (425). Another seriously disabled couple, Willie and Margaret, allow us to share in their growing relationship through a poignant British film called *Like Other People* (248). In this deeply moving document that deals with the sexual, emotional, and social needs of the mentally and physically handicapped, the two overcomers evolve. Their capacity to communicate their love helps the viewers to understand that, even though someone is physically handicapped and even out of communication with many of us, he or she is not mentally or emotionally beyond the reach of loving and being loved. The vitality of this very touching relationship helps us to consider many other issues raised in the film about the quality of life, the desire to marry, the facets of care in residential homes and institutions, as well as the "pursuit of happiness" in the face of very great odds.

TAKING ACTION: CHOICE AND COMPROMISE

As Fromm points out, narrowing the word sexuality to the act of coitus in the adult is

as foolish as for a person to say that although he has never looked at a subject, handled a paintbrush or mixed paint, he knows that he will be able to execute a masterpiece in paint as soon as he feels like it. Full adult sexuality has a long history (as has full adult knowledge of language, craftmanship or anything else) of growth through play, experiment, inquiry, instruction and application (345).

Adult sexuality has taken many forms in the many cultures that make up the backgrounds of Americans. However, there is one unifying factor, and Sherrington expresses this best when he points out that "Man is Nature's beginning to be self-conscious; he is the only recognizer of values" (390). As the only recognizer of values, it is incumbent upon each of us to make choices and compromises that are not only compatible with our own development, but in harmony—if at all possible—with the needs and trends of our fellow men. The able and disabled have equal responsibility for this—if they claim adult privileges. Many need guidance in the fundamentals of behavioral alternatives and consequences, however. As in music, one has to learn the basics of harmony and counterpoint before learning how to bend the rules, or play within them, for more personally dynamic results.

Many observers of the handicapped have remarked upon it, but Smith and Bullough say it more clearly than the others: "the sex act itself is not the chief difficulty—the real problem is finding a suitable partner" (398). As they point out, disabled persons have to find ways of getting out independently, have to learn how to initiate conversation and to be even more open verbally than most people, and have to find ways acceptable to themselves and their partners of getting around the mechanical barriers to sex that are imposed by their disabilities (162). There are, however, many patterns of relationships with another individual, and persons with impairments have a fairly wide horizon to consider, even though available choices may be more limited at one time or another (167).

SEX AS A SUBSTITUTE

Sex is not an antidote for loneliness, feelings of inadequacy, fear of aging, hostility, or an inability to form warm friendships, etc. in spite of what the movies, television ads, and tall stories of our peers may tell us. As a substitute for a warm, continuing relationship with another person, it fails—even to the point of provoking suicides among the seemingly most desirable of Holly-wood's sex symbols. And those locker room stories of conquests by the "penis athletes" are appreciated only by those who have never known sex as the "natural spontaneous accompaniment of a warm, loving relationship between two people" (197).

Holbert, himself a respiratory polio quadriplegic is among those who point out that the well-known Puritan ethic of our society has greatly distorted our individual reaction to our normal healthy feelings. As a result, attitudes range from total rejection of sex as a nasty, unwholesome thing to a total preoccupation with it. Failure to develop a great big sexual relationship is equivalent to total personal failure in the eyes of those totally preoccupied with sex. "The psychosociologist from abroad is completely aghast at the ingenuity and preoccupation of the American ad man, who can make phallic symbols out of hot water heaters and appeal to a sick kind of narcissism in selling breakfast cereals" (197). Holbert advocates developing a healthy realistic feeling about our own sexuality. He emphasizes the fact that the inability to develop a regular sexual life does not mean any failure of a masculine or feminine personality, nor does it mean that the individual has failed as a valuable social being. To illustrate this, Holbert cites the hundreds of thousands of individuals of all ages who have chosen a monastic life, or for whom circumstances have chosen asceticism or total sexual denial. With a sexual life submerged in the background, these people contributed enormously by devoting their lives to the care of the sick, aged, to the relief of poverty and ignorance, etc. And these people are thereby as happy as most and realistically content with the outcome of their lives . . . We all have two choices in this business—we either find ourselves in an on-going sexual relationship with another person or we must make the best of life without it (197).

Becoming a "sex salesman" to the disabled population is not a valid substitute for professional services that usually are rendered to forward functional capabilities. Regardless of whether the professional in contact with a disabled person has been trained as a physician, psychologist, social worker, educator, or any other of the helping personnel, it is more than likely that sex education and counseling were not included in their graduate studies. While many writers refer to problems which arise when contact care personnel avoid the subject of sex, the opposite is also true. There are misguided people in every profession who seem to get a vicarious feeling of accomplishment by encouraging any disabled person, even those who are unprepared emotionally and who are socially incapable of assuming such responsibility, to add sex to their limited experiences. Some of these self-elected counselors do not realize how vulnerable a sheltered disabled person can be when a subject as intimate as sex is mishandled. One possible result is that they may awake to find themselves the object of the patient's affection. As Smith and Bullough point out, it is important to "let the patient know early that the relationship is a professional one rather than a personal one . . . make clear that she or he is off limits sexually . . . persons who are love objects should always be focused outside the nurse–patient dyad" (398).

It is even more important not to jump into sex counseling of the disabled just because it looks so easy and there is as yet no generally accepted standard of proficiency. As Loring points out,

A non-handicapped person may think, that because he has a sex life, however it is, he knows everything about sex. The misconceptions he eventually has, sex educated or not, are transferred to his view of the handicapped's sex life, mixed with stereotypes he has about handicapped people in general, depending upon lack of contacts, fantasy and understanding (304).

Some members of the helping professions seem to assume that being healthy themselves and having attended a sexual consciousness-raising seminar wherein they spoke freely to their colleagues about sex topics and sex jokes automatically qualifies them to "push the sexuality of the disabled." A caution is raised here to alert professionals to seek more information and qualified guidance into the complex psychosocial and legal ramifications of sex with the same vigor that they have investigated some of the technologic aspects of sex. Two excellent articles to start with might be the ones aptly called "Are We Trying to Solve Too Many Problems With Sex?" (241) and "Legal Issues in Family Life Education and Family Planning for Mentally Retarded" (318).

SEX AS SATISFYING IN ITSELF

In the wide horizon of human appetites, there are individuals to whom the physical act of intercourse, of itself, is satisfying. Among them are both able and disabled people. The following frankly shared reactions of a severely physically disabled young man illustrate how some people are able to enjoy sex initially as an erotic experience and to feel that it contributes toward their personal goals of psychosocial development. We are fortunate that this well-educated individual, who shares his developing feelings about sex, is able to express strong emotions and tensions that many other people cannot recognize or put into words (328). He writes

I endured this tortuous, pent up sexual tension throughout my college years. I was inhibited for two reasons: first, I still embraced the Victorian morality of my parents. Second—and much more important—I still had grave doubts regarding my own sexual adequacy. I had had no chance to experiment and also actually no opportunity even to discuss the subject with a knowledgeable adult. Therefore, in spite of my advanced education, I was still in complete and total ignorance.

This all changed when I started my Master's work at Columbia University. There, I was attracted to a fellow sociology student. For a while, I know that she was as attracted to me. I had my own hotel room on campus, so there were plenty of opportunities. Yet, I was still so insecure that I was scared to death even to bring up the subject. As a result, I never even got around to kissing her and finally lost her to another man.

I was crushed. My emotions had received a body blow to their entire structure, and paradoxically, it was that very emotional structure that had prevented me from achieving at least sexual and possible marital fulfillment. Fortunately, however, I possessed both the intellect and the knowledge to execute a thorough house cleaning of my psychic castle. I was determined not to suffer another romantic Waterloo. I completely overhauled my masculine sexual image. I became assertive and agressive with women; at times, perhaps too assertive and too agressive. At times, perhaps I grossly over compensated for my mistakes of the past. Yet, I was now a mature man, freed from all irrational inhibitions.

Oh man, did I ever overcompensate. I remember driving one of my young secretaries right up a wall! For two years, I chased that poor girl. She could find no peace. Gradually, though, I learned to accept rejection gracefully and like a man. I learned that if I expected a woman to disregard my disability and to respect me for what I truly was, then I must respect her wishes and feelings.

At that juncture in my life, I became capable of rationally looking for a socio-sexual partner. First, via my contacts I had developed in Harlem, I tried to find a prostitute who would render me my first initial sexual fulfillment. But the lowest offer was $150 per hour plus $25 for the hotel room. This is a very good index of just how substantial the socio-sexual distance was between a disabled man and the prostitutes in the area. My second attempt was to place an advertisement in two newspapers. I received over 75 responses. To each one of these responses, I sent a three-page description of what I was looking for in a woman. An excerpt is below.

A little girl is made of sugar and spice, and everything nice! But of what is a mature, fullbloom woman composed? Even as each human being has his own unique finger-prints, so does each individual have his own unique personality. In addition, to be a woman endows a person with that much more uniqueness, that much more grace, that much more charm. Consequently, women have different patterns of needs.

Deep within her psyche, these patterns of needs merge into an underlying mosaic of motivation. These need motifs, then, are the driving force behind her actions. That is, in order to find self-fulfillment, the woman must find a man whose need motifs compliment and supplement hers, as well as vice versa. The meshing of need motifs, then, is the concept of Plato's twin halves, with the prototype being the sexual embrace. For, in the sexual embrace, does not certain need motifs of the man and certain need motifs of the woman fuse, thereby satisfying each other? However, sex is just one dimension of the total spectrum of life. Indeed, the greater number of dimensions on which the need motifs of a man and woman mesh, the greater their compatibility: in turn, the greater their compatibility, the more self-fulfillment the woman—as well as the man—will find.

Upon the above criteria, I screened all 75 applications, and finally chose a Junior College Professor in Puerto Rico. I flew to Puerto Rico to meet my new mate. Although the relationship went well for several months, it finally fell through. Words cannot express how depressed I was; just then, in walked a new homemaker. Her name was Terry. Since we were both looking for sexual gratification, we had a common ground from which an enduring, loving relationship sprang. As a result, now, a woman has a husband, two children have a father, and two babies have a grandpa. In addition, I could have never become Editor-in-Chief of my new magazine if it had not been for the constant assistance of my loving wife. Again, this all sprang from a simple sexual gratification. Therefore, to those who still contend that sex is dirty and ugly, I say, "Reorder your system of values."

The high priority given to what is often called simple sexual gratification is not confined to men. The following letters written to the Editor of *Accent On Living* by two of its disabled women readers speak for a growing audience (249):

To the Editor:
Regarding "Sexuality and the Disabled Female," I thought this was the best article I've yet to read in ACCENT.
ACCENT has always left me with the feeling that it holds back a little on articles regarding sex (to date, only sex and the disabled male). These past articles always left the most important questions unanswered. "Sexuality and the Disabled Female" did not.
I commend Ms. R . . . for her insight, sensitivity and frankness. Any further detailed questions regarding sex and a disability would have to be answered by a specialist as each individual varies.
To feel like a total woman, one does not have to jump in bed with every Joe that passes by; but one does have to know that option is available.

J.P., Wisconsin

To the Editor:
Mrs. R . . .'s article was certainly refreshing, it's about time the female was recognized as having needs and that neither man nor woman lives by bread alone!
She made many excellent points, particularly about female sexuality being more than the act of sex, and equating self-worth with desirability and functioning. The rest of the article, however, was more of a "how to" guide and came close to becoming a double standards article.
The S . . . article for men was extremely good and helpful to both sexes. Nowhere in that article did it say if you don't have a partner at hand, join a church group or do volunteer work. The majority of this article is helpful to the person who already has a partner or may be likely to and needs to know "how." What about the female who doesn't have that partner, has no prospects of a partner, and isn't able to join a church group?
This is where the double standard effect comes into play. The men's article discussed

normal desires, even the use of prostitutes as a possible solution. Once again, despite Mrs. R . . .'s initial statements, the female has been brushed aside unless she's got that proper "partner."

Now let's have an article for "humans without partners."

P.Z., Connecticut

These excerpts illustrate that sex can be satisfying in itself when used as an introduction to sexuality. Lest we assume that this is limited to individuals with disability, a quote from *The Sex Scene—Understanding Sexuality* by Race, Leecraft, and Crist, which is addressed to normal populations, will put this aspect of sexuality into better perspective (336):

In a previous generation it was quite common for boys to be initiated into heterosexual activity by using prostitutes. Today, with increasing frequency in sexual activity, such initiation is no longer prevalent, but it still happens. Many boys would rather find out with a prostitute or casual pickup how they'll perform sexually than to expose their insecurities to their best girl. And some just may not want the responsibility or the close relationship that intercourse with a girl friend would entail.

Psychological or physical problems may result from the practice of using prostitutes. Those who have used them for initiation purposes have sometimes had subsequent trouble with premature ejaculation as a result of being hurried through that first time or being made to feel awkward or inferior by an insensitive and business-like partner. And, with many boys or men, the "pay for" kind of sexual encounter causes a guilt feeling which is hard to handle later. In the physical area, there is always the possibility of acquiring venereal disease, probably greater from a casual pickup than from regular prostitutes whose business generally benefits from frequent medical check-ups.

There are girls as well as boys who choose sexual experimentation with someone they don't care about, often just from the fear of being found to be virgins by their sophisticated boyfriends. Some girls who are looking for a close warm relationship with a guy mistake sex for closeness and spend years of promiscuity without fulfillment. Even some marriages are undertaken with the same mistaken expectation that a good sex life will automatically produce a rewarding psychological intimacy, and the desired result is often not achieved.

Sociologists indicate that the concept of sex as strictly a "fun thing" is gaining adherents. Toward the end of the next 25 years, they feel that the shift of sexuality into the sphere of play—sex as satisfying in itself—will diminish in many instances the emotional investment that has previously been connected with sexual experiences. They do point out, however, that, while this trend is growing, it is by no means predominant in today's society (400).

PARTNERSHIPS WITHOUT KNOTS

In discussing the growing number and the increasing quality of recreation and education programs for handicapped adults, Nigro (300) brings to our attention the fact that one element frequently avoided "is the pairing off of people into romantic alliances and love affairs and sexual activity at many levels." She provocatively points out that, if we are going to bring adults together, stimulate growth, bombard them with social experiences, increase self-esteem, and promote self-awareness, we must be prepared to deal with the resultant behavior. Staff members in adult programs frequently panic at the first sign of overt affection. Nigro, however, feels it is essential that anyone involved in programs for severely disabled adults should expect and perhaps even encourage such affection, even though the expression of love and the conduct of romances in such a setting may be less mature than would be expected. For instance, if two people in their 40s are behaving like teenagers, it must be understood that love, romance, and sexual expression are developmental processes. These people may not have been through the usual stages yet and may have to go through the whole process before learning to express themselves in a mature way.

In response to these needs, Nigro designs programs to include an element of sex education and sex counseling for both the disabled themselves and for the staff who work with them. She strongly believes that

It cannot be stated emphatically enough that the people we are concerned with are adults and have to be thought of in that context, regardless of how they might behave or how retarded or dependent they might be. They are adults, and we must remember to treat them like adults. In a good many cases, they're probably not behaving like adults, because they haven't been treated that way. An extension of this concept is the very important principle that the participants in the program must be included in the planning. If they are truly to be treated as adults, they must have a voice in planning their own lives. Obviously, we work with a tremendous range of adults, not only intellectually but experientially, and their capability of being part of the planning process is something that has to be developed in many cases. Some of the people will continue always to need a great deal of direction from the staff, and others will be able from the very beginning to assume a great deal of responsibility, but the program ought to be designed to encourage them to assume an ever-increasing responsibility for making choices, planning programs, and being responsible for their own lives.

It is Holbert's experience that the handicapped person often hopes for marriage or at least for a satisfying sexual relationship. Whichever alternative is chosen depends less on the sexual capacity of an individual than upon his development as a total person. This development must include steps to become outgoing, interested and concerned about the lives and interests of others; he must be growing continually in knowledge. As he obtains pleasure in Nature, in the intellectual world, and in meaningful relationships with other people, Holbert predicts that he will become an interesting, "deeper," and a more attractive person "without really trying" and, as such, he also will become sexually more attractive. Frequently, a more normal sexual life can develop.

A good friend of mine, going to the University of California in a wheelchair and a Huxley breathing belt, has more girlfriends than he can handle and, believe me, they don't spend their time playing Monopoly! A common fallacy exists that often a disabled person is physically inadequate or incompetent sexually as a result of his injury. Most always this idea is completely untrue, and not uncommonly a nearly normal and quite satisfactory sexual life is possible . . . (197)

Unfortunately, Holbert's popular wheelchair-bound friend is still more of an exception today than a rule. However, Nigro's observations of the developmentally disabled indicate that the difficulties that they have are also mainly interpersonal in origin (302). She advocates more active participation of trained staff members when moderately to severely handicapped young persons look to staff for assistance in convincing parents of their right to an opportunity to establish romantic alliances. These romances usually involve other disabled people since those are the only friends with whom time is spent away from the family.

And he does have this right, I hope you'll agree. Parent's objections to their handicapped children's dating (and probably our own objections as well) usually have to do with the fact that the young adult "child" will only be hurt in the long run, because where can a romance lead to but to an eventual breakup and heartbreak. Certainly it can't lead to marriage. Or can it? (299)

Nigro considers this the real crux of the matter: Who has the right to marry, and who sits as judge to make such decisions? Who decided whether you should marry and whether you would make an adequate parent?

I would first like to say that relationships between two people which don't necessarily lead to marriage can provide enough pleasure to offset the pain of the eventual demise of the relationship. So there is some justification for establishing such relationships at all. Furthermore, many long term alliances or engagements which I have witnessed have given the couples involved, who feel that they could not manage marital life, a semblance of normalcy and many years of satisfaction and emotional fulfillment. Also, of course, not all handicapped people want to marry or find suitable mates, just as is true for ablebodied people (301).

MARRIAGE FOR THOSE WHO DIG IT

While the term "dig it" is popularly used for "like it" or "want it," it can be used in some instances with justifiable logic. Lasting marriages take considerable digging, comparable in many ways to the type of discipline, hard work, and interpersonal responsibility that at one time led to rewards of gold or diamonds for pioneer mine diggers. The diamond and gold veins of those early mines were often found to lead far away from the surface, to be erratic in their course, and occasionally to peter out unexpectedly, so the analogy is not too farfetched. The marital diggings among so-called normal populations in our country recently led a liberal minister to observe (185)

I see the sexual relationship of the husband and wife as the key to the soundness of the family's life together. If it isn't right, nothing is likely to be. A recent survey indicated that 87% of those questioned saw lack of communication as their primary problem, 46% checked conflict over the children, 44% sex problems and 37% financial quarrels. Yet I suspect that many of the communication problems had a sexual component.

Constructive study of marital sexuality and sex is still a "first-generation" exploration among the general population, and valid research or observation among the disabled populations is even more primitive. There are complex physiologic, psychologic, and social reasons for this. A marital candidate may be mildly, moderately, or severely disabled, and some of the psychologic stresses upon such an individual depend on whether the onset of the disability was associated with early development or later occurrences (see Special Needs and Special Concerns). Furthermore, the lifelong handicapped may be divided into three other general categories. Some handicapped people, such as some spinal cord injured, may have physiologic dysfunctions resulting in direct impairment in sexual functioning. Others who are multiply disabled, such as the cerebral palsied, are not hampered by genital malfunction, as far as we know. Still others may have mental deficiency with or without a physical handicap that is usually not related to any impairment in sexual functioning (23,58). Each of these groups has quite different problems to face in dealing with sex within a marital partnership (259,292,300, 302).

Poling (328) observes that descriptions provide adequate physiologic commentary, but they do not provide an adequate sociologic description. Although most people make the ipso facto assumption that severely handicapped people only date, court, and/or marry other severely handicapped people, this is not necessarily true. Poling, who is himself disabled, comments,

In my case, it was almost the direct opposite. Hence, we need to develop a typology that will indicate the different types of relationships that handicapped and non-handicapped individuals may form. For this purpose, I tentatively propose the following typology:

Typology of Sexual Relations between Handicapped and Non-Handicapped Individuals

N–N   H–N
N–H   H–H

KEY: First letter in the typology indicates the status of the male, while the second letter indicates the status of the female.

N—Non-handicapped.
H—Handicapped.
NN—Both partners in sexual relationship are non-handicapped.
HN—Male is handicapped, while female is non-handicapped.
NH—Male is non-handicapped, while female is handicapped.
HH—Both partners in sexual relationship are Handicapped.

Even at first glance, a typology such as this reveals certain interesting differences among the four types. Of course, we are not at all concerned with type NN. In type HN, the handicapped male has certain social advantages, because he can take the initiative in attracting the female. However, at the same time, the male must operate under certain physical disadvantages, because he has extremely limited mobility. For example, if the couple went to a motel, would the female be strong enough and understanding enough to help her partner out of the car and into the bed? In type NH, the situation is practically the direct opposite. The female has certain social disadvantages, because she cannot take the initiative in attracting a male; however, once a male is attracted to her, he can remove most, if not all, of the physical obstacles. In type HH, it is an entirely different ball game altogether; since both partners are severely disabled, third party involvement will probably be required. In types NH and HN, the concept of "socio-sexual distance" becomes critical.

Even as a person can be varying distances away from a point physically, so a person can be varying distances away from another human socially. Furthermore, the greater the social distance between human beings, the greater the ignorance and the greater the prejudice between them. Sociologists have developed scales to measure social distance between ethnic groups. One of the pioneers in this field is Louis Guttman. Below is an example of a Guttman scale that appeared in *The American Soldier.* Although this scale does not measure social distance, it does demonstrate the general principle involved:

1. Are you over six feet tall?   __YES __NO
2. Are you between 5 feet 6″ and 6 feet tall?   __YES __NO
3. Are you between 5 feet and 6 feet tall?   __YES __NO
4. Are you under 5 feet tall?   __YES __NO

Note how a person can only answer a specific number of successive questions in the affirmative. Also note how a person logically cannot skip around; that is, if a person answers one question negatively, he is automatically forced to answer all successive questions negatively as well. (In the Guttman type of scale, there is only a 10% margin of error.)

Guttman developed a similar scale to measure anti-Semitism. The first question in this scale was something like "Do you object to Jews immigrating to this country?" The scale became progressively harder with such questions as "Would you mind having a Jew in your firm?" or "Would you mind having a Jew as your next door neighbor?" The scale concluded with the question, "Would you object to a Jew marrying your daughter?"

I propose that a similar scale could be constructed to measure socio-sexual distance between handicapped and non-handicapped individuals. I further propose that socio-sexual distance is a single continuum, with sexual relations being at the extremely intimate end of the scale. For, sexual relations is one form of intimate communication between two human beings, between a man and a woman. Therefore, the intimate end of the ten point scale would read something like the following:

8. As a one shot deal, would you go to bed with a disabled person? __YES __NO
9. Would you be willing to establish a stable and prolonged relationship with a disabled person? __YES __NO
10. Would you be willing to legally marry a disabled person? __YES __NO

Although the exact wording may need refinement, it is hoped that the general concept is apparent.

With one exception, my contacts with the opposite sex were of the HN type. The one exception was a mildly handicapped woman, who had one atrophied leg, and therefore, had to walk on crutches. The rest of my social relationships were with non-handicapped girls and women; and, because of this fact, the concept of socio-sexual distance played a critical role throughout my developing manhood. Parenthetically, the reasons for my unusual access to non-handicapped girls and women were three in number: first, since the eleventh grade, I attended school with non-handicapped students. Second, I have done over ten years of social work in urban racial ghettos, and all of my secretaries have been nonhandicapped. In fact, my female secretaries had been my greatest reservoir of dating and courting material. Third, as I became more and more independent, Welfare provided me with non-handicapped homemakers. Indeed, this is the way in which I met my darling wife, Terry.

With Nigro's and Poling's very human and frank commentaries as a background, it is now possible to look with a more wholesome skepticism at a few well-known surveys and professional observations made during the past 10 years. Hopefully, these will provide impetus for more in-depth insights in the future.

Disability Subcultures

Sociologist Myers (291) finds a higher degree of social interaction among the disabled than occurs among adults in the general population. As a result of personal or social isolation, the disabled frequently develop subcultures or communities of their own. This tendency for disabled persons to seek social satisfaction with each other has produced a complex system of social organization. Myers contends that research is needed on how and why social groups arise among the disabled, who joins them, and what functions they fulfill for their members and for the larger society. The effects of the subculture and its social institutions on the disabled person also need study. Furthermore, Myers asks,

Are the consequences of disability different for those who participate in the disabled subculture than for those who do not? How does the subculture exercise social control over its members? Looking ahead to prognosis, is rehabilitation more or less successful among members of the subculture than among non-members? . . . The deaf, to give an example, have developed national fraternal and professional associations, and there are newspapers and journals operated by and for the deaf. Within this context, it should be noted that a high rate of intermarriage prevails among deaf persons. However, not all disabled persons, nor all deaf individuals for that matter, associate with each other to such a high degree.

Professionals at the New York University Deafness Research and Training Center (100) state, "Not a group homogenized by their common disability, deaf people differ as much from each other as they do from all other individuals." However, the staff still essentially support Myers's findings. Their studies indicate that deaf persons marry less frequently than their age peers in the general population. When they do marry, they are more apt to pair with deaf spouses, but their marriages tend to be somewhat less stable than marriages in general. While there are many contributing factors to this instability, it is Elliott's contention that some of these deaf adults come to the marriage relationship biologically mature but—because of deficiencies in early meaningful communication—are sexually naive as well as emotionally and experientially deprived (121). Consequently, the marriage counselor's therapeutic approach to such deaf couples must be fairly eclectic. In some instances, helping a couple to verbalize their thoughts and to communicate with one another may be the key. In others, more intensive therapy may be required to build a client's self-esteem, since self-deprecation and the history of early rejection by others can have adverse effects on marriage. In still other cases, the hearing mate of the couple may have married the deaf partner in order to perpetuate a "parenting" role, or the deaf partner may have sought to preserve the dependent child role. Elliott points out the importance to any eventual marriage of developmental experiences and family life—education for growing youngsters who are deaf, as well as the need for specific sex education for deaf adults.

With the controversy over deemphasis of heredity has come wide parental and professional differences of opinion regarding marriages of mental retardates. Morgenstern (284) reports that the question of marriage for retarded offspring evoked great emotion in parents. Parents wish that their children could marry normal partners, yet they are fearful that normal partners would reject their youngsters. Many deep-seated feelings and attitudes, obviously, are tied to this. The parents by and large felt that the youngsters were capable of marriage. However, some parents had serious misgivings about any children born to disabled couples — their well-being, upbringing and possible dependency upon the grandparents themselves.

Professional opinions concerning retardates and marriage cover a wide horizon. The President's Committee on Mental Retardation states that the retarded have a "right to be free from restrictions on the sanction to marry" (347). This "right" condemns blanket invalidation of a marriage because one or both of the partners happens to be retarded, but it has been greeted with varied responses. On the positive side, Maddock (255) states that the few studies done on handicapped or retarded persons who are encouraged and guided in establishing paired relationships (including marriage) have

indicated quite positive results (Mattison, 1973 [259] Shaw & Wright, 1960 [389]). Similar findings are reported by institutions which have instigated programs encouraging peer group interaction, including male–female relationships (Edgerton & Dingman, 1964 [114] Scheer, 1967 [375]). This is not difficult to understand. Experience with relationships and with handling sexual feelings is itself a socializing factor that encourages responsibility. It helps the individual move toward a more independent, effectively functioning role in society. These individuals, despite their handicaps, are more likely to contribute positively to society and less likely to remain dependent upon it.

Although Wallin (441) sees the emphasis toward increased environmental aids to combat the deficiencies of mental retardation as a constructive change, he thinks differently about the deemphasis on the prohibition of marriage of the mentally retarded. "In fact, there are those [professionals] who frankly espouse their [the mentally retarded] right to contract the marriage bond. The writer has not yet reached that stage of liberalism, or conceptual maturity, if that is what it is." Furthermore, Wallin points out that there are many social and economic reasons why persons who, at best, will have a hard time supporting themselves should not be encouraged or permitted to assume additional complicated burdens which they could only discharge imperfectly in a highly competitive industrialized society. He believes that if retardates are allowed to marry at all, they should be allowed to do so only under conditions of reliable birth control, such as is afforded by sexual sterilization.

Sterilization today is frowned upon by many humanitarians (but not all) except as a measure of population control. Because of the population crisis, the advocates of permanent birth control (which is what sexual sterilization is) for large masses of people have become numerous and lusty. But sterilization for eugenic purposes still has a place on a selective, voluntary basis.

In addition, the freedom from such burdens as care and support of children often allows a couple of borderline mental capacity to sustain marriages that seem to have very fragile bases (292). To outsiders they may even look badly mated, but as Nigro perceptively points out, they seem to want to play the role of married people in imitation of adults around them. These marriages of habit and convenience seem to endure, affording ample contentment to the partners. This may be related to modest level of expectations on the part of the couple, as well as to the lack of demands each places on the other (302).

In contrast to the emphasis on social concerns surrounding marriage for retarded individuals, the major question about persons who are physically disabled involves their capacity to fulfill a partnership in marriage. For example, in a government sponsored booklet addressed to paraplegics, Bundy writes (57):

—If you were married before your illness and if the marriage was a good one, it will probably be a good one.
—Some paraplegics have their marriages break up after their injury. In most cases the illness was not the reason. It was just an excuse. Love does not fly out the window, when you have trouble. Usually it grows stronger.
—If you are not married, you will probably get married. Other people will be more interested in the kind of person you are than in your illness.
—You are probably wondering about sexual relations. Have a good honest talk with a doctor that you like and trust about this problem. There are many ways of having good sexual relations with your husband or wife. Be sure you understand these ways.

Morgan (283) approaches the question of marriage of disabled people from a developmental point of view. He assesses the potentialities of people who may have emotional and psychologic blinders put on by a society which has not offered sufficient preparation. He writes, "This means that many handicapped people never learn about adult responsibilities and duties, and marriage is seen as a highly desirable and respectable state to be in, with no concept of the giving and taking and additional responsibilities that one has to take on when married."

In a discussion on sexuality and multiple sclerosis Horenstein carries this perspective a step further (393). He refers to three bases for marriage: 1) sexual gratification, 2) companionship and mutual interest, and 3) reproduction and continuing interest in children. It is his contention that a marriage can be held together with any two of the components but not with one alone. According to Horenstein, what often happens with multiple sclerosis patients is that not only are they physically ill, but in addition their psychologic preoccupation with their illness and the consequences of the disease on the cerebrum interfere with two of the three hypothesized bases of marriage. Bidgood (35) takes all arguments full circle, back from emphasis on disability to emphasis on marriage as a "role, a relationship, and a behavior. It requires as a minimum, a degree of independence—both psychological and physical, of support—both psychological and financial and a certain level of emotional maturity."

Nigro carries the logical approach of Bidgood a step further by applying this logic with human tenderness to people she is best acquainted with, namely, the multiply handicapped (299). She feels that, although sex is one part of marriage, and a very important part, marriage is far more a way of fulfilling the couple's emotional needs. Establishing a meaningful intimate relationship with another human being can be the difference between a solitary, empty life and a rich, sharing partnership which makes the lives of both people so much more rewarding. She questions whether anyone has the right to deny this experience to the disabled, who already have been denied so many other routine experiences which most of us take for granted. It is her conviction that marriage can be a very satisfying way of life for disabled people who are too handicapped to participate in many other human endeavors, such as work. Some of the couples whom she knew before they were married were dependent or semidependent on their families, felt useless, were isolated, and in general were living life in a very marginal way. In their marriage they have found a meaning and a purpose far beyond that which marriage holds for the average person. Because such a marriage is so central to their existence, frequently it is a much stronger, more binding union than many among able-bodied persons. Nigro illustrates this as follows:

One couple I know, both quite handicapped but very resourceful and far from helpless, keeps house together, shops for groceries, prepares their food, all, I might add, without regard for the usual male–female roles. They do all this at a snail's pace, because they are so handicapped, and it consumes their day. They take care of each other, share their chores, and when they are finished they relax and make love. What could be more beautiful?

Making love is, for handicapped people as for others, a very private and uniquely worked out practice. If their disability is such that they can engage in sex in the standard or conventional way, they have no more problems than able-bodied people in working toward a good sexual adjustment. If their physical disability prevents them from the usual practices, either because of physical distortions or because of impairment in sexual function, this need not be a barrier to achieving sexual satisfaction. Our book stores and libraries are filled with manuals which detail an infinite variety of methods of achieving sexual pleasure and which tell us repeatedly that no practice which is acceptable to the two parties involved ought to be overlooked. In addition, there is a growing body of literature [and responsible counseling services—Ed.] which rather explicitly describes the methods disabled people with sexual dysfunction have found for achieving success in finding and giving sexual satisfaction. I don't want to imply that no serious problems in this area may arise, but it is apparent that a loving, determined and resourceful couple, regardless of their handicap, can find an acceptable way of fulfilling their sexual needs.

Some of the objections to marriage between handicapped people have to do with their inability to support themselves and their inability to responsibly bear and raise children. With regard to financial support, most handicapped people who cannot support themselves are entitled to public assistance. This is true whether they marry or not. And simple arithmetic will prove that it is cheaper to support two people in one apartment than two people in two apartments (and certainly less than two people in a chronic hospital or nursing home). Aside from the simple facts stated here, consider the fact that many people whose circumstances have nothing to do with physical disability are being supported by public assistance. Can we honestly deny marriage to physically handicapped people because they are not self-supporting?

Mobilizing Factors

While Nigro's experience with the multihandicapped is a rich one, her contacts are mainly among those who also struggle against economic and housing problems in an impersonal urban megalopolis. To maintain perspective, let's look at the college-bound and, in some instances, those who are not the economically pressed multihandicapped. The best examples seem to come from individuals with cerebral palsy. Muthard and Hutchinson report that in their admittedly small study of college students the cerebral palsied student group included fewer married persons than did the comparison group of nonimpaired. The cerebral palsied had markedly fewer marriages than married college students in the general population as reported by the 1960 U.S. census. Of the four cerebral palsied students who were married, none was married to another cerebral palsied person, and only one was married to a person described as disabled. As might be anticipated, substantially more of the nonimpaired graduates had married after college than had members of the cerebral palsied alumni group: two-thirds of the nonimpaired group married, compared to 31% of the cerebral palsied. In the 6 years intervening between the two surveys of this study, an additional 20% of the latter group had married. When the two married groups were then compared with respect to number of children, no differences were found, but eight of the ten in both groups did not have children at the time of the follow-up study (290).

Group studies of small populations in selected areas lead to generalities which must be carefully analyzed, and their contribution to individual situations is questionable. On the other hand, individual reports illustrate how some people, who are not generally assumed to have a relish and capacity for life, defy our stereotypes. Admittedly, this is a Christmas letter from a well-to-do, well-educated, multiply handicapped young woman who is planning to be married (238). But notice that all is not sweetness and light; many practical hurdles had to be coped with, and this letter shares these, as well as the bride-to-be's good humor:

I wish you could meet and get to know Harry; if you could, you'd love a very brilliant, sensitive, corny guy!! We met 2 years ago when he transferred from Kendall Junior College to Southern Illinois University. Five days after our marriage, we will receive our B.A.'s; mine will be in English; and Harry's will be in Spanish and French. So you'd better watch your language. He plans to teach high-school Spanish after we complete our Master's work. SIU made its mistake of accepting both of us for graduate school. Harry will continue studies in Spanish and French while I do work in Linguistics. . . .
After our marriage, we plan to live in an apartment at Southern Hills, the University's complex for married students about 4 miles from campus. We hope to get one of the several modified apartments for handicapped students, so I'll be as independent as possible. The master bedroom, living room, kitchenette, and bath are furnished very untastefully, but at least they are furnished. The spare room is unfurnished, and we want to make it a study room just in case we ever get the urge to study. All we will have to do will be to go into the Study Room to get rid of the urge. Harry and I just ordered a 1969 Dodge Dart. Our wedding present from my parents will be installed

in the car, so we can keep it cool. Mom and Dad are giving us an air conditioning system for the car. We'll have the car by March in time for Harry to start his student teaching. I'm also getting a new electric wheelchair that is supposed to be delivered last October. The Stork evidently didn't do very well in Geography because my chair is wandering around the Country. So if you happen to see a lonely electric wheelchair, meandering around, I would appreciate your steering it in the right direction toward Carbondale.

I first became interested in Linguistics two summers ago when I took the introductory course in Transformational Grammar from Mr. Epstein who encouraged me to take more advanced courses in the field. Fortunately, SIU is privileged to have on its faculty one of the leading Transformationalists, Dr. Katranides. He sold me on the merits of this new, highly controversial method for constructing grammars. Briefly, Transformational Grammar purports to generate the infinite set of possible sentences from a very strict finite set of rules. (HUNH?) Anyway, Linguistics involves quite a bit more than T.G. and T.G. involves quite a bit more than I know about it or anyone else knows about it. I hope to be able to add something to the world's knowledge of Linguistics after completing my Master's. To make it possible for me to continue work in Linguistics, I'm getting a new I.B.M. Electric Typewriter (which is supposed to be delivered last November). The typewriter will have special phonetic symbols used in Linguistics. In other words, the typewriter will have special characters for a character.

Eleanor Thomas, who "has the honor" of sharing my room at school, is a very good kid, if you like kids. El has one problem: she's boy crazy, but I really can't blame her because I was a Boy Scout, too. I just hope she does her duty so that she will have the honor of finding a guy like Harry.

Probably the most influential person in my life is Dr. Horecker. Dr. H. is helping me solve many unsolvable problems of life. I think his help and his teachings will be the key to a successful marriage between Harry and me.

May 1969 be your best year yet, and may you be as happy as I am.

                                                                      Love, Barby

According to four young couples who were interviewed by Kanton for *Accent on Living* marriages between able-bodied and disabled persons do not differ greatly from other marriages when hurdles are recognized and tackled by mutual concern (217). One wheelchair-bound wife who uses a pole with a hook on the end for turning on the stove and for lifting items such as a teapot reports that, "I can cook, wash dishes and keep the apartment fairly neat. Steve helps by doing the heavy chores such as vacuuming and washing the floors." In the case of the wheelchair-bound husband of a couple who have two daughters, age 7 and 3, marriage has given the husband the opportunity he sought for greater independence: "I can do just about anything in my wheelchair—even drive. I couldn't assert this independence, however, until I left home to get married." As one young wife explains, "It takes a certain type of person to marry a person in a chair. He must be responsible and empathetic." Her husband claims, "It just depends on if you can live with another person's differences. I have handicaps that Marilyn must live with. . . . The only difference is that people don't see mine when I walk down the street; but we're really not different."

From a statistical point of view, the most recent state survey to include prevalence of marriage among severely disabled persons was made in Iowa (330). As Table 3–2 indicates, among severely disabled, employment per se

TABLE 3–2. MARITAL STATUS: TOTAL AND BY EMPLOYMENT STATUS

STATUS	TOTAL		EMPLOYED		UNEMPLOYED	
	N	(%)	N	(%)	N	(%)
Single	269	(41.3)	140	(42.5)	129	(40.4)
Married	259	(39.9)	129	(38.7)	130	(41.0)
Widowed	61	(09.4)	31	(09.4)	30	(09.3)
Separated/divorced	61	(09.4)	31	(09.4)	30	(09.3)
Total	650	(100.0)	331	(100.0)	319	(100.0)

has little effect on marriage; marriage per se has little effect on employment. Whether the source of income is from the nondisabled partner or other resources is not covered in this survey, which indicates that more in-depth information is needed before statistics are used as a basis for planning.

To ask the questions — Should the disabled marry, or should a disabled person marry another disabled person or a normal person? — is completely to overlook the individuality of disabled individuals and the uniqueness of partnerships into which they enter. As Table 3–3 attempts to show, there are 240 different partnerships that are possible between individuals, if one identifies the *severity* of the physical impairment (mild, moderate, or severe or none—normal) and *onset* at birth or later.

For example, male A was born with a mild disability. If he chooses partnership #2, he will have a partner who also was born mildly disabled; but, if he chooses #26, he will have a normal female partner who is not the carrier of a recessive gene (#30) that might jeopardize a future child. Female H acquired a moderate disability in her teens. She might choose partnership #100 with a fellow who has a mild disability from birth, or she might choose #120 who has a severe disability acquired by accident long after birth. And a final example from Table 3–3 is Female P is normal but carrying a recessive gene of hemophilia; she seeks a relationship #224 with a partner whom she nursed during a recurrent but mild kidney disability which started in his twenties. Table 3–3 gives some indication of the many possible partnerships that defy smug solutions, that is hardly complete since the disability that is called mild, moderate, or severe may be, physical, mental, or emotional!

The wide variety of choice and of possible partnerships should point to the many needed directions and opportunities for research (260). What needs are satisfied when a disabled person marries another disabled person? When a disabled person marries someone able-bodied? What special problems are experienced in these partnerships? The following experiences are cited as necessary for a physically handicapped young person to mature socially and vocationally. Are they equally important to a healthy marriage? (330).

1. Possession of enough information about one's disability to understand it
2. Opportunity to associate with nonhandicapped of the same age
3. Opportunity to have some experience of living on one's own

4. Opportunity to learn about different occupations and careers
5. Chance to talk with someone about a personal problem
6. A work experience
7. Opportunity to participate in an educational program at each individual's level
8. Opportunity to do household tasks
9. Chance to talk with someone about physical abilities and disabilities
10. Opportunity to learn social graces
11. Opportunity to earn money
12. Opportunity to develop a hobby
13. Opportunity for a comprehensive sex education program

Items on this list were rated as important and very important by former student patients of a midwestern hospital school facility. It behooves both service and research personnel not to give them short shrift.

SAME SEX PARTNERS

The open spirit of the past decade has made it possible to discuss homosexuality in various public forums (111,258). Homosexuality is no longer classified by the American Psychiatric Association as a mental illness (439). The works of Marmor, Hopkins, and Hooker; the Walfenden study and report; cross-cultural studies by Beach and Ford; and Gould's work with adolescents, hippies, and college students all substantiate classification of a group of homo-sexuals as the normal (165,166). To this, Singer (394) would add that homosexuality is essentially a minority interest for humans, as it is for all other species. As long as it remains a minority interest, it cannot function as an equally viable means by which everyone may express his or her sexuality. " . . . While some people may be able to achieve their optimal satisfaction through homosexuality, others will not. . . . the choice of a sexual object will depend upon a great many variables, including innate disposition, hormonal tendency, psychological development and social conditioning." This corroborates Sagher and Robbins's position that homosexuality has an infinite number of origins (368). The common sense approach of Race, Leecraft, and Crist is worth repeating here:

Homosexuality is the consistent choosing of a person of the same sex for a love object. (When the partners are female, they may be called more specifically, Lesbians.) A person who has engaged in homosexual practices is not necessarily a homosexual; most persons at one time or another have fantasies and longings and, occasionally, behavior involving the same sex. But unless they consciously choose this type of sexual expression *in preference to* others and call themselves *homosexual,* society is on shaky ground to make that pronouncement for them. It is well known that sometimes people under certain stressful conditions (prisons, distant outposts, etc.) resort to homosexual behavior, but when they return to normal environment out of stress, they revert to their previous sexual orientation. Many adolescents experiment with homosexual behavior, but this is not a fixed choice until they decide it to be (336).

With the many stresses placed upon individuals having disabilities, including those who are segregated not only from the unimpaired majority but are isolated from companionship of the opposite sex by communication barriers, it would not be surprising to find an adult homosexual minority. The sparsity of information in this area indicates the very real need for empathetic research and greater understanding. Unfortunately, the recent Supreme Court decision to delegate authority to the states has thrust a legal issue into an area that heretofore has rested within the privacy of the individual—or individuals, namely consenting adults. Until this is resolved appropriately to the needs and concerns of a multicultural population, counseling will have to include the possibility of imposed restrictions by some state laws. Meanwhile, an early article by Holbert is worth remembering in order to keep our equilibrium during times when the social pendulum swings wide:

How about the homosexual relationship? This depends entirely upon the basic personality and sexual identification of the individual concerned. If a male person finds that he truly sees himself as a female and finds a genuine sexual response of a female type to another male, then a happy, satisfying lasting sexual relationship is possible, assuming again that there is a real loving, caring feeling between the partners. However, if one accepts a sexual relationship with another of the same sex, merely as a substitute, because "the real thing" is not apparently possible, then all sorts of difficult and damaging effects are bound to occur. A homosexual relationship should be accepted only if this kind of relationship would have developed in spite of the disability.
The outlook for a completely happy, normal sexual life for the disabled is therefore seen as difficult and complicated, but I think that we have all slowly and painfully learned to accept what we must and take that which we have and turn it into the best possible good (197).

IN CONCLUSION

The disabled young man and woman, like their able-bodied counterparts, have to arrive at some solution regarding the level and type of success that each can comfortably strive for, and live with, in the adult male or female role. In present day society a wide variety of sexual behavior patterns exist. Some disabled persons who have chosen heterosexual relationships, whether married or unmarried, develop a variety of patterns agreeable to their partners as well as themselves. Others choose sexual abstinence or rely upon masturbation or homosexuality for relief of sexual tensions. As far as possible, each individual should be given the opportunity to choose his or her own way of expressing sexuality compatible with personality and life-style (169).

On the other hand, empathetic counselors will help both the developmentally disabled and those experiencing onset of disability after childhood if they can communicate the options, the capabilities required for each choice, and some examples from the experiences of others in similar situations. However, there are several levels of counseling for which professionals must prepare themselves. Whether a counselor is prepared to provide limited services or extensive skills, an important part of his knowledge should include *when* to refer a disabled person to *another* colleague who *can* meet the immediacy of a specific need. Thoughtful planning is needed. But as an unidentified wag has said, "Planning is what you do before life takes over!" In life as it is lived, many individuals, whether able-bodied or disabled, entertain the hope of being fulfilled by another person. They attribute much of their loneliness to not having found the "right" mate. It is a very human truth that not having found oneself and one's capacity for life and for love is actually the barrier confronting most of us. *Being the right person*, right for oneself, is the essential step toward finding fulfillment. If then the "right" person comes along—the cup runneth over!

TABLE 3–3. VARIETY OF RELATIONSHIPS

		FIRST PARTNER							
		MILD				MODERATE			
		@ BIRTH		LATER		@ BIRTH		LATER	
		♂	♀	♂	♀	♂	♀	♂	♀
MILD									
@ BIRTH A ♂		1	2	5	6	9	10	13	14
B ♀		4	3	8	7	12	11	16	15
LATER C ♂		33	34	37	38	41	42	45	46
D ♀		36	35	40	39	44	43	48	47
MODERATE									
@ BIRTH E ♂		65	66	69	70	73	74	77	78
F ♀		68	67	72	71	76	75	80	79
LATER G ♂		97	98	101	102	105	106	109	110
H ♀		105	99	104	103	108	107	112	111
SEVERE									
@ BIRTH I ♂		129	130	133	134	137	138	141	142
J ♀		132	131	136	135	140	139	144	143
LATER V ♂		161	162	165	166	169	170	173	174
L ♀		164	163	165	167	172	171	176	175
NORMAL									
AVERAGE M ♂		193	194	197	198	201	202	205	206
N ♀		196	195	200	199	204	203	208	207
RECESSIVE									
PROBLEM O ♂		217	218	221	222	225	226	229	232
GENE P ♀		220	219	224	223	230	227	232	231

SECOND PARTNER

FIRST PARTNER							
SEVERE				NORMAL			
@ BIRTH		LATER		AVERAGE		RECESSIVE	
♂	♀	♂	♀	♂	♀	♂	♀
17	18	21	22	25	26	29	30
20	19	24	23	28	27	32	31
49	50	53	54	57	58	61	62
52	51	56	55	60	59	64	63
81	82	85	86	89	90	93	94
84	83	88	87	92	91	96	95
113	114	117	118	121	122	125	126
116	115	120	119	124	123	128	127
145	146	149	150	153	154	157	158
148	147	152	151	156	155	160	159
177	178	181	182	185	186	189	190
180	179	184	183	188	187	192	191
209	210	213	214				
212	211	216	215				
233	234	237	238				
236	235	239	240				

Even numbers=male-female partnerships between a first partner
and mate [second partner]

4 PRIORITIES FOR PARENTING:
Genes and Judgment

Parenthood is the only profession that has been left exclusively to amateurs.—Anonymous

The survival of mankind no longer depends upon reproducing as many people as possible. Indeed, there are those who feel that the quality of life around the world is at present threatened by uninhibited quantity (Table 4–1). In our society anyone who wishes to enjoy sex that is separated from reproduction has the general sanction and opportunity to do so. Parenthood need no longer be an accidental outcome of intercourse.

PARENTS AND NONPARENTS: MODERN PERSPECTIVES

The question of bearing and raising children is a complicated one for *all* members of our complex society. "Parenting" is not an instinct in the human race; it must be learned (115,337). Until recently, it was learned through the social and cultural cues passed from one generation to another. But society has changed to a mobile, multicultural entity, housed and transported haphazardly within teeming urban megalopolises. Since the new cultural cues are seen differently between generations, as well as within the childbearing generation, many new problems affecting parenting are seeking solutions:

1. the care of surviving *dependent* persons (for example, those developmentally deficient infants whom medicine has saved from death at birth by extraordinary procedures, and those adults who will survive long years in coma or extreme senility);
2. the increase in divorce, in illegitimate children, and single parent families. Approximately 210,000 girls age 17 and under gave birth in 1971, and the divorce rate of those married in their teens is 3–4 times higher than that of any other age group (115);
3. the shocking rate of child abuse, plus inadequate resources for those children and their abusing parents. Some 300,000 cases of child abuse are reported annually to authorities in the United States and some 60,000 result in death or severe disability (70);
4. the improved, but still less than optimum and not universally available birth control, abortion, and sterilization techniques.

TABLE 4–1. WORLD POPULATION
(August 7, 1977 at 2:00 PM)

4,014,426,686

One birth every ¼ second
One death every ⅔ second

which means:

145 more people a minute

207,000 a day

1,500,000 every week

(From Computer, Boston Science Museum Department of Population Science, Harvard School of Public Health)

During these turbulent times, some couples have consciously turned away from childbearing. Actually, a recent news report corroborated careful surveys showing that, among the nonimpaired population, 1 out of 25 married couples in the United States have decided not to have children because they 1) prefer their careers and uninterrupted intents, 2) don't want that type of overbearing responsibility, and 3) know older couples who have fulfilled their lives without children and don't feel that they need to *own* children for fulfillment, since they get many satisfactions from living and enjoying other peoples' children (429).

It has been suggested that this voluntary childlessness is an outgrowth of the tremendous demands experienced by working mothers as a result of the combined responsibilities of a job, a family, and a home. Movius believes that career oriented wives may increasingly consider the child-free state as a liberating alternative (307). Freed from child care responsibilities, a career oriented woman may benefit by greater mobility, fewer family commitments, and more time for professional development. The flexibility and freedom that accompanies this child-free alternative may be necessary for a career woman to meet today's competition and inflation (287).

The reasons for *having* children are also varied among the general population. Innocence, accident, loneliness, a need to create a love object that can't get away, an attempt to trap a mate or to "save a marriage," etc. vie with more mature reasons such as the realization that a child can add a dimension of growth and development to a satisfying marriage wherein the partners are willing and able to assume the needed responsibilities (265).

The fact that many people in today's society are not prepared for parenthood has only recently gained attention. With youth living in broken homes, going away to college, or seeking career opportunities in cities far from home, they become biologic parents with few models for parenthood around them. Even the experience gained in a home with both parents may not have provided them with the understanding necessary to become effective parents. As these needs have surfaced, it has become obvious that adding sex education to the three "Rs" is still not enough. Therefore, in recent years, HEW's Office of Education and Office of Child Development have sponsored a new program called Education for Parenthood. In conjunction with private agencies and schools, this program is designed to increase adolescents' awareness of the social, emotional, educational, and health needs of children and of the roles parents play in satisfying these needs (Table 4–2).

Concurrently, young adults are questioning the roles traditionally assigned to parenting. The old-fashioned domineering father is out. Some claim that his roles have been usurped by mother, teacher, policeman, social worker, and therapist, but a new brand of fathers is appearing (28). In like manner, the old-fashioned home-body mother is found less frequently today. Some women claim that this role can be condensed within a managerial scheme that includes wifing, childing, and careering. But a new brand of mother is also emerging who is willing to arbitrate. Androgeny is on the increase. Its exponents claim that parenthood is a time for men and women to share

TABLE 4-2. EDUCATIONAL MATERIAL ON PARENTING AND RELATED
RESPONSIBILITIES

Parenting Guide: Selected Resources and Materials 1965–1975. National Alliance Concerned
  With School-age Parents, 7315 Wisconsin Ave., Suite 211–W, Washington, DC 20014
Education for Parenthood Curriculum Materials. Director of Special Programs, U.S. Office of
  Education, 400 Maryland Ave., S.W., Room 2013–G, Washington, DC 20002
Family Life and Child Development—Annotated Bibliography. Child Study Association of
  America/Wel–Met Inc., 50 Madison Ave., New York, NY 10010
Films, Pamphlets, Educational Materials:
  1. Planned Parenthood—World Population, 810 Seventh Ave., New York, NY 10019. Re-
     gional Offices:
       Great Lakes—234 State St., Suite 1001, Detroit, MI 48226
       Midatlantic—255 South 17 St., Suite 2005, Philadelphia, PA 19103
       Midwest—406 W 34 St., Room 725, Kansas City, MO 64111
       Northeast—810 Seventh Ave., New York, NY 10019
       Southeast—3030 Peachtree Rd., NW, Room 301, Atlanta, GA 30305
       Southwest—4928 Burnet Rd., Room 204, Austin, TX 78756
       Western—680 Beach St., San Francisco, CA 94109
  2. American Association of Sex Educators & Counselors, 5010 Wisconsin Ave., N.W., Suite
     304, Washington, DC 20016
  3. American Association of Marriage & Family Counselors, 6211 W. Northwest Highway,
     Dallas, TX 75225
  4. American Institution of Family Relations, 5287 Sunset Rd., Los Angeles, CA 90027
Informational Materials to Control, Prevent or Terminate Pregnancy:
  1. Association for the Study of Abortion, 120 West 57 St., New York, NY 10019
  2. Association for Voluntary Sterilization, 708 Third Ave., New York, NY 10017
  3. CHOICE Religious Coalition for Abortion Rights, Box 381, Scarsdale, NY 10583
  4. Clergy Counseling Service on Abortion, 55 Washington Square South, New York, NY 10012
  5. Planned Parenthood and its affiliates. See above.
  6. Wickersham Voluntary Sterilization Service, 133 East 48 St., New York, NY 10022

values and responsibilities equally, including child care. Proponents of androgeny hold that the old inflexible male and female family roles were false;
parenthood to them is partnership at all tasks for the mutual benefit of all
members of the family (133,150).

IS THIS INHERITED?

As disabled young adults enter the mainstream of society and consider the
acknowledged pros and cons of parenthood, some of them have an additional
responsibility. They wish to rule out the fact that whatever has impaired
them or their spouse will not threaten any child of their union: is this inherited? There are few workers in the field of rehabilitation who have not been
asked this earnest question.

It is estimated that some 12 million Americans suffer impairments which
are wholly or partly due to defective genes or chromosomes (409). This figure
does not even include those mentally ill who are afflicted with major psy-

choses. With present-day confusion caused by precipitous deinstitutionaliza-tion, the increased reproduction of thousands of schizophrenics and others who could not bear children in custody settings is now an additional threat to the gene pool (14). As a result of research consensus on the genetic-environmental factors involved, Rosenthal suggests that "future generations may include many more mentally ill and those predisposed to mental illness than exist today" (358).

Medical authorities estimate that 1 in every 150 babies is born with a genetic defect which will result, for most, in serious lifelong physical or mental impairment (202). According to the National Foundation—March of Dimes—genetic mistakes are responsible for some 2.9 million Americans with mental retardation; 1 million with diabetes; 1 million with congenital bone, muscle, or joint disease; 500,000 with complete or partial blindness; 750,000 with impaired hearing; and some 6 million others with imperfect organ systems. In addition, genetic factors are said to be responsible for at least 40% of all infantile mortality (409). Progress in detecting, diagnosing, preventing, and treating genetic diseases, together with descriptions of vari-ous genetic diseases and the effects that they produce, are included in a 32-page publication, *What Are The Facts About Genetic Diseases*, which may be obtained free of charge from the Office of Research Reports, National Institute of General Medical Sciences, National Institutes of Health, Be-thesda, MD 20014.

GENETIC COUNSELING RESOURCES

While a knowledge of the basic facts about genetic disorders helps to remove the mystery and paralyzing fear that has been associated with them until recent years, individual questions require consultation with specially trained genetic counselors (223a). Genetic counseling and related services have nearly tripled over the last six years (202). In the United States, in 1977, there are 389 laboratories offering various genetic services, according to the *Inter-national Directory of Genetic Services* published in March by the National Foundation. Of these, 272 offer genetic counseling. Further information is available from

The National Genetics Foundation, 250 West 57th Street., New York, NY 10019

The National Foundation—March of Dimes, P.O. Box 2000, White Plains, NY 10602

Information Office, National Institute of General Medical Services, Na-tional Institutes of Health, Bethesda, MD 20014.

Since 1972, ten universities and medical schools have received funds from the National Institute of General Medical Services to establish human ge-netic centers to conduct research on the diagnosis, treatment, and preven-tion of human genetic diseases and disabilities (202). The basic focus of re-search at the University of Pennsylvania is on hereditary disorders of the nervous system and chromosomal disorders, while research at the Indiana Center, located in the James Whitcomb Riley Memorial Hospital for Children in Indianapolis, includes studies dealing with hereditary deafness, identical twins and their families, the effectiveness of genetic counseling, and the recognition of new genetic diseases and their causes. Other centers have been established at the Yale University Medical School, New Haven; Albert Einstein College of Medicine and Mount Sinai School of Medicine in New York; the Johns Hopkins University, Baltimore; University of California School of Medicine, San Diego; University of California Medical Center at San Francisco; University of Texas Graduate School of Biomedical Sciences; Houston; and University of Washington School of Medicine, Seattle (202).

CANDIDATES FOR COUNSELING

Research has brought us to the current situation in which virtually all aberrations of the chromosomes of the human fetus can be detected while the fetus is still in the womb. These abnormalities are in the basic hereditary material and generally presage serious, sometimes fatal, developmental defects. Those who seek counseling may themselves be afflicted with or may already have a child afflicted with a birth defect, mental retardation, or hereditary disease. Or they may have a racial or ethnic background that puts them at risk for a certain disorder. As Ebben explains, "In many races and ethnic groupings there are abnormal genes that occur predominantly in that group and rarely in others. Typical examples of such disorders are cystic fibrosis in whites, Tay–Sachs disease in some Jewish people and sickle cell anemia in blacks" (152). Another threat to an unborn child may be sex-linked defects; the most widely publicized of these has been the hemophilia of European royalty. This disability may be carried by a female but strikes only the male offspring.

For nine months, pregnancy has heretofore kept the secret of chromosomal hazards to a child's well-being as well as the secret of its sex. However, inroads are being made into Nature's secretiveness in both of these areas. One approach to determining the sex of a fetus is suggested by a European research team who analyzes a woman's urine for testosterone hormone excretion early in her pregnancy (250). Another research unit has developed a saliva test to be taken during the middle three months of pregnancy. They claim to report the sex of the fetus with 98% accuracy (382). However, the most widely publicized approach in the United States is the microscopic observation of the X-chromatin and/or Y-chromatin of fetal cells. These cells are obtained by amniocentesis, the process whereby a physician takes a sample of the protective amniotic fluid surrounding the unborn fetus in a woman's uterus (44). One study, based on examination of the X-chromatin, proved to be 97% accurate. Examination of the Y-chromatin gave a 99% accuracy. This led investigators to conclude that this process, using fresh amniotic fluid cells, is a valuable, rapid, practical method for prenatal sex determination (213). Therefore, at present it may be claimed that maleness and femaleness of the unborn can be identified with fair certainty. However, the methodology has not yet been achieved whereby parents can *predetermine* sex from external or internal manipulations. Claims of success are made for separating the X-bearing and Y-bearing sperm and selecting the desired sex sample for artificial insemination (243). Others advise a supervised do-it-yourself preselection technique based on the timing and position of intercourse (243). Still others try interventions such as acid (for girl) or alkaline (for boy) douches, or special food. As with all 50–50 chances, those who win the child with the wanted sex feel that they have the system mastered. For better or worse, there is no statistically sound system at present for preselecting the sex of a child.

One sociology professional who believes that sex determination will be available five years from now or sooner also predicts that at least 55–65% greater preference in our society for male children (399). However, Westoff, among others, claims that, if effective sex controls were universely available in the United States, the immediate temporary effect would be a surplus of male births in the first couple of years, followed by a wave of female births. Oscillations of male birth and female birth periods would eventually be used to "facilitate the marriage market" (445). But, who can say for sure? Scientifically, it is more and more conceivable that the biologic state of the fetus, including its sex, will be increasingly available. While this may offer great benefits to families threatened by sex-linked hazards, the impact this will have upon society with its preferences, prejudices, cultural hangups, and learning lags remains a future challenge.

Another group seeking genetic counseling, or recommended for counseling as a risk population, are women over the age of 35. It has been found that 60% of all babies with Down's syndrome are born to mothers over that age, for example (43,297). There are tests to predict the possibility of some diseases in offspring of prospective parents. If a woman is already pregnant, it is often possible to identify certain defects by analyzing a small amount of the amniotic fluid. This fluid can be analyzed biochemically, or its cellular content can be examined cytochemically, either cultured or uncultured. Technicians look for chromosome alterations in the cultured cells. When viewed in conjunction with a relevant clinical history, diseases such as Lesch–Nyhan syndrome and Tay–Sachs can be strongly suspected if the amniotic fluid shows elevations of uric acid and a deficiency of hexoseamidase-A, respectively. Cytochemical evaluation of *un*cultured amniotic fluid cells may reveal such disorders as Pompe's and Tay–Sachs disease; evaluation of cultured cells can reveal as wide a variety as galactosemia, metachromatic leukodystrophy, Niemann–Pick disease, or cystic fibrosis. Chromosome alterations may reveal Down's syndrome, D-trisomy, or X-linked disorders (108).

In previous years a great deal has been written about the risks of amniocentesis, but in 1975 the National Institute of Child Health and Human Development reported at the American Academy of Pediatrics on a controlled study that showed conclusively that amniocentesis, in the proper hands, is safe for both the pregnant woman and the fetus (11). An abstract of the study in nonscientific terms reports:

Of the 1,040 women who had amniocentesis, 34 were found to have fetuses with defects—19 with chromosomal anomalies and 15 with metabolic disorders. In addition, 11 male fetuses were identified as having a 50% risk of a sex-linked disorder. Of the 45 women, 35 elected to have abortions. Eight of these aborted fetuses were affected with Down's Syndrome. Among the women in the control group, seven gave birth to infants with Down's Syndrome—the overall accuracy of the procedure was determined to be better than 99% (10,44,331).

In a very few instances, it has been possible to give treatment to alleviate a problem detected by amniocentesis, but more often the biochemical or enzymatic changes detectable in early fetal life may have already caused irreversible damage to the fetus. In the larger proportion of cases, the information concerning the fetus has either assured the parents that the baby will be free of gross genetic defects or, when such defects have been revealed, has given them the chance to decide whether or not to end the pregnancy by an abortion (108).

PREGNANCY: HAZARDS FOR WHOM?

Loving relationships expressed sexually are important to many individuals, including disabled persons. Under varying circumstances and agreed upon accommodations, a disabled woman can take part in intercourse provided that she has a vagina to which access can be gained. She can reproduce by natural or artificial insemination if she ovulates and has a uterus. But a key question remains. What hazards will pregnancy bring to her or to the child that she may carry to term? Although this is an area which will require much more study as more of the disabled come into the mainstream of life, scattered bits of experience have already been collected. They indicate one present surety in the field: pregnancy is not precluded just by the *name* of a particular physical disability. Rather, it can be considered in terms of remaining functions and compensations, as well as in terms of the potential mother's mental and emotional well-being, and life-style.

PARALYSIS AND PREGNANCY

Ordinarily, pregnancy presents few problems to a woman with a spinal cord injury, including one with a cauda equina disorder (fundamentally a lower motor neuron lesion). If her menstrual periods have been interrupted by the accident, they will usually return within 6 months. Ovulation continues, and she may be impregnated. Although weight gain is gradual enough for the woman to compensate for it on a day to day basis, the guidance of a dietician is suggested to ensure sufficient calcium intake. "Sufficient" is the amount needed for fetal development which will, on the other hand, not provide too much ash for the mother to handle (356). Care should be taken to avoid renal infection, and it must also be remembered that breathing will be largely diaphragmatic in women whose cervical lesions cause abdominal and intercostal weakness. Therefore, when the mother-to-be is sitting, she may experience respiratory insufficiency at times because of the resistance offered by the enlarging uterus to the downward excursion of the diaphragm. Due to sensory loss and resultant freedom from painful labor, pregnant paraplegics are at times advised to accept hospitalization prior to the offspring's due date. This is to avoid giving birth without even realizing it, as has occurred! (371)

The average paraplegic woman may have a headache, perspire during contractions, or may feel some general discomfort, but the majority are able to deliver their babies normally. However, in the second stage of labor, many will require use of obstetric forceps to counteract the paralysis of those muscles ordinarily used in the expulsive efforts (371). There are times when additional precautions must be taken: during the latter part of pregnancy when Braxton Hicks contractions have begun, or in the first or second stages of labor when autonomic dysreflexia secondary to contraction of uterus muscles may induce paroxysmal headache, hypertension, and retinal or cerebral ischemia. At such times, Horenstein suggests interrupting the dysreflexia by administering spinal anesthesia or an autonomic blocking agent. Pregnancy or labor is then terminated by cesarean section (201). In general, however, babies born to paralyzed women are just as likely to be born healthy as babies born to the nonparalyzed (371).

SURGICAL REPAIR AND PREGNANCY

Women ostomates have different problems and different solutions. They have had surgery to remove malfunctioning parts of their intestines (ileostomy or colostomy) or of their bladder (urinary ostomy). In these surgical repairs new outlets (stomas) are made for emitting body wastes, and exterior appliances are worn to collect these wastes. However, these patients are free to go about ordinary activities. Often a person feels so much better, physically, after years of suffering that there is a new enjoyment of life. With the exception of a very few women who might have required pelvic exenteration which includes removal of the vagina, most female ostomates with a sympathetic partner find their condition does not interfere with sexual function (385,387).

The United Ostomy Association publishes newsletters, booklets, papers, etc. in which many professional and personal references to pregnancy are made. They are clearly written with a touch of good humor and a wealth of common sense. Through them one learns that, unless other abnormalities are present, the number of children a female ostomate can have is a matter of individual preference. In fact, one report indicates that only be getting relief from the condition which made an ostomy necessary could some women consider childbearing. One woman, previously barred from considering children due to ulcerative colitis, had a baby 4 years after ileostomy and traveled during pregnancy; another, childless for 12 years of marriage, became pregnant 6 years after surgery. Yet another, whose ostomy was performed 5 months before marriage, had a child 2 years later.

Although it is considered advisable to wait at least 2 years after ostomy surgery, a survey of 20 mothers varied widely in the number, timing, and spacing of pregnancies. The course of the pregnancy varies as it does in any population. For example, in any population there are blood incompatibilities that threaten a child rather than the pregnant mother. One ostomy mother "with an Rh-factor incompatibility had her baby transfused three times while he was still in her uterus, but his birth was normal, as was her second baby's" (387). Although there may be occasional reason for cesarean section at time of birth, it is strictly for obstetric reasons having nothing to do with the presence or absence of an ostomy. In summary, pregnancy is neither harder nor more dangerous for the average ostomy mother or for her child than for the unimpaired mother and child as a result of the growing number of physicians who are experienced in care procedures (384, 385, 387).

WHAT ABOUT THE CHILDREN?

Another question frequently asked by young disabled couples, wherein one or both of the partners are disabled, is "Will we be able to take care of a child . . . how have others faced this?" They are not the only ones concerned or involved. Parents of these couples who elect to let nature take its course, or who anticipate added problems and responsibilities with the advent of grandchildren, also seek other opinions. Professionals are slowly abandoning blanket decisions based on whether "the disabled" should or should not have children. More experience with individuals having varied capacities is giving content to the pros and cons (260).

Nigro claims that to a large extent the multidisabled couples she knows have given more thought to this question of children than the average couple. She finds that what they can honestly and realistically accomplish and be responsible for has been much more carefully analyzed. Their decision to have children or not to have children has actually been made

in relation to the total soul-searching self-examination they have put themselves through in making a decision about whether they could function in a marriage together. Those whose disability is related to heredity have had the best professional advice and are acting in accordance with the facts as they perceive them." (302)

DIAGNOSIS DOESN'T DECIDE

It is well to realize at this point that those multidisabled couples to whom Nigro refers have had the advantage, under the guidance of her staff, of planned social development and sex education, as well as marital and vocational counseling—combined with training to develop a sense of responsibility. Not all disabled individuals have had this guidance toward responsible decision-making. Too often, professionals who are quick to espouse sex education are slow to add planning for (or against) family life and parenthood to their repertoire. As a result, misinterpretations are propagated. For example, a 1975 newspaper carried an article, "Can Love Find a Way Despite Retardation?" Considerable space in the article was given to a retarded engaged couple, ages 22 and 26, who stated that they want the right to marry, to live together, to bear children, and to lead private lives.

They will look for an apartment, the couple said. They will learn to budget and they will have a family. If their child were mentally disabled (the hereditary factor varies in the case of retarded parents), they would accept him—and if he were normal, "We'd be tickled to death—that's what we want. A normal life."

This article romanced the couple's "rights" without exploring their capacity for responsibility and their capability for carrying out possible goals (97, 247).

In contrast to this type of eye-catching and slanted reportage is an English report of a Symposium on Marriage and the Handicapped (182). Several of the participants' observations on childbearing and child-rearing are well worth repeating here:

Morgan: I think I should now turn to the question of children and whether there are any circumstances in which a handicapped couple may decide that it is not appropriate for them to have a family. Clearly, most married couples see a baby as a logical fulfillment of their union and the completion of their family. Clearly, too, most girls and women want to have a baby. . . . but with handicapped girls the desire could be even more intense, because this would prove to everyone, and perhaps especially to themselves, that they really *are* women. I think this also applies to handicapped men, [although] perhaps to a lesser degree, but it is obviously very important to be able to demonstrate your sexual potency by producing a child. Is it not important, however, for some handicapped people to face this and then perhaps make the decision that it is best for them not to have a child, especially if it seems likely that they would not be able to provide or care for the child adequately? Do we consider deeply enough the feelings and very real problems of a child who has one or possibly two handicapped parents? How can we help both the children and the parents to face the difficulties that will undoubtedly arise?

Groups at this symposium discussed different aspects of this crucial problem.

Martin: It was agreed that whether or not handicapped people should have children depended on the degree of handicap. It was felt, however, that the severely handicapped should not have children, especially if they are wheelchair cases, as this would only put an extra amount of physical strain or mental stress on the parents and might have a bad influence on a child's upbringing . . . the decision as to whether or not the handicapped couples should have children should be left with the parents, but they should be able to seek the advice of Doctors, Marriage Guidance Counselors . . . they should take into account the economic factors, whether they would be able to provide a good upbringing for the child, their degree of handicap and its effect upon the child's upbringing. . . .
Wright: Some of the group said that if the handicapped couple decided to have children and were living in a hostel, it should be the responsibility of their hostel to provide for their children. Someone, I think the older ones, felt this was not a tenable line, because there was a lack of resources, lack of money and, above all, the Spastics Society or whoever sponsored the hostel had a responsibility not only to the other occupants but to people on their waiting list and why should a married couple get priority just because they were handicapped.

Perry: . . . We were asked what we thought regarding a married couple having a child and who should take the responsibility to decide whether they should or shouldn't. It was mentioned that this could be discussed with a Doctor and the couple, with the Doctor's advice, could sort this out, but we thought, generally speaking, you can't expect anybody to involve themselves with a personal thing like this—you have got to decide for yourself and weigh up your own situation and then go ahead accordingly as to whether you are ready or not. If you have got very expensive accommodation, then obviously you've got to consider this as well, because if you are going to have another mouth to feed, then you have got to get some money from somewhere, and if its going basically on accommodation with what is left over on food, then somebody is going to go short and we didn't think it would be the child . . . there were a lot of views aired and they were some for and some against.

Hargreaves: [in reply to the question of what the child's reaction will be to his parents during adolescence, and whether there will be any loss of affection:] I remember only too well, up to the age of five B_____ was quite happy to walk out in the street with me, but as soon as he went to school, he no longer wished to hold my hand, he no longer wished to be seen walking with me, and he has been very frank, and I am delighted B_____ that you have, and he will not mind me repeating part of a conversation he had with me. I am delighted, and I am sure you are delighted too, that he is able to talk about it to me. One day I asked him, "Why don't you bring your friends home?" and he replied, "I'm ashamed of you. I don't want my friends to hear you thumping around the house." Now, let's get all this into perspective. B_____, as he said, is now a mature young man; he has got things into perspective. I know that at school, the school teacher told me, my daughter went through two very bad years from the other school children, [who asked] "Is your father soft in the head?" Well, toward the end of this conference I am feeling a little soft in the head, but to get it into perspective, ladies and gentlemen, every parent has some idiosyncrasy—if you have a long nose, other children say. . . . "Hasn't your Dad got a long nose?" or if you have a bald head, "Your Dad's bald." Well, you know I can't win—I mean being spastic with a long nose and a bald head? I am sure that you wish me to thank B_____ very much because it must have been quite difficult.

Nigro has some interesting comments on attitudes relevant to childbearing and child care by multiply disabled couples (302). She claims that most of the couples she has known have felt that the most they could expect to accomplish was mutual self-care and that children were out of the question. Even where the desire for children was strong, some decided to establish strong ties to the children of relatives and friends instead of having their own. However, she cites some interesting exceptions: One couple whom she knows has two very young children and are managing quite nicely now. They realize they may need help when the children are more active, and they are responsibly planning for the future. But they are loving parents, and their children are healthy and happy. On the other hand, a young woman whom Nigro has followed for a long time, who had a stormy relationship with her own rejecting mother all her life, married and had a baby. She had expected that she and her nondisabled husband would be able to take care of the baby, but the marriage did not last. The baby was placed in a foster home and is doing well. The mother sees her child regularly, and the child knows she is her mother. The fact of having borne this healthy child (which is something her own mother was not able to accomplish) is probably the single most important event in this young woman's life. She has achieved a kind of peace within herself and a purpose for existence she never had before (302). Another couple cited by Nigro had a baby which, by prearrangement, was to be raised by a childless sister of the wife. They had a beautiful daughter who now knows them as aunt and uncle. The child is happy with her adoptive parents whom she knows as her own, and the handicapped couple takes pride in the addition they have made to their extended family.

Some mildly retarded couples are raising happy, healthy children. In Nigro's opinion, the children of such couples whom she has followed are no worse off than hundreds of thousands of children born to parents of marginal intelligence, undiagnosed as retarded, whose limitations are known to us all and who are sometimes classified as culturally deprived. She believes that the children of these well-adjusted retarded couples who keep in touch with developmental resources are, in fact, better off by far, "for the retarded parents know they have deficiencies and know they must avail themselves of professional advice"(302).

As in all major life situations, the *diagnosis* of the impaired person has less to do with the question of whether or not to have children than the balance between a couple's capabilities and inabilities, mentally, physically, emotionally, and socially. Horenstein's reply to the question "Do doctors most often recommend that a female [with multiple sclerosis] not conceive children after she has been diagnosed?" contains practical and empathetic points for persons in many situations.

Oh, I don't know what doctors most often do, but I can tell you what I do, though I am not sure why I do it. It just seems to make sense. I suggest that if a patient has had a lot of new symptoms in a short period of time, that this is not a very good time to take on an additional physical or mental responsibility. Those of you who have had children know that the first six or eight weeks after the child is born is really a very exhausting time. If one talks with the ordinary woman who has had one child or more, she will often say that the first six or eight weeks after the birth of the child, unless there is lots of help, is a very busy and tiring time. As a matter of good practice, it seems to me that a patient with multiple sclerosis who has been having a lot of recent difficulty should not take on an additional physical or emotional responsibility. I do not believe there is any reason for saying that a patient with multiple sclerosis who is otherwise well, or who has been stable for several months or years should not conceive and bear children if that is her choice. When families come to see me about this, I try to obtain agreements about postpartum assistance in terms of not requiring the patient to be up for night time feedings. I think there should be a formula service and the use of disposable diapers so that as much of the load should be taken off the patient as possible. I believe that patients who do not become exhausted are less likely to suffer decompensation of function. Patients with multiple sclerosis suffer frequent transient increases with fever, anxiety, the use of drugs and just being very tired. If the patient with multiple sclerosis is the mother and she is chronically exhausted and unstable in walking, chronically disturbed and with frequent flexor spasms, this is hardly an environment in which to raise a child. I think these are important things to explain to the husband and wife and obtain their concurrence. I come back to the point which I made in the beginning, that sexuality in the family is a transaction between two people. (393)

ADOPTION

There are instances, however, when even the most responsible and mature couples having a disabled partner should not, or cannot, conceive a baby. It would be foolish to identify this with any specific condition, since individual factors of each case must be reviewed by one or more competent physicians who can judge the risks to a severely disabled young wife or to the wished for child. There are also instances when a disabled male partner is unable to impregnate his wife even by artificial insemination. Some couples facing these barriers have surmounted them by passing the requirements of stringent adoption regulations. For example, an ileostomate and her husband had no trouble meeting the requirements of an adoption agency and adopted a newborn baby boy (385). A proud father whose disability precluded conception writes, "After one year at Michigan State University, I broke my neck at the C-5 level in a diving accident in 1952. In June 1956, I married a wonderful girl I had gone with in high school. In 1964, we finally got a four-day-old girl. She is one-fourth American Indian and cute as a bug's ear" (410). The summer 1977 issue of *Accent On Living* contained the following letter to the Editor:

As a disabled person who adopted a baby boy 12 years ago, I can certainly speak about this with some authority. First, if your own doctor can arrange a private adoption vs. going through an agency, it may be easier. Agencies are very difficult to work with. The disabled person who can care for him—or her—self will have an easier time of it.

After adoption the child learns to accept every family member as "normal," even though each one is different, and as he grows up he is able to help the disabled parent to some extent. The child also likes freedom and so should never be burdened with *extra jobs* in the home. He should be encouraged in normal studies, sports, and to have playmates, parties, etc., just as other children have. It is also important to be friendly to other "normal" families and to fit in with other programs such as church-going, club activities, boy scouts, picnics, etc.

Name Withheld By Request

Contrary to many popular notions among the unimpaired, as well as the disabled, children per se do not hold a marriage together. For example, of 333 marriages reported in a recent study of males with spinal cord injuries, 73.9% had children prior to the accident. Of these, 32.1% turned to separation or divorce while only 20.7% of families with no children sought these alternatives. Furthermore, of those having children pre-injury, 15.4% had additional postinjury children. They still had a higher divorce–separation rate than those without postinjury children (153). Obviously children have not had a statistically stabilizing influence on these marriages.

LONG-TERM QUESTIONS

There is no simple solution related to the question of whether a couple, having one or two disabled partners, should or should not become parents.

However, society at large is concerned and has some reason to be cautiously watchful of would-be parents who have problems which will require *prolonged social solutions*. Careful consideration must be given to questions regarding carriers of critically defective genes or environments which threaten children (71, 97, 292, 459). In addition, the mating of irresponsible mental retardates, psychotics, and drug-dependent persons must be viewed even more from the perspective of the innocent child victims than from the point of how society can function adequately as a proxy parent. In many respects, people of all abilities and disabilities have a right to get married, but doubt is growing about a couple's "right" to bring a child into the world when they cannot adequately care for it mentally, physically, or emotionally.

One of many studies on marriage of adult retardates reveals how often the major responsibility for their offspring has become the problem of someone else (321). Furthermore, despite the importance of the question, there have been few valid long-term studies of the children of psychotic parents. However, there is enough data to lead current investigators to regard such children as a high-risk group for some form of psychiatric disorder at some point in their lives. Consistently, the studies of children of psychotic parents show higher rates than those for the general population not only of schizophrenia and manic–depressive psychoses, but of other types of psychologic behavioral disturbances (14). It is also well documented that babies born to alcoholic women show a marked pattern of defects (small heads, stunted body size), and almost half are found to be of below normal mentality. Given the rate of chronic alcoholism among women of childbearing age, it is estimated that 1 out of 2000 babies is born with fetal alcohol syndrome, making that the third leading recognizable cause of mental deficiency in the United States (8). As for babies born to drug addicts, one needs no substantiating study—they are seen writhing with symptoms of drug withdrawal in every hospital nursery where they are born.

An equitable answer to the question of parenthood for the disabled frequently cannot be reached just through disability summation (90). It is more reasonably approached by assessing the capabilities possessed by each couple. Each must ask themselves whether they can meet the responsibilities and the growth requirements of the child who would depend upon them.

5 PROBLEMS AND POSSIBILITIES: Impacts and Enablers of Sexual Function

It's not what disease the patient has but which patient has the disease.
—William Osler

STRESS AND DISTRESS

The sexuality of individuals with disabilities has been grudgingly granted in recent decades by professionals and by the disabled themselves. It has been recognized slowly because of the few definitive studies in this area and the confusion of opinions which were drawn from the unique perspective of limited clinical impressions. "The disabled" are not an entity, although we are far too prone to speak of them as a homogeneous group (82, 95, 134). "They come," as Chigier points out, "in as many varieties as do all other people, and this fact should be the starting point of rehabilitation policy and programming" (69). Even the same condition leaves wide individual variations, dependent upon the extent of tissue damage or dysfunction, its location, and what this *particular deficit* means to this *particular person* at this *particular time* in life. When stresses and distresses that are related to an individual's sexuality are physical in nature—affecting motor and sensory functions—they also may have emotional impact upon the individual's psychosocial development.

If one reads journals to which the disabled themselves contribute, such as *Accent On Living* or *Rehabilitation Gazette,* one becomes more aware of actual people and their immediate problems and resources, as a few quotes may illustrate(5, 341):

—I was born without arms or legs—attend a college—what I want more than anything else is to meet college people similar to myself, and especially a nice cool girl.
—My son . . . is very bright and studious and would like to exchange letters with other boys his age. Because he is a dwarf we have problems . . .
—I found I had multiple sclerosis (1950), and soon after I went to a wheelchair . . . I know what real love and feeling are. My wife and I have been married 48 years . . .

Today most of us know someone who limps, who lumbers along awkwardly, or who may be in a wheelchair as a result of polio, cerebral palsy, multiple sclerosis, stroke, spinal cord injury, etc. How often do we consider the private life behind the disability? When we talk of a "para" (paraplegia—two limbs involved) or a "quad" (quadriplegia—four limbs involved) with paralysis caused by spinal cord damage, do we see this person as a statistic or as a real person?

According to Singh and Wagner, spinal cord injury has many present day causes (395). While they list automobile accidents as the leading cause of spinal cord injury in the United States, motorcycle and motor scooter accidents are increasing alarmingly. Different ages experience different threats. For example, falls from heights and sports, such as diving (into shallow water), football, and skiing, cause many spinal cord injuries in young people. On the other hand, industrial accidents contribute to the number of spinal cord injuries among employed men, while older persons are prone to injury from falls or from not being cautious enough as pedestrians. Although combat injuries cause a relatively small percentage of spinal cord injuries, they have been significant in inspiring improvements in care for patients. Diseases cited by Singh and Wagner as leading to paraplegia, for which causes or cures are as yet undiscovered or are incompletely known, include cancer and other tumors of the spinal cord, infections and abscesses of the spinal cord, multiple sclerosis, congenital defects, including severe forms of spina bifida, and other rarer neurologic disorders.

Estimates from various sources of the number of Americans with paraplegia range from 60,000 to 100,000, and new cases per year have been estimated at 4,500 to 10,000 (395). When one considers that paraplegia affects only part of the 40 million disabled persons in our country, the enormity of the problem is self-evident. At that, 40 million is a conservative figure taken from the 1970 U.S. census, which was the first nation-wide count to ask about disabilities—and it did not include the handicapped in institutions! Fifty million could be closer to today's reality—quantitatively (273).

Qualitatively, there are disabled persons in all sectors of our society whose sexuality is threatened by stress and distress. Some stagnate in confusion, despair, self-pity, etc. Others with similar difficulties refuse to submit. They strike out for solutions and find respite either by trial and error or by imitating what has worked for someone else. However, what may have been a best solution for someone else still has to be tailored to fit a new personality and a new setting. Therefore, the following examples of initiative in problem-solving are not offered as solutions, but as possible catalysts from which to launch individual efforts towards a richer life.

WHAT PRIVACY WITHOUT INDEPENDENCE?

Genital satisfaction, love, marriage, and reproduction all require a certain amount of privacy, which in turn requires a modicum of independence. One cannot generalize about "the disabled" and "their" capacity for the independence which allows for various degrees of privacy. Obviously, the different stages at which and situations in which persons become disabled (birth, prepubescence, adolescence, adult, elderly; single, married, separated, divorced, or widowed)—as well as such factors as intelligence, adjustment, socioeconomic status, and resiliency—produce many variations. What are the concerns of severely disabled persons and the concerns of those professionals who strive to remove barriers on their behalf?

The recent conclusion of a 15-year, follow-up study of some 1000 persons with cerebral palsy (disabled from birth) showed the following range of independence among the living (where mean age is 25 years (421):

14.7% have own home
67.9% live with parents, friends, and relatives
17.4% live in institutions (private and public)

An educated guess for others who have been handicapped during the bulk of their lives would lead one to believe that a larger percentage of retarded persons are in institutions or group residences, but about the same limited percentage (15%) may have their own homes. Long-term follow-up studies about the independence of persons with disabilities occurring after childhood are few and far between. Suffice it to say, the unemployment statistics for moderately and severely disabled individuals indicate major social and economic dependency. Through recent legislation, HEW is giving priority to rehabilitation of severely disabled persons and to incentives that will counteract employer resistance. However, with dwindling job opportunities during economic retrenchments, no great inroads to independence are yet evident. Shifting from large institutions to community based residences and from social isolation to affirmative action has been verbalized in the last 10 years, but implementation still remains at pioneer and project levels (239).

PRIVACY SETTINGS

While sexuality is getting fairly wide debate among professionals associated with institutions and group residences for young adults, the quality of independence needed and the nature of privacy settings are only recently coming to concerned attention (304). Hospital and institutional settings are usually designed to make it easier to give and to supervise care. The architectural plans are generally drawn from the staff's point of view, where efficiency takes priority over such humanizing aspects of life as esthetics or privacy. Even if lovely private rooms exist, in how many institutional settings may an adult lock the door without evoking staff criticism? Even if visitors' parlors or lounges exist, in how many can friends, relatives, or lovers meet without sharing space with other residents? Even bathrooms have been invaded by misguided and overconscientious staff seeking to curb masturbation (122, 161).

Fortunately, rehabilitation personnel are beginning to realize that if independent living is an accepted goal for many patients, some opportunity for privacy must be afforded even during training stages. On the positive side, "privacy rooms" are appearing in institutional settings. In as widely separated areas as the Netherlands, England, and Cincinnati, Ohio, Bidgood (36) points to apartment units designed for disabled couples that are staffed by compassionate professionals. Another step ahead are the apartments developed in and near the Spinal Cord Injury Centers of the Veterans Administration. In these, patients receive functional training that is directly transferrable to their own home setting—and to their personal need for privacy. For a comprehensive overview of the progress being made in this area, the reader is referred to *Housing and Home Services for the Disabled,* by Laurie (239). Among many creative pointers therein is the experience of a Canadian couple who proved that it is less expensive for two wheelchair-bound individuals to share an apartment than to live in an institution. Since many administrators may consider privacy a luxury but could be influenced by cost–benefit, it might be more useful to go that route in the arrangements for deinstitutionalization and take privacy as a spinoff!

PRIVACY ROLES

What privacy really means to a disabled couple—in this case both are deaf —is charmingly expressed by the young bride who confesses that she thought her wedding day was the happiest in her life, "but our happiness keeps growing. We get along even better since we're married. I suppose it's because of the complete privacy of being alone together, being two people who can share totally. We believe in each other, care for each other and help each other" (407). As LeShan perceptively indicates, even among the nonimpaired in our society, "It is important for each partner to be aware of social sensitivities and to find ways to respect each other's needs for both privacy and intimacy. . . . happily married couples strike the balance between intimacy and privacy in various ways" (246). Among the disabled, there are no fewer considerations; in fact, there are many additional ones. For example, how does the disabled person carry off the role of "lover" when it is also necessary to depend on a "caretaker" for basic physical needs. Impaired college students who have caretaker–roommates or companions are dependent upon the subtle capacities of these buddies to fade away at the "right" moments; youth and intelligence generally favor these arrangements. But it takes practice and perseverance to be the resilient lover, while needing special transportation and help in and out of it. This very situation, wherein a permanently disabled young man needed male nursing during dates to get in and out of his car, led to the invention of a now frequently used piece of equipment—the car lift! Few people are that inventive or have the resources to carry an invention to fruition. Most have to accept intimate help that directly affects their partnership role.

On a still more intimate role level, Romano points out how difficult it can be for a sexual partner to have sexual feelings about a disabled person when the partner must fulfill the role of nurse as well as lover, while the disabled fulfills roles of both patient and sexual object. For some people, moving back and forth between these roles can be confusing. In such instances, perhaps the couple should consider hiring an outsider to assume the caretaking roles, e.g., bowel and bladder care. Local visiting nurse groups, student aides, private nursing registries, or a willing neighbor may be able to fill this need (239, 354).

Unfortunately, there are times when partners are so physically disabled as to be unable to help one another. Extension of the privacy role may have little precedent and requires considerable thought. Such was the case when the following question was addressed to members of the helping professions at a meeting of persons with permanent disabilities:

If two intelligent but severely disabled persons living in a group residence are deeply in love as a result of a long-term friendship and compatibility, would you help them obtain contraception and assist them in getting into bed together and finding a mutually compatible sexual posture and satisfaction?

There were wide differences of opinion among the few who felt prepared to respond. There were no pat answers, but study of reasonable and possible alternatives under various contingencies will undoubtedly widen the horizon of responses as this gains more consideration. However, Loring's observation at the 12th International Rehabilitation Congress on the topic of "Assistance in Sexual Intercourse" may throw some light on the subject:

There is the question of the extent to which grossly handicapped spastics should be assisted in the act of sexual intercourse. Many require specific physical handling in order to achieve satisfactory intercourse. In some Scandinavian countries, it seems that such help is regarded as part of the nursing function, but the extent to which this can happen depends upon the culture and the current moral standpoint of the nation concerned in matters of this sort. Many staff would find the proposition repellent. Others who have achieved a close friendship with the spastics concerned would find it acceptable; some staff might find it acceptable, but for perverse reasons. In my opinion in the majority of countries this must be a matter for the staff and the handicapped persons concerned, and no pressure should be put on the staff to undertake duties of this sort against their own instinct and wishes. It would be more acceptable in the case of some members of staff to take a negative viewpoint and do no more than secure the privacy of the two handicapped persons concerned. However, supervisors and other staff should use their common sense and their compassion in these matters, taking into account the long-term happiness of the handicapped. (251)

PRIVACY ACTS

In addition to privacy settings and privacy roles, it is necessary to look with compassionate objectivity at privacy acts. Diamond points out that one must not only think of genitals or bathroom activity when one considers sexuality. Two broad areas must be considered—public and private sexuality. These he defines as follows:

Public. How does the person act in public; what role is played by these actions? Will a handicap interfere with the individual's personal or public appraisal of his or her masculinity or femininity? For example, can a telephone lineman with a paralyzed leg accept, without loss of masculinity, the job of a telephone operator? Can the arthritic housewife accept the loss of her hands and deft touch without considering it a reflection on her femininity?

Sexual patterns and roles are our public demonstration of socially recognized sexual expressions. Public concerns may manifest themselves in the choice of how the individuals interact with society.

Private. Here we refer to the genital sexual responses and those inner problems not usually discernible. This includes the ability to maintain an erection, have orgasm, receive and give genital and sensual pleasures, and reduce sexual tensions in oneself or partner. (104)

The private acts related to private aspects of sexuality include communication as well as physical relationships. In Diamond's opinion

There are practically no sexual concerns or situations that cannot benefit from increased communication by and between the individuals involved. Expectations and preference capabilities can be more realistically appraised with good communication and false impression can be minimized. The handicapped, as do many able-bodied, often attach a magnified value to certain suspected deficiencies without ever testing the reality of the situation with the "second person." For example, in the realm of sexuality, most of us are concerned with something in our physical makeup. In this regard the handicapped and able-bodied again are alike. Consider that an individual may be concerned personally with being bald, having small breasts, or being deaf, blind, or elderly. Only by communication with the "second party" can one find out if the concern is mutual or the magnitude of the concern. Communication between the individuals involved will reduce hesitancy in finding out just what is and is not possible and what is or is not acceptable. (104)

The private consenting acts which bring mutual satisfaction to two people who are disabled are as varied as those among the nonimpaired population. Professionals must train themselves to be nonjudgmental in terms of client preferences and resolutions. Nor should the personal preferences, practice, or point of view of any professional be forced upon a client who may find it incompatible with his feelings, ethics, or religious convictions. Lewis Mumford, social scientist, philosopher, and author is quoted by LeShan as observing:

The more dehumanized we feel, the more frenzied we become in trying to reveal everything. The less we experience genuine love, the more we talk about sex; the less alive we feel, the more we spill our private thoughts to anyone who will listen and the more helpless we feel about control of our own destinies, the more willing we are to allow others to rob us of our privacy. (246)

A professional has the obligation to inform adult clients about all possible alternatives, with their pros and cons. What a client chooses with the mutual consent of his or her partner remains within the treasured domain of privacy.

SIDE-EFFECTS OF CHEMOTHERAPY

As a result of constantly improving chemotherapy, people are living longer and more comfortably than in any previous generation. Medication can correct a body deficiency if it is carefully chosen by a physician, is prescribed in selected dosage, and effectively produces the desired change, be it freedom from seizures, diabetic shock, muscle spasms, etc. But now new demands are being made on the very medication that is doing what it was originally expected to do. Among these new demands are requirements that any side-effects of medication which may interfere with sexual performance be removed. Since there is always some price to pay for any benefit of medication, how much are we willing to pay in demanding its added safety? There is no set answer; each case warrants individual consideration. In fact, what is really known about medications and their various effects—on efficient sexual function, on the fetus of a pregnant patient, or on the action of chemical contraceptives—is that their use demands continual vigilance and research.

Sometimes we become too comfortable with a little knowledge and a partial solution. For example, most of us are familiar with the normal life that diabetic friends are able to live as a result of proper insulin intake under continued medical recheck. How many of us have given consideration to the fact that coitus is a fairly vigorous exercise, although pursued in the horizontal position? Actually, a diabetic on insulin injections has to learn how to balance injection dosage, food intake, and exercise. If the exercise happens to be coitus, he or she may have to try to regulate likely times of intercourse for optimal well-being and sexual satisfaction. Sexuality imposes an extra demand on drug function that few of us may have recognized heretofore (135). The enormity of the lack of needed facts is overwhelming. It should be a caution to those who glibly espouse the sex "rights" of all members of this childbearing generation. The right of the disabled to live a properly medicated life, even though they may have to renounce reproduction, has to be weighed against the right of an unborn child to be protected against violating chemicals.

IMPACT ON MALE SEX FUNCTIONS

Since erection is largely dependent upon parasympathetic innervation, drugs interfering with the parasympathetic function may cause erectile impotence. On the other hand, the ejaculatory system derives its nerve supply from the thoracolumbar sympathetic outflow, so drugs having peripheral sympathetic blocking effects are likely to disturb ejaculation.

Beaumont points out that in the past reports in the medical literature of suspected drug-induced sexual side-effects have tended to be imprecise (27). Impotence in the male has often been reported without specifying whether the problem is failure to achieve satisfactory erection, inability to ejaculate, or both. The distinction is important. For example, drugs most likely to interfere with ejaculation seem to be those with alpha-adrenergic receptor blocking properties. The best known of these are used in the treatment of hypertension. Many antihypertensive agents have been found to produce ejaculatory impotence: guanethidine, bethanidine, bretylium, debrisoquine, clonidine, and methyldopa. The so-called psychotropic drugs are another group of drugs likely to interfere with ejaculatory function.

Tricyclic antidepressants like imipramine, desipramine, amitriptyline and particularly clomipramine will cause it. Thioridazine is a well-known inhibitor of ejaculation and similar effects have also been reported with chlorpromazine, chlorprothixene, chlordiazepoxide, perphenazine, trifluoperazine, butaperazine, butyrophenones, and mono amine oxidase inhibitors. (27)

Threats to erectile potency have different origins. Beaumont indicates that in the case of those drugs which exert their effects principally on the peripheral sympathetic nervous system, erectile potency is usually maintained. In some cases, however, he finds this effect is dose-dependent. For example, smaller doses of drugs like chlorpromazine or clomipramine produce only ejaculatory impotence, whereas larger doses also interfere with penile erection. Erectile impotence has also been reported with imipramine, protriptyline, mebanazine, and desipramine. This effect is presumably due to anticho-linergic action and has been compared with that of methantheline bromide, which has been known to produce impotence, presumably by its action on the parasympathetic neurons.

Ganglion blocking drugs like hexamethonium, mecamylamine, pen-tolinium, and pempidine cause total impotence in the male, and there have also been reports of erectile impotence with drugs like propentheline. Therefore, Beaumont suggests that it would be worthwhile to look for sexual side-effects among patients receiving antispasmodic, anticholinergic prepa-rations. In addition, he calls our attention to other drugs such as ampheta-minelike substances which may cause male impotence. Appetite suppres-sants like fenfluramine also bear watching (27).

The greatest number of observations, surveys, and studies on the sexual function of disabled men have come from records of spinal cord injured patients (171, 356). Among these, the influence of medication has received minimal definitive research, even though systemic drugs for relief of spas-ticity have been observed to have effects on the reflex of voluntary sexual activities of some patients (171). Romano and Lassiter (356) claim that their patients

report that the presence of spasticity does not interfere with sexual activity, and in fact for some male patients, spasticity potential means effective potential. In this case, we might caution the male patient to avoid central nervous system depressants, be they drugs (e.g., diazepam) or alcohol, prior to intercourse, if erection might be eradicated.

Griffith et al. (171) point out that in earlier studies a high percentage of cord injured males had spermatogenic arrest related to the level and degree of spasticity, but more recent reports point to the decreasing incidence of testicular atrophy and the improvement in spermal qualities with repeated ejaculation. Spira (405), and Guttman and Walsh (174), instilled neostigmine (Prostigmine) intrathecally to produce ejaculation, generally with erection. Of these patients 33% with complete flaccid lesions and 67% with incom-plete flaccid lesions ejaculated. Although ejaculatory capabilities improved, impregnation rarely followed—with the exception of a few successful cases of artificial insemination. These few are enough to invite a wider horizon of research.

IMPACT ON FEMALE SEX FUNCTIONS

The effect of medication on female sexuality has complications not found in the male. Medication may or may not affect female sexual behavior, the efficacy of any chemical contraceptives taken by women, or, finally the vul-nerability of a fetus carried by a woman on medication. At present, one must say "may or may not affect" any of these three areas, since these are rela-tively new aspects of research. Beaumont reminds us that a woman's sexual behavior often shows cyclical changes related to the stage of her menstrual cycle, and this should be considered before attributing reduced or accelerated performance to any short-term chemical therapy (27). Actually, the peripheral pathways relevant to satisfactory orgasm in women are not as well understood as in the male. Since the parasympathetic system seems to be more involved, yet most drug-induced problems concern the sympathetic system, Beaumont hypothesizes that "peripheral drug effects leading to disturbed sexual function would appear to be less likely in the female, although there have been reliable reports of orgasmic impotence which was probably drug induced peripherally. . . . drugs like clomipramine have been reported to do this" (27).

The central nervous system is less involved with sexuality and reproduction in the female than it is in the male. This should make it as possible for a spinal cord injured woman to conceive, gestate, and deliver in the same manner as her nondisabled counterpart. Actually, the resotration of female hormonal regulation following cord injury is supported by the evidence that most women resume menses within 3–6 months postinjury and are susceptible to pregnancy (171). In response to this potentiality, Romano and Lassiter raise the question of chemical contraception for some of these patients. It is their contention that significant correlation exists between birth control pills and thrombophlebitis, as well as between the latter and spinal cord injury. As such, these relationships serve to make oral contraceptives questionable as a means of contraception for women with spinal cord injury (356).

Another disability for which oral contraceptives are held in question is cystic fibrosis. Taussig believes that preliminary evidence suggests some patients with this disability experience deterioration of pulmonary function while on the pill, and he advises other birth control methods for them (423). On the other hand, when asked whether he would give the pill to women patients having multiple sclerosis, Horenstein replied that the only patients he discourages from using birth control pills are women who have one of the well-established contraindications: "Over forty, hypertension, established blood vessel disease and the occurrence of neurological deficits while taking the pill" (393).

Information is extremely meager on the chemical interaction of the oral contraceptives with other drugs, and more research is needed. For example, oral contraceptives may necessitate an increase in insulin dose of women diabetics but do not appear to be more hazardous than in nondiabetics (451). Only recently have scientists at the University of Arkansas brought to our attention the interaction of birth control pills with a drug having widespread use—alcohol! Intoxication lasts longer among women using oral contraceptives. When alcohol metabolism was measured in pill users, other women, and men, it was found that pill users took 1.2 hours longer to metabolize the alcohol, possibly because of increased hormone levels (326). Other drugs, less well known than alcohol and generally considered medications, also interact with oral contraceptives. O'Malley reports that antipyrine metabolism becomes 31% slower and phenylbutazone metabolism becomes 41% slower for pill takers than for controls (308). It is his contention that the effect of oral contraceptive steroids on antipyrine metabolism is a reflection of decreased activity of hepatic drug-metabolizing enzymes. Therefore, "It is to be expected that in women taking oral contraceptive steroids, the intensity and duration of effect of many concomitantly administered drugs might be increased" (27). As yet, there are no definitive studies of young women on the pill who are also taking medication which is metabolized in the liver. This could be a useful research and may eventually help to determine optimum individual dosage.

A completely different situation among those who use birth control pills is found in the experience of female ostomates. Some women having ostomate repair found that pills, especially capsules, sometimes passed whole through the intestine and were not absorbed. Sparberg investigated and reported that birth control pills seem to be absorbed in his patients with ileostomy; nor did he learn of any such problem in the literature about ostomy (403). However, the United Ostomy Association cautions that each patient should discuss absorption with her own physician and, of course, has the alternative of other contraceptive methods.

The most careful consideration must be given to those medications prescribed for women, with or without disabilities, who may become pregnant or who are already carrying a child (432). While no drug used in therapy has shown the very destructive effect on a fetus as thalidomide, it may be that damaging effects of a lesser degree have still to be recognized. Drugs which have been mentioned as having a possible slight teratogenic effect if taken early in pregnancy are barbiturates, aspirin, phenytoin, and dexamphetamine. Drugs suspected of affecting the fetus late in pregnancy are narcotics (if the mother is addicted), possibly inhalational and local anesthesias, barbiturates, and alcohol(143).

According to a recent California study, the widely used tranquilizers meprobamate (Miltown, Equanil), and chlordiazepoxide (Librium) [a close chemical relative of diazepam (Valium)] have been found to cause serious birth defects if taken during the first 6 weeks of pregnancy (271). This study examined 19,044 live births and is believed to be the first study on humans to indicate that nonbarbiturate tranquilizers may damage the fetus. Conducted by Milkovitch and van den Berg of the University of California (Berkeley) School of Public Health in conjunction with the Kaiser–Permanente Medical Care Program, it compared the incidence of birth defects among the offspring of four groups of women, all of whom had been diagnosed by their physicians as suffering from anxiety or tension. One group had received meprobamate; a second group, chlordiazepoxide; the third group, other drugs; the fourth, no drugs at all. Study results revealed that serious birth defects occurred more than four times as frequently in the offspring of women taking meprobamate and chlordiazepoxide than in those whose mothers had no drugs for their anxiety. The incidence of defects was twice as high and fetal deaths were more frequent among the two tranquilizer groups as among the group that had been given other drugs. While the study findings cannot be considered conclusive, the researchers believe results indicate that "meprobamate and chlordiazepoxide may not be safe during early pregnancy." They suggest that these drugs should be prescribed for women of childbearing age guardedly, with the assurance that the women are taking precautions against pregnancy (271).

At the 1975 annual meeting of the American Academy for Cerebral Palsy, the question of the effects of maternal anticonvulsives on subsequent offspring was raised. Whether there may be a subpopulation of women sensitive to the hydantoins taken to control convulsions or whether pregnancy itself —or the pill—affects the metabolism of diphenylhydantoin (Dilantin) with subsequent danger to the fetus was a topic of considerable concern. At this meeting, Hanson and Smith reported on the fetal hydantoin syndromes. They claim that through epidemiologic studies over the past six years evidence has accumulated which indicates that hydantoin anticonvulsives have a serious teratogenic potential. While numerous dysmorphic features have been reported, most focus on individual defects of major medical significance. However, eight unrelated patients of Hanson and Smith shared a broad multisystem pattern of abnormalities suggesting a specific fetal hydantoin syndrome: craniofacial features include a broad depressed nasal bridge with short upturned nose, epicanthic folds, hypertelorism, ptosis, strabismus, minor ear abnormalities, wide mouth with prominent lips and sutural ridging. Limb defects include hypoplasia of distal phalanges and nails, digital thumb, and alterations of palmar creases and dermal ridges. Growth deficiency is usually of prenatal onset and appears to be permanent. Mental or developmental deficiency is common, as are other defects. However, major defects such as cleft lip and/or palate and cardiac defects are less frequent.

Hanson and Smith suggest that recognition of the broader syndrome may serve to identify children who could have a problem not apparent in infancy. They caution that this syndrome has been misdiagnosed in individual cases as Coffin–Siris and Noonan's syndromes. To clarify this and associated problems, an epidemiologic study using records from the NIH Collaborative Perinatal Project is currently underway. It will attempt to define the frequency of this syndrome among the infants of women taking hydantoins during pregnancy. Meanwhile, potential risks arising from the use of hydantoins should be discussed with exposed epileptic women who may be considering a pregnancy (179).

Comments of physicians responding to the report by Hanson and Smith included: "All four children of a mother controlled by Dilantin had a fetal syndrome." . . . "Tridione is much worse." . . . "Women taking related medications should be made aware of its effects on the fetus." . . . "Women relying on this medication should seriously consider whether or not to have children." . . . "studies of this nature suggest the wisdom of cautious observation of all medication, including the interaction of chemical birth control with medication . . . research and chemical observation must be stepped up."

The United Cerebral Palsy Associations are sponsoring Tennyson's studies on the effects on the fetus of drugs which the mother takes during pregnancy. Tennyson is looking into the possibility that some drugs may cause sublethal assaults on nerve cells at critical periods of fetal development, predisposing the fetal nerve cells to early aging or impaired growth and thus causing neuromotor disorders. She is testing many drugs, including agents commonly used in treating various medical and psychologic disorders. One particular area of the nervous system that Tennyson is studying consists of a group of dopamine-containing nerve cells in the midbrain that make connections with other areas. It is known that, if these cells are damaged and dopamine is not present, a movement disorder such as Parkinson's disease will result. Whether loss of dopamine-containing cells also may cause cerebral palsy is the crux of her inquiry (110).

Once a problem is recognized, the research not only requires careful design, but also new technologic approaches. A recent example of the latter is an apparatus used by the Epilepsy Center of Michigan to analyze the blood level of anticonvulsive or antiepileptic drugs—to determine whether patients are using these medications at optimum levels to prevent injuries and whether other medication is affecting these blood levels. The determination is made by a method called gas–liquid chromatographic (GLC) analysis. To obtain this analysis a physician need only forward a completed request form furnished by the Epilepsy Center and mail it with a sample of the patient's serum to the Center (181). At present, a GLC analysis can be made for five anticonvulsive medications: dipheny/hydantoin (Dilantin), phenobarbital, primidone (Mysoline), tegretol, and ethosuximide (Zarontin). Other drugs will be added to the list in the near future. The GLC service provides a convenient way for a physician to obtain an opinion on the dosage of a particular anticonvulsive medication for the patient without having the patient travel away from home for the determination.

PHYSICAL CHANGES AND SEXUAL FUNCTION

Sexual function is a complex matter. How do physical aspects of disability relate to the physiology of sex and to the remaining possible choices of sex acts? To provide a more solid background for this discussion, let us review Trieschmann's clearcut distinctions between sex, sex acts, and sexuality (430):

Sex is one of four primary drives, the others being hunger, thirst and avoidance of pain. The drives originate in the subcortex but are modified by learned responses in the cortex. Thus the cortex governs the methods, occasions, opportunities and expressions of the primary drives. A majority of these learned patterns are regulatory, inhibitory and prohibitory, deriving historically through church and state laws.
Sex acts are behaviors involving the secondary erogenous zones and genitalia, sexual intercourse being only one kind of sex act. The term *sex act* does not indicate the relationship of the people involved, their emotions or their attitudes.
Sexuality is the combination of the sex drive, sex acts and all those aspects of personality concerned with learned communications and relationship patterns. This learned, regulated communication and relationship process occurs at many levels, for example, conversation, shared activities and interests and various expressions of affection, including sexual intercourse.

Disabled adults do not need anyone to tell them about their sex drive. They are the ones best informed about its past and present impact. But what they most often lack is information about their physical potential for sex and the alternatives remaining for them (84, 220, 322). Even individuals who suffer no direct physiologic impairment of their sex organs—as in stroke, polio, spasticity, amputations of extremities, arthritis, etc.—are often required to learn new patterns of sexual behavior to compensate for the deficits imposed by their gross disability.

Sex education and sex counselors have found a great many adults (disabled and unimpaired) seriously lacking accurate information about normal human anatomy and sexual physiology. Therefore, counselors as experienced as Romano and Lassiter emphasize that a first step in providing sexual counseling to the disabled is to call upon a physician (in their situation it was the physiatrist) to review the anatomy and physiology of the human reproductive system. They used the word *review* because "we find that our patients can more readily accept this information with minimum anxiety if we ascribe to them them the knowledge we wish they had and present it with a 'now you will recall that' approach" (356). Finally, every adult with a disability should be aware of the range of sex acts within the human repertoire which could contribute to sexuality if any are found mutually compatible to the disabled individual and partner.

Sexual problems cluster in areas of organ dysfunction, sensory changes, and secondary interferences. In each of these areas the whole solution is greater than the sum of its parts—that is, sexuality of a couple will reflect not addition of each reaction, but the newly developed resolution which they deem compatible to a lasting relationship.

ORGAN DYSFUNCTION

Historically, the study of sexual capabilities among disabled populations found its impetus in the rehabilitation wards of soldiers who had been injured during World War II. At first, neither patients nor rehabilitation personnel paid attention to sex since there were too many unknowns to be tackled that were related just to keeping the patient alive. But as techniques to maintain well-being were developed and became routine, studies in sexual function were pursued.

Disabled Men

By 1973, Griffith and his colleagues could review nine surveys covering over 2000 male spinal cord injured subjects (172). From these, he reports that erection occurred in 54%–84% of subjects. In fact, as few as 7% of men with complete lower motor neuron lesions and up to 99% of those with incomplete upper motor neuron lesions reported erections. While most men attained capability of erection within 1 year following the spinal injury, ejaculation only occurred in 3%–20%. Specifically, as few as 1% of patients with complete upper motor neuron injury reported ejaculation while up to 70% of those with incomplete lower motor neuron injury reported it (172).

Statistics are one way of opening the doors of investigation; rationale is another. Rusk and his colleagues set out to teach rehabilitation personnel and clients the logic behind function, in other words, what had to be known in general to understand practical approaches (360). It was not accidental or mysterious that some cord injured had spontaneous erections when giving no thought to sex, and others could elicit erections by touch and/or sexual fantasy. The circumstances made more sense when one learned that erection occurs when the blood vessels of the cavernous bodies actively dilate by parasympathetic stimulation to engorge and stiffen the penis. The center for erection is located in the sacral portion of the cord (lower back) and may be activated reflexly by sensory impulses reaching the center over the pudendal nerve from the numerous sensory nerve endings in the glans and prepuce of the penis. Erection is also often activated by psychic stimuli descending from the cerebral cortex through the spinal cord (360).

Ejaculation is not an automatic concomitant of erection. True, a male may be able to have erections and ejaculate if the spinal cord, cauda equina, and thoracolumbar sympathetic outflow are intact. However, since two centers are far apart, a lesion may affect one and leave the other intact, which means that many times an injured man can have erections but cannot ejaculate (360, 361). Cole adds another dimension to considerations of the sexuality of the male with complete cord transection by pointing out how many aspects of his sexual response remain *normal,* even when erection and ejaculation may be unusual. Like most able-bodied males in response to sexual arousal, the paraplegic or quadriplegic may find that his nipples may erect; his muscles may develop spasms; his blood pressure, pulse, and respiration may increase; the skin of his scrotum may tense; and he may develop a skin flush. Indeed, he is capable of many of the sexual responses of the able-bodied (79).

Although the experiences of cord injured paraplegics and quadriplegics are the most heavily documented, there are other conditions which threaten erection temporarily or permanently. Only recently has information about a very few of these conditions reached the general public. For example, the impotence experienced after radical surgery to wipe out cancer of the rectum and of the sigmoid colon is frankly discussed in understandable terms in pamphlets of the United Ostomy Association (384). More communication along these lines is needed for other disabilities, now that members of the health and helping professions are gathering and reporting reliable data at professional conferences. Cumming's work on amputees, which includes the biologic and psychologic impact of amputation on erection (93), and Tobis's findings on cardiovascular patients (427) await dissemination through popular media. Also, more professionals, as well as the educated layman, should become aware of the excellent chapter, "The Effects of Illness on Sexuality," in Kaplan's book *The New Sex Therapy* (220). While much of her material may be found in scattered scientific studies, she has brought it together for further study. It awaits translation for the general public. Her work not only includes the impact of psychophysiologic states such as depression, stress, and fatigue, but also encompasses such direct threats to impotence as may be indicated by the following relevant quotes:

—Diabetes is notorious for affecting the erectile response in men very early, often before any other signs or symptoms appear.
—Hypertension does not directly affect erection; however, many forms of antihypertensive medication cause impotence in many patients by impairing the neurovascular reflexes.
—Vascular diseases: Leriche's syndrome, thrombosis of veins or arteries of the penis, leukemia, sickle cell disorders, trauma impair erection only; ejaculation and libido remain intact.

Although impotence or ejaculatory problems *may* be a presenting symptom in multiple sclerosis, the following summary of a careful analysis will act as a warning for those who hear the name of a disability and jump too quickly to generalities and conclusions. Horenstein uses several important findings to evaluate the ability of patients with neurologic disease to complete coitus. First, he checks for the presence or absence of sensation—response to pinprick—on the skin of the penis, scrotum, and the saddle area, or that part on which the person sits. Sensation is often intact in persons with multiple sclerosis. Then, a second significant check is whether or not muscle tone of the anal sphincter is present. If so, it is considered a positive prognostic feature. Finally, the capacity to contract muscles of the pelvis, particularly the ability to contract the buttocks voluntarily and tighten the anal sphincter classifies those who succeed as having "partial upper motor neuron lesions." Horenstein has found that about 98% of the men who can satisfy these criteria achieve and maintain satisfactory erections. These erections differ only in the sense that they may have been produced by mechanical or tactile stimulation of the skin of the pelvis, lower abdomen, or some other parts of the body. About 80% of these men are capable of completing coitus if they can work out satisfactory positioning with their partners, and some 40–50% are capable of ejaculation, with about a 10% fertility rate. Horenstein also discusses the optimal duration of intercourse, with or without orgasm, and the elements of the personal relationship which may give important cues to the physician and counselor (393).

Disabled Women

In contrast to the number of studies on organ dysfunction in male populations, Cole points out that research on the paraplegic woman is abominably lacking. No available literature describes the secretions from the wall of the vagina during sexual arousal in a woman with complete cord transection. Nor are there existing reports on what happens to the swelling and opening of the labia, contracting of the uterus, and ballooning and expanding of the vagina. "We know that the clitoris may become reflexly tumescent; the nipples may indeed swell, as may the breasts. Breathing, blood pressure, and pulse rate may increase, Muscles may go into spasm and a characteristic sex flush can occur" (79).

Although published information on organ dysfunction of women is sparse, Griffith documents a few facts obtained from his observations of cord injured females. He found that most women had no major alteration in hormonal function and thus resumed menstruation and their fertility seemed relatively undisturbed. He attributes the more facile sexual adaptation of disabled females to their traditionally more passive coital role and continued fertility (172).

As for women with multiple sclerosis, Horenstein reports that they, too, continue to menstruate in spite of severe spinal lesions. This, of course, means that they are continuing to ovulate, which in turn indicates that pregnancy is possible. He finds that women with multiple sclerosis have few problems with pregnancy other than some bowel and bladder dysfunction, and labor is generally uncomplicated. However, if the adductor muscles are tensely spastic, tending to cross the legs, this poses a mechanical barrier both to intercourse and to delivery. The problem of adductor muscle spasms not only interferes with sexual function,but also with personal hygiene, standing, and walking. Horenstein's discussion of remediation includes considerations of nerve block, surgical alternatives, and drug actions (393).

Acceptability vs. Availability

In considering the sexual aspects of organ dysfunction, divergent opinions exist regarding feasible solutions or alternatives. However, all counselors agree that the specific choices among any suggested solutions should be left completely up to the couple involved. As Hohmann points out, a couple should be "encouraged to engage in whatever types of sexual activities are physiologically possible, pleasing, esthetic, gratifying and acceptable *to both*" (195). This point that the activity should be *acceptable to both* is not to be dismissed lightly. Nor is a verbal agreement on the part of partners always to be taken at face value, since deeply hidden or unrecognized emotions may exist within the partnership.

A rather dramatic example of such a conflict arose when one couple agreed to accept a penile prosthesis for the paraplegic husband. Although some other couples had made this decision uneventfully, within 72 hours of this husband's return home with the prosthesis, his wife left their house to seek a divorce (413). Although husband and wife had both agreed that their sex life prior to the operation fell short of their premarital expectations and both had admitted that they spent too much time together in an isolated home, they also had expressed positive expectations for the outcome of the procedure. However, an unforeseen factor working against this particular solution for this particular couple was the fact that the prosthesis made the wife feel less involved and less important to her husband than she had before. In addition, the psychiatrists in attendance were of the opinion that this woman, who had married *after* the onset of impotence in her husband, was likely to be fearful of sexual penetration in a setting of genuine intimacy. In reviewing this and other cases, Stewart and Gerson suggest that couples who marry *after* the male partner has become impotent should have careful psychiatric evaluation prior to installation of a prosthesis (413). In their experience, couples whose sexual relationship was stabilized *prior* to the onset of impotence are often more able to look upon the prosthesis as a "welcome reacquisition of the lost ability."

Some Accepted Approaches

Since sexuality is interconnected with personal needs, family traditions, cultural values, and religious beliefs, solutions will be varied in a country with so diversified a population as the United States. The disabled need no longer settle for general physical rehabilitation without facing their sexual limitations and learning about the possible ways of realizing full sexual capacity (189, 192).

For Men. Where the barrier to a couple's regular sexual activity is the disabled male's inability to have or to sustain erection, not only should counseling about sex include positioning and special techniques of foreplay and stimulation, but it should also help individuals and couples to assess their feelings on such matters (267). Whether or not a paraplegic male loses his desire for sex may very well depend upon whether he feels he will be able to perform satisfactorily. The many and varied physical problems of sexual adjustment are no greater than the very subjective psychologic problem of the patient's self-concept. "If he thinks he cannot perform, chances are that he will be unable to adjust to whatever ability he retains. His self-concept will influence his sex life, just as his sexual adjustment will play a role in determining how he feels about himself" (170). This influential feeling is best illustrated by a direct quote from a client who recognized that with him,

it was a problem, I believe, of creating a new self-image. I thought that I had to be the virile male and live up to my wife's expectations (which she didn't have) of me. She was perfectly satisfied with what I was able to give her after the accident, but I was always trying to do more. And, finally, I just sat back and enjoyed it—and it was great! (104)

Important as feelings are, they must be based upon whatever facts are available. Unfortunately, many people, able and disabled, are sadly lacking in information about the physiology of sex. Counselors find that ignorance in this area provides a fine vehicle for discussion of the mechanics of intercourse where organic problems exist. Appropriate stress can then be placed on the importance of foreplay and the range of "normal" activity involved therein (*e.g.,* kissing, caressing, licking, oral–genital contact), and on the various positions of intercourse and the importance of adequate positioning. Patients may also be encouraged to explore their own erectile changes through attempts to trigger erections both psychically and reflexogenically, the latter by rubbing or scratching the insides of the thighs and lower abdomen (172). Some have found the application of hot towels to the penile shaft useful for facilitating or maintaining erections (171). Another simple mechanical device that may help is a rubber band placed around the base of the penis. However, *its use requires considerable caution and should not be attempted without full discussion with the individual's family doctor or urologist* (384).

Another more complicated mechanical method of maintaining erection employes an artificial phallus. A number of special devices are available to help with problems of impotence caused by disease, operations, and injury. However, it should be remembered that the prosthesis is only an aid to enable the phallus to be inserted in the vagina. It assists, but does not replace other factors necessary for successful copulation (413). In fact, men for whom a major part of the rewards of sexuality comes from body contact and closeness may find that the imposition of an apparatus within this relationship diminishes it (195).

Many couples will find their own solutions: sexual gratification by noncoital methods such as mutual hand stimulation of the genitals or oral–genital contacts; the use of positions not usually employed in coitus; sexual relations outside the marriage, with or without the consent of the handicapped partner; or the use of masturbation by the nonhandicapped person (438). A disabled man with organic dysfunction may use prostitutes or other casual sexual partners as experimental vehicles for determining his capability of performing various sexual activities. Counselors find that once uncertainty is satisfied, few paraplegics without orgastic potency have been known to frequent prostitutes. The consensus of counseling opinion seems to be that satisfying sexual activity must exist in the context of a close interpersonal relationship (195).

The results of sexual activity are most often experienced in terms of giving and getting pleasure, of reducing tension, of sharing intimacies. If this is kept in mind, the stereotype that "good" sex involves only an erect penis in a vagina can be eliminated (104). Actually, gratification from sexual activity reported by most patients is found within pleasing one's partner. In any mature sexual relationship, satisfaction of the sexual partner becomes almost equal to, or in some cases more important, than self-gratification. Studies show that the paraplegic man who is able to bring his partner to orgasm gains great satisfaction out of her pleasure. Empathetic gratification also may be present since, at the time the partner achieves orgasm, paraplegics often report a "sort of para-orgasm. If strong empathy is felt with the partners, the cord injured person may show many of the psychological and physiological changes associated with detumescence, such as profound muscular relaxation, decreasing respiration, slower heart beat, drowsiness" (195). Where physical solutions are no longer possible, reports from life, such as the following, have much to say for sexuality:

. . . . Before my husband died, he was for the last two or three years, so very ill that for us there was no more sex, as most people think of it. But there was still a deep affection between us. I built my life around different types of activities so that I can't say that I really felt too great a lack in my life because he was still very affectionate, very sweet to me and showed me lots of love and attention, and I tried to do the same for him. That was important. The fact that we no longer had typical sexual relations just ceased to be of any importance to either one of us. (104)

For Women. There are fewer threats to the sex organs needed for intercourse in women than in men. However, intercourse for women with organ dysfunction merits consideration qualitatively, if not quantitatively. Colostomy surgery does not interfere with sexual function, but more extensive surgery, as a pelvic exenteration that includes removal of the vagina, could prevent genital sex relations (385). Nowadays, it is recognized that one does not need a well, functioning vagina (or penis) to express oneself sexually in a satisfactory way. If standard intercourse is not possible, what one needs is a cooperative mate, a relaxing of inhibitions, and mutually satisfying love play. Some choose mutual masturbation, some choose oral sex, and many enjoy the wide range of pleasuring afforded by touching, licking, and kissing. As Money so often reminds us, "Sexuality remains as long as feelings and imagination are in touch."

Hemicorporectomy. In this day and age, people are living through experiences that have never before been survived. Take the example of a young man who was crushed between two railroad trains and cut in half. Everything below his fifth lumbar vertebra had to be amputated. Yet, as the highest amputee known, he lives a full life as head of his family, husband, and father. Since both he and his wife wanted a large family and had only one child previous to the accident, their major resentment, besides the fact of the accident itself, was their inability to have more children. Sexuality itself proved no problem to this couple who could say after the shock of the first hard year, "We've gotten closer . . . we talk more on a basic level." But for a couple whose life revolves around children and who could provide love and basic needs, a way had to be found. It was—artificial insemination. When they shared their solution with friends and relatives, the father-to-be reported not only general acceptance but rejoicing. As he puts it, "They really enjoy the idea because they know I want kids. I told her [his wife]: I wish you'd have twins!" (458) Half of his body was cut away—but his heart is quite whole.

SENSORY CHANGES AND SECONDARY INTERFERENCES

In addition to the results of disability which directly affect the sex organ complex, other complications may interfere with satisfying sex activities. Logistical problems may be introduced by sensory changes in parts of the body, by pain and discomfort, by motor changes (excess of spasticity or mobility limitations), or by urinary and bowel problems (172, 430).

Sensory Changes

Sight, sound, smell, and touch are so taken for granted as secondary sexual gratifications that the general population is often used as a pawn in the exaggerations of the advertising market: smoking is pushed by good-looking couples, "wolf whistles" follow the passing glamour girl, perfumes proclaim romance, and everyone strives to get the skin she or he "loves to touch." Variations from these artificial sensory norms are threats to the self-image of many an immature person in so-called normal society. So it is little wonder that many of the able-bodied feel that individuals with actual sensory losses are hopelessly bereft of some basics for sexuality and might as well devote themselves to concerns about restoring function. The unimpaired make these assumptions, and many disabled adopt these conclusions also. But not all! There are those professionals and those disabled persons who constantly explore the nature of their loss and seek ways to get around it in order to maximize remaining sexual capabilities.

Sightless and Soundless Sex. If the normal population think at all of the sexuality of blind and deaf young adults, they express differing opinions about their marriage potential or about the quality of home life that a child of theirs could experience. But there are other more immediate challenges. What hazards threaten their intimate experiences? For example, at a large meeting held at a country residence, a lovely and loving young blind couple thought they were slipping away from the crowd and proceeded to make love at a distance that was out of hearing, but not out of sight. How many of the onlookers who were tolerantly amused gave serious thought to the young couple's need for more assured privacy, and what provisions are ever made for it? How many persons witnessing the tender exchanges gave consideration to the tactual aspects of sex education which must be taught to young people as is done in some European residential schools?

Similarly, in considering the sexuality of the young adult deaf, how many people ever consider the visual and tactile cues that had to be learned by the deaf to replace the loving spoken exchanges used by unimpaired couples? How many of the normal population really know young people who experience major sensory losses such as deafness and how many professionals are equipped to be helpful? Elliott brings useful insights to the problem of sensory impairment in her overview of some special studies about deafness; she reports specific adjustment patterns and the formidable communication barriers that face would-be counselors of young deaf persons in high school or college (121). There is good evidence in her article, "Marriage Counseling with Deaf Clients," that because of defects in early meaningful communication, some deaf adults come to the marriage relationship biologically mature, but sexually naive as well as emotionally and experientially deprived. Often the communication mode of such couples is idiosyncratic, and while they may have similar (that is, similar to the normal population) academic levels, their social life has probably been restricted and, in many cases, they have not faced the real world and its stresses.

What it means to "face the real world" is told poignantly by a young woman who was born deaf and at one time almost felt trapped by it. Stamper shares with us how she felt when hearing fellows whom she dated would forget her handicap and sometimes turn their heads away in conversation—or speak so rapidly that she would miss words. At other times, she would have problems with dates who were deaf, and, although intelligent, they were more used to sign language and had limited verbal ability. As she confided in this revealing article, "We just couldn't talk to each other. It was very frustrating and I felt caught in a double bind" (407). Much of this was resolved when her present husband came along with similar problems and coping skills. Their continued efforts to educate themselves to capacity and their realistic search for work which would allow them to shoulder the responsibilities of marriage, as well as its privileges, are heartwarming illustrations of how one couple challenged the stresses facing marital goals of individuals with as severe a sensory deprivation as total deafness.

Many professionals debunk the idea of teaching "logistics" of sexuality, but man does not come by these instinctively and might well profit from the experience of others. As Cole indicates, "There is a need for practical information which can help people develop the competence which is an important part of human sexuality" (79). Although his original reference was to the physically disabled, his point is equally valid for the sightless and the soundless. Their sensory limitations often deprive them of cultural cues or of the scope of cultural sex options available to young adults in the general population.

Sensation Gaps. Although a loss of sensation to touch occurs in several disabilities, the relation of this limitation to sexuality has been studied more frequently in individuals with spinal cord injury—where paralysis may or may not be present (79, 322). To appreciate better the adjustments that must be made by a person who experiences cord injury, one must realize that this is greatly influenced by the location of the injury and the corresponding extent of sensory loss. In one patient the damage may consist of a totally irreversible paralysis with loss of sensation from the breasts down. In another, an incomplete lesion may spare the sacrum and such a person—male or female—may be sexually stimulated by caresses to any area where normal sensation remains (195). In fact, in women, if sacral sparing of pinprick sensation is present literally in the clitoris, vulva, and perianal dermatomes —and if such a female has experienced orgasm prior to spinal injury—she will also be able to do so after injury (83). Even in the case of more extensive injury, Hohmann cautions against relegating one's concept of sexuality exclusively to the genitalia and related tactile areas. His argument is based on the fact that "much of sexual arousal, excitement and gratification comes from the stimulation of secondary erogenous zones . . . stimulation to the lips, nipples, neck, ears [will be found] quite as erotic [by the injured] as by anyone else." Romano's study with women corroborates this. Her patients reported that sexual pleasures came from "sweet words and stimulation of other nerve-laden areas such as the breasts, mouth, neck and ears" (354).

With respect to surface stimulation of the body in both men and women, Horenstein observes that, in patients with spinal cord injury and somewhat less often in patients with multiple sclerosis, sensation may become more acute at the body level just above the sensory loss and this area may become an area of eroticized skin. Tactile stimulation of this area by a partner produces erotic feelings, just as stimulation to sensitive parts of the body of healthy people gains erotic response. Horenstein points out that most of these secondarily eroticized sensations depend upon preservation of the spinothalamic sensory pathways, which are usually substantially spared in patients with multiple sclerosis (393). Since numbness involving the perineum is not rare in multiple sclerosis, heightening secondarily eroticized sensations will go far to counteract lack of feeling in the genitals of both sexes (396). Important as these cues are to physiologic sensation in individual cases, it may be that Griffith holds the key to generalized feeling in recognizing that sexuality is more than a sex act; it is the entire repertoire of tender, loving gestures that form a basis for a relationship. It will be essential to study these factors in order to investigate postdisability sexual functioning (171).

Pain and Discomfort. Any condition which causes pain or discomfort in carrying out sexual activity may inhibit the sexual response of both the disabled person and partner. Therefore, it would be wise for all concerned to anticipate this possibility and plan preventive strategies. Complaints of this nature are likely to be made by individuals with severe arthritis, lower back problems such as those caused by herniated vertebral discs, or large inguinal hernias (220, 451). These seem almost self-evident in view of the general information available about these conditions. However, less obvious are the painful incidents or anticipated pain associated with recovery periods of amputation, ostomy, and spinal cord injury. For example, Cummings reports that phantom sensation, whether painful or not, is almost always present in patients who have undergone amputation. While literature abounds on the therapeutic approaches to phantom sensation, Cummings is one of the first to bring our attention to the disturbing effects of phantom pain on sexual activity and the need for further investigation (93).

Until recently, little was known about ostomy care, so that the victims of those problems that arise from intestinal tract excisions had to form a society (United Ostomy Association) for the purpose of informing the professionals, each other, and the public. One of their booklets on the female ostomate indicates that immediately after an ostomy operation there is some sensitivity and pain, but once the abdominal incision has healed, normal sexual relations can be resumed (387). In case of a more serious complication, optimism still appears in such recommendations as "Where the rectum has been removed, the perineal area may be sore for some months. This varies with individuals. But this should pose no problems. Just ask the partner to be gentle with that area." To prove further that none need consign himself to a sexless life because he has lost some intestinal tissue, the booklet for male ostomates suggests, "If you're still draining and need to wear a pad, the White Knight perineal pad-holder for males will hold the pad in place and leave the genitals free for action" (384).

Although spinal cord injury is associated with loss of feeling or sensation, as Gregory points out, "many do not realize that paraplegics frequently suffer intense pain" (170). More specifically, Meirowsky identifies the types of pain in the presence of paraplegia. One is burning pain that is usually intermittent and varies in degree, and it occurs in virtually every paraplegic. Ambulation and activity are claimed to help considerably in combatting this burning pain. The other is intractable root pain, commonly seen in lesions of cauda equina. Meirowsky believes that in these cases surgery is necessary if drug addiction is to be prevented (267).

Fortunately, great strides have been made since 1954 when Meirowsky made this report, and these extreme forms of pain are restricted to fewer and fewer cord injured patients with each new treatment procedure. Also, attitudes are slowly changing so that these patients are being taught to accept the inconvenience of intermittent and mildly painful experiences within the larger pattern. Sadoughi's study of some 55 physically disabled men and women is an illustration of this (366). After discharge from the hospital, the subjects were asked whether or not they felt uncomfortable in carrying out sexual activities. Sixteen men and ten women indicated some discomfort due to disability related physical limitations. The women identified these as shortness of breath, fatigue, and pain. This group suggested that the hospital staff counsel patients prior to discharge, a suggestion which is contained in many follow-up studies. Counseling should cover many needs: physical relief via medication, understanding the nature and frequency of discomfort, postural alternatives and variations of satisfaction during sexual activity, and better communication with the sexual partner. As a result of her many experiences in sharing the confidences of the disabled who turn to her for counseling, Romano has this to recommend to those who may fear the possibility of pain during intercourse:

The kinds of communication that are most effective are the ones that give information about and approval of desired behavior, rather than ones that scold. Thus it is more effective to say, "I love it when you hold me so gently," than it is to say, "Ouch! Cut that out! You're hurting me!" For some disabled women who have constant pain or discomfort, it may help to explain to a partner that the partner should not be afraid of hurting them. Many people are, in fact, afraid that they will accidentally hurt a disabled person and it is up to the disabled person to give reassurance that injury to themselves is not likely ... trying to relax and helping one's partner to relax increases the likelihood of enhancing sexuality and good sexual function. (354)

For those who feel that it's easy enough for an able-bodied counselor to talk about relaxed communication, confirmation of its importance can be found among those disabled who are actively breaking down related barriers. In a delightfully frank article, a wheelchair romantic outlines how to avoid turning a partner off by treating him to communication with a capital "C." In other words, she wisely points out that a partner may at first be frightened by so novel an experience as intercourse with a disabled person and may be overconcerned about hazards of pain and discomfort. Her solution is to tell him to relax, "I'm no masochist. I'll let you know if you're hurting me." She recognizes that her partner is no "mind reader" and can be made comfortable by casual introduction to "foreign objects" (catheters). She also makes a convincing argument for her contention that the greatest suffering is not with physical actualities, but in suffocated romantic hopes (334).

Bowel and Bladder Nuisances. Our culture has taken the outhouse indoors, and the privacy of our concern for bowel and bladder functions is only relieved by the candor of radio and television ads which deftly skirt reality. But disabled persons who have bowel and bladder complications added to the original insult to their well-being are constantly faced with the reality of these bodily needs. For those who are not only interested in sexual activity, but have a willing partner, the logistic complications of bowel and bladder routines can be devastating; or they can be tolerated, as physiologic and psychologic resolutions are tried. Many of the rehabilitation centers and hospitals have worked out varieties of techniques which may satisfy physiologic requirements, but the need for personal counseling is acute (393). Gregory suggests that the most shattering blows to self-concept that a paraplegic must face probably are concerned with the established ideas relating to excretory processes (170). This is a highly charged, irrational area, not just for persons with spinal cord damage, but for everyone. In our culture, privacy is required and elaborate rituals are set up around excretory functions. Also, as Siller observes, strong infantile elements influence our behavior as adults, e.g., people giggle, make jokes, and otherwise show their tension and anxiety. "When there is a distinct disturbance in this area, the individual feels responsible, regardless of the physical facts, and much shame, guilt and anxiety are aroused" (170).

Romano also refers to urinary or bowel incontinence as "one of the most embarrassing logistical complications." When bowel incontinence is a problem, she cautions that it is usually wise not to engage in sexual activity when one's bowels are expected to move, as the stimulation and activity can cause accidents. Furthermore, disabled women on regular bowel programs would do well to wait either until their routine is completed or to choose another time altogether for sexual activity. However, in her usual common sense approach, Romano adds, "Accidents can happen, though, and if one does, it need not spell the end of all sexual activity, especially if it can be dealt with verbally by the woman and her partner."

The United Ostomy Association takes a very matter-of-fact attitude from both the male (384) and female (387) points of view, as their frank booklets indicate (63).

Cleanliness is a must [for the male ostomate]. Uncleanliness and bad odor would most likely turn off one's mate. Bathe and be sure the appliance or other stoma covering is clean, secure and neat. Appliances should be emptied prior to lovemaking

Then appealing to the esthetic question of many individuals, the message continues

While few attempt to cover appliances, this can be done by boxer shorts, a cummerbund, or a light-weight girdle with crotch removed or removable.
A woman should not expect, after ostomy surgery, any decrease in the sexual ability or enjoyment. The surgery does not alter the physical structure of her uterus or vagina . . . prior to intimacy you may wish to avoid eating or drinking anything that may give you trouble . . . Cleanliness, of course, is a must. Uncleanliness and bad odor would naturally turn him off. So bathe and powder. If you wear an appliance, be sure it is secure and empty it. If you have a colostomy, be sure your stoma is clean and make it as small and neat as possible. Now, if you wish to conceal your appliance or other stoma covering, you may cover it with a decorative sack or a frilly cummerbund.

For an ostomate with a sense of humor, they even suggest a decorated girdle with crotch removed that is called none other than "anticipants" (387).

While general medical references to bladder problems and their related therapy are extensive, the field of bladder problems *related to sexuality* awaits research (393). In her level-headed approach, Romano opens the door to further investigation as she reports the results of trial and error. For example, she has found that the woman who has an indwelling catheter that cannot be removed safely for sexual activity, in many cases, can leave it in. However, it should be taped to her stomach temporarily so that it will not be pulled out during intercourse. For women paraplegics without catheters, Romano cautions that it is generally wise to empty the bladder as fully as possible before starting sexual activity. However, a woman who has urinary diversion can usually just empty her collecting gear and simply push it out of the way without disconnecting it (354).

The importance of these few commentaries lies in their illustration of how practical pointers combined with constructive psychologic attitudes may overcome odds that initially seemed insurmountable. In short, yes, there are real problems in sexual activity for those with bowel and bladder conditions, but that has not stopped some victims of these disabilities from approaching sex with the same positive attitude that they had prior to their disability. It is also important to note that now there are people talking openly, without guilt or shame; there are people who have experienced these secondary disablements who have not succumbed to despair. In fact, a few lucky ones can relate turning what might have at one time been considered an embarrassing catastrophe into a humorous incident. The number of competent counselors in this area is increasing as seminars are introduced into all professional disciplines (see Appendix C) and the taboos of old-fashioned silence are lifted.

One additional consideration must be mentioned. That is the problems and attitudes of the disabled individual's sexual partner. This partner may also need to learn the importance of seeking resources to allay anxieties which arise out of both ignorance of what is really involved and knowledge which may at first seem threatening (39). Compassionate understanding does exist among qualified counselors as this quotation from Hohmann's illustrates so well:

Many wives (of disabled men) have told us that it is nearly impossible to routinely provide bowel care, feeding, nursing their husbands and still retain an interest in, and image of, their husbands as sexual objects. If such tends to be the case, the wise counselor will try to preserve the sexual aspect of the relationship by encouraging the use of outside resources, such as visiting nurses and part-time attendants, in doing these unesthetic chores. (195)

Mobility Limitations

The forced acceptance of helplessness and dependency that is part of the initial phases of recovery must give way to the acquisition of new forms of locomotion and positioning before the newly disabled individual can make a meaningful sexual adjustment. The individual must face his physiologic and anatomic limitations and, while acknowledging what he can no longer do, learn new activities that he *can* do. The individual with life-long or longterm mobility limitations must also make a realistic assessment of how to function in order to give and receive sexual pleasure. As Cole indicates, "There is a need for practical information which can help people develop the competence which is an important part of human sexual expression" (79). Experience has shown that a patient's competence is a combination of gaining optimal action through the physical therapies and of modeling activities on what has been learned by others who found ways to outwit their limitations. For example, the victim of spinal cord injury at first experiences an abrupt and total loss of movements in all muscles innervated by motor nerves at and below the point of injury. Muscle wasting, impaired circulation, and tissue breakdown are constant threats. To combat this, self-care in activities of daily living, in brace and crutch-standing techniques, and in getting around in a wheelchair all require concentrated effort under direction of the therapists. While general use of a wheelchair may be less strenuous and look less awkward, the secondary value of some crutch-walking is quite important. It enhances bowel and bladder function, provides keep-fit exercise, and helps reduce spasticity (170). To the casual observer, the secondary values are more often thought of as contributing to locomotion and general well-being, but patients themselves indicate that mastery of these activities also lays a better physiologic basis for sexual activities. Then, having taken stock of remaining physical resources and having arrived at the decision to make use of available counseling, the client (no longer a "patient") is ready to review such practical information as may be presented in the range of sexual options (75, 78, 222, 281).

Motor changes in cord injured women parallel those of men, and they compromise the pelvic and hip movements ordinarily used in sexual response. However, most references to the "kinesiologic aspects of coitus are confined to the generalizations that women may be expected to adapt well to the passive supine position because of its similarity in many instances to a premorbid coital role" (172). Actually, a cooperative partner and pillows placed strategically for support allow for such variations as lateral positioning or rear entry. For those disabled women for whom intermittent spasticity is a problem, it is helpful to find a position where spasms will be limited—lying on one's stomach has been found useful to some (354).

The "kinesiologic aspects of coitus" are greater challenges for men. The more conventional position of intercourse for most men is to be above the partner. However, this is nearly impossible for many men with spinal cord injury or other disorders that present severe motor limitations. Therefore, a man must be willing to accept new positions, such as lying on his back or side, or sitting while straddled. For some men, as Romano and Lassiter point out, positional changes require new behaviors specifically designed to get the sexual partner into the appropriate position, e.g., saying "You'll have to climb on top of me," whereas before his injury, the man could take both verbal and physical control of the sexual situation (356).

When a man with erectile dysfunction and motor limitations has good rapport with his partner, there is likely chance for mutual satisfaction. For example, in the female-superior position, some couples find it easier to use the "stuffing technique." That is, the female can stuff the semisoft penis into her vagina and by voluntary contraction of her pubococcygeal muscles, she can hold her partner's penis within her vagina. Similarly, in situations where the disabled man is capable of erection but not capable of ejaculation during intercourse, the female-superior position with the woman thrusting in a stimulating fashion has proved helpful (237, 281).

Brief sexual encounters have been enjoyed by some couples in sitting position where the disabled male positions his partner on his lap with her back toward him. Another option is removing the arms of the man's wheelchair, allowing his partner to sit astride, facing him (78). This sitting position is not only helpful in cases of male paraplegia, but during pregnancy the wife of either an able-bodied or disabled man may find this a useful change in position.

The mechanics of body positioning during sex play and intercourse have also presented problems to individuals who are not paralyzed—for example, amputees, cerebral palsied, arthritics, or the obese. Balance or movement may be a problem for amputees. However, some amputee problems have relatively simple solutions, such as switching sides of the bed so that an upper extremity amputee has the normal arm free in a side-lying position. Then again, change of position during the sex act might be necessary for others with more extensive disability where change from the male superior to the female superior might be indicated (93). As for the cerebral palsied, heightened reflexes and spasms in some spastics, as well as increased involuntary motion in some athetoids may frustrate both masturbation and coitus (190). The few existing American references to sexuality and the palsied fail to make note of this. They seem to emphasize the social and interpersonal immaturities that hinder sexual relationships. It is likely that the Dutch physicians who have remarked upon the observed frustrations and who have suggested appropriate doses of diazepam (Valium) to be given 1–2 hours prior to intercourse may have had a more severely involved cerebral palsied population and therefore have paid attention to these needs years before they were realized to exist in the United States (190). Another overseas group, this time British, bring to our attention the difficulty that some arthritic and obese men have in getting an enjoyable degree of penetration. They suggest hand or oral sex—or lateral positioning with both partners on their sides and the woman with her thighs up as far as possible and entered from the rear (351). Another suggestion of theirs is a "Love Stool." Its padded and slightly inclined seat is adjustable for height and width. It straddles the recumbent's lower abdomen and permits the missionary position for intercourse while supporting the weight of the male.

These illustrations of some resolutions to *some* people's mobility problems are cited not as prescriptions, but as examples of experiments that have worked for the experimenters. They tell those who may still be wondering whether they stand a chance of overcoming mobility problems that the answer is: Could be! Could be, if you get the helpful guidance of professionals willing to scan the information available and willing to add to it after earnest research and demonstration.

There is one aspect of mobility limitation which is brought up at national and international meetings, but rarely reaches print. That is what to do if both members of a couple are so disabled as to require assistance with sexual activities. For years, this topic was discreetly avoided, but now that counseling for sexual dysfunction has taken on research recognition, its realism can be faced. Mooney and his colleagues point out that, if partners are unable to assist one another (weak hands, paralyzed lower limbs, involuntary movements), a discreet and *trained* assistant can help remove clothing, assist with contraceptives, remove and replace appliances such as catheters, and transfer a couple to bed with whatever pillow support or positioning is needed. While dismay at the lack of privacy is the initial reaction of all involved, couples who have been able to surmount this difficulty report a deepening of their relationship (281).

As has now become more obvious, positioning is of sufficient usefulness and importance to warrant consulting books devoted to it (75, 281). However, communication remains the ultimate attainable skill for optimal positioning and satisfaction (222). Comfortable functional positions have to be talked over by the couple involved. Romano and Lassiter have a particularly meaningful way of emphasizing this. They feel that their counseling time must be directed toward helping their patients to assert themselves verbally with confidence. They base this on the theory that, if the disabled person has an aura of confidence in what he or she is doing and asking of someone else, this confidence will be transmitted to the partner. They point out that some assertions may be verbal, such as "Please put that pillow under my right leg at the knee" or "Please turn around." Other assertions may involve limited body communication "such as that used by a young quad man who indicated to sexual partners his need for unzippering his pants by moving his partner's hand with his arm down to his zipper" (356). As Cole so often points out, inability to move does not mean inability to please nor does inability to perform mean inability to enjoy.

IN CONCLUSION: COLD FACTS AND WARM FANTASY

About one of every ten persons of the general adult population has a disability which produces a physical handicap. Some of these handicaps had their onset at birth or in early childhood. Others have had an abrupt onset, while still others have had chronic progressive courses, starting before or after puberty and affecting the life-style of those so afflicted. However, in spite of common belief to the contrary, many disabled people report that their disabilities do not alter their sexuality or their libido (78). As so many careful observers are beginning to realize, sexuality remains as long as feelings (emotions) and imagination are intact. Persons of both sexes report achieving orgasm even in the presence of complete denervation of all pelvic structures. Fantasy apparently plays a large role. Some patients claim to be able to reassign sensation from a neurologically intact part of the body to their genitalia and to experience orgasm from that sensation in their fantasy. Many report that this type of orgasm is entirely satisfying and leads to a comfortable resolution of sexual tension (82).

FANTASY AS A TURN-ON

Libido is the desire to copulate and does not depend upon the presence of body sensation. Animal experiments in cats and dogs of both sexes confirm this view (25, 26). In human beings, fantasy is one of the infinite number of libidinal turn-ons that can be developed for giving and receiving sexual pleasure. Due to the extent of injury, some men and women cannot feel the genital contact of intercourse, nor can they directly experience an orgasm. However, those who may remember the physical sensation prior to injury may try mentally to recreate and intensify the feeling—and may thereby enjoy a mental orgasm (phantom orgasm, fantasized orgasm). Even among individuals with no sex experience prior to injury or among individuals having developmental disabilities, there are those who report fantasizing orgasms that give satisfaction (281). This would seem to confirm Cole's contention that fantasy is both the ability to recollect and/or the inventiveness of imagination.

It joins the elements of what actually happened to those that almost or never have occurred. It is often exaggerated or unreal, when examined within the context of our daily lives. However, it lives as a real and important part of all of us. People who masturbate understand fantasy, for masturbation is virtually impossible without it.

Early in life, fantasy becomes an important adjunct to sexual expression for people who are alone or in a relationship (80).

The young adult who wishes to use this very human capacity of recollection and/or imagination to achieve a higher level of sexual satisfaction, and possibly a mental orgasm, may employ

1. Sensory amplification, or the act of thinking about a physical stimulus, concentrating on it, and amplifying it in one's mind to an intense degree
2. The substitution or mental transfer of sensation from an area of the body that has retained feeling—as the inner surface of the arms, the breasts, neck, ears, buttocks, or around the anal area—to the genital area where physical sensitivity is absent
3. The substitute satisfaction of one's partner and the use of one's partner's physical and sensory experiences for one's own sexual fantasy, sexual excitement, and sexual satisfaction (81, 281)

WHAT FANTASY CAN TEACH

While many more physicians and disabled clients are now discussing aspects of penile–vaginal intercourse, few such discussions cover options among pleasuring techniques, oral–genital stimulation, the use of devices to heighten excitement, etc. It is still extremely rare for physicians to instruct patients in the use of fantasy (78). Since this is an extremely intimate area of the personality, it is just as well that "instruction," per se, is lagging behind empathetic inquiry; much remains to be learned. However, it is useful for members of the helping professions, as well as for clients, to be aware of some of the constructive uses of fantasy. For example, Cole has found that able-bodied professionals who fantasize that they have a physical disability often develop a willingness to consider the sexuality of those who do have a disability. The professional who fantasizes about such varied disabilities as a colostomy, amputated leg, loss of sensation, painful deformity, or a life-threatening health concern and then tries to superimpose one of these disabilities onto recent sexual activities "can then begin to feel vicariously the significance of your body in an intimate relationship with another person whose approval is vital to your self-esteem" (82).

The practitioner who has learned to acknowledge his or her own fantasies (to self, if not to others) can best appreciate Kaplan's observation: whatever their nature, fantasies are normal and very useful in sexual functioning since not only do they serve to stimulate but they also distract the individual from anxiety which is a frequent early reaction (222). In a step to encourage fantasizing as a part of sexual experience, Hartmann and Fithian employ a Fantasy Trip throughout the body. It is used in their counseling therapy for sexual dysfunction in an attempt to help people get in touch with related emotions and their feelings toward themselves and toward their partners— existing or desired (186). The newcomer to the field of sexuality for the disabled would do well to read the 40-page outline of what Hartmann and

Fithian consider a complete sex history and the 16-page outline of a Fantasy Trip (186) which encourages a modest approach to so intimate a facet of personality as fantasy that is related to sexuality. It should also convince those who are too hasty with answers and generalities that there is a great need for more study under competent guidance.

With increasing recognition of the relationship between the disabled person's sexuality and adjustment to other aspects of life, it behooves our society to prepare professionals to deal with the biopsychosocial aspects of sexuality (329), their own and their clients (13, 82). One of the common myths, cited by Pomeroy, is that sex problems "can be cured very easily. All you need to know are a few mechanical tricks which have become well known, such as the 'squeeze technique.' " Growing research and valid inquiry should be the ongoing concern of all those persons who wish to collaborate with the disabled in making life more meaningful. "The capacity for some sexual fulfillment is present in everyone and perhaps we should see to it that the handicapped are not necessarily frustrated within the limits now acceptable to society at large" (350).

6 MATURATION OR MATURITY?

Truth never is, it is always becoming.—Ralph Waldo Emerson

There is a question implied for everyone in Maturation or Maturity?—whether to begrudge the inevitable aging processes after the peak of youth is over or to accept them with an inquisitive attitude toward the rest of one's life span. This holds for sexuality, as well as for one's personal philosophy. In fact, they are the two sides of the same coin. Today, that coin is in an open market. In a multicultured, youth oriented society, the options for spending this coin are many. According to Lerner, "Our society has shifted from acting as though sex did not exist to placing the most emphasis on sex of any society since the Roman" (244). So those of us who relate to the disabled, or who are disabled, must take a hard look at the range of adult senior sexuality to be sure that we neither shortchange ourselves nor spend recklessly.

EXPECTANCIES: A KIND OF LISTENING

If we accept Pater's clue that "all life is a kind of listening," we hear some rather exaggerated claims for senior sexuality in the general communication media. While some resign themselves to ascetic meditation, others—the "performing addicts"—express their conquests in "quantities of the number of orgasms achieved and the time to go from arousal to orgasm" (167, 340). Money's comment that "there's a lot of sex that goes on that isn't healthy sexuality, just as there's a lot of eating that isn't nutritional" is most apropos (277). It is also quite to the point when Novak remarks in a recent popular magazine that in medieval paintings, children looked like miniature adults whereas in tableaux from life today, adults appear as wrinkled adolescents (306). One must go to the professional literature for more balanced perspectives.

After reviewing relevant material, Sadoughi finds that relatively little is known of the sexual behavior of healthy individuals and what is known tends to be concentrated on the age group below 50 years. One of the few exceptions is the 1968 research at Duke University by Pfeiffer, Verwoerdt, and Wong that studied 254 men and women between the ages of 49–90. Within this group the median age for stopping intercourse was 68 for men (range to 90) and 60 in women (range to 81) (451). This corroborates the Kinsey as well as the Masters and Johnson contention that regular coitus may continue into the 7th, 8th, and even the 9th decades (366). However, while the potential for erotic pleasure may be present from birth to death, Kaplan's studies recognize that "Age shapes the biological component so that intensity and quality of response varies at different ages" (220). The following excerpts introduce her thoughtful writings on the shaping processes that accompany aging:

—By the time a man is over 40, the quality of sexual pleasure has often begun to change noticeably from intense, genitally localized sensations of youth to the more sensuous but diffused and generalized experience of middle age and later life. . . . Men between 50 and 60 are usually satisfied with one or possibly two orgasms per week —the refractory period of penile erections lengthens, though this varies individually.

... After 50, far longer and more intense stimulation is required to achieve erection and ejaculation—older men require intense physical stimulation and time in order to enjoy sex fully.
—For the woman over 40. . . . The fate of libido depends on a constellation of factors including physiological changes (associated with menopause), sexual opportunity (i.e., a dwindling supply of men and the possibility of a middle-age husband avoiding sex) and the diminuation of inhibitions. . . . After the 50's, the post-menopausal years, women may also show great individual variation. . . ."

Accompanying the gradual physical decline in sex "drive," Kaplan has found that, while there may be less preoccupation with sex during the middle years, both men and women may enjoy, seek out, or respond to sex opportunities. At these times, "fantasy and ambience become more important in lovemaking and there is relatively less preoccupation with orgasm." In fact, the onset of age related physical changes can be either a liability or an asset to sexual interest and responsiveness. Kaplan sees them as providing potential for individual or marital stress or, on the other hand, they may be utilized to enhance a love relationship (220).

ATTITUDES TOWARD SENIOR SEX

With the fluid family relationships of modern societies and the frequent relocation of retired people, the opportunity for new interpersonal relationships is always present. If any of these develop into serious attachments, some senior citizens consider this to be one of life's later bonuses. However, many of society's attitudes toward senior sexuality in general are harsher (263). Studies by Butler and Lewis reveal that the idea of people making love in their 70s or 80s is astounding to younger associates or relatives. Many of the general public are inclined to, or wish to, think that older people 1) do not have sexual desire, 2) could not if they wanted to, 3) are too fragile and sex may hurt them, 4) are physically unattractive and therefore are assumed to be sexually undesirable, and finally, 5) the whole idea is shameful! Actually, healthy sexuality is a part of good mental health (61). True, the 80-year-old man is no longer able to produce the intense and multiple orgasms of his youth or experience a distinct phase of ejaculatory inevitability. However, according to Kaplan, he can still have some enjoyable erections when he is effectively stimulated, and he is perfectly capable of experiencing occasional orgasm. Women, on the other hand, remain capable of multiple orgastic responses, essentially without a refractory period, throughout life. Acceptance of potential sex techniques for older persons is important—both for the professional and the involved couple. As one practical example, Butler and Lewis suggest considering such alternatives as having sex in the morning for those older persons who fatigue early. They also mention the importance that masturbation may have for those "who do not find its practice personally upsetting." Many people do not realize that masturbation helps preserve potency in men and the functioning of Bartholin's glands in women, releases tensions, stimulates sexual appetites, and contributes to general well-being

(60). While many older people were brought up to think differently about masturbation, counselors of the elderly believe that some may be flexible and responsive enough to accept such new information, if presented on a take-it-or-leave-it basis.

SENIOR SEX EDUCATION

Although younger people now feel relatively free to discuss sexual relationships, this may not be so for older groups (374). Discussing body parts and habits related to sexual or eliminatory functions may not be within the cultural pattern or verbal competence of some senior citizens. While counselors of varied professions and different sexes are becoming more comfortable with such material and more knowledgeable about sexual options; communication barriers may occur. An older man, for example, might feel quite uncomfortable relating details of urinary dysfunction and sexual impotence to a young female nurse or doctor. Conversely, the young professional's vocabulary may not reach the person for whom it is intended.

It has been found that for this age group, questions related to sexual activity produce more revealing responses if they are indirect. For example, asking how a person found sex most pleasing, often gets more response than asking whether or not the patient had or has a sex life. Again, "How often do you engage in sex?" or "How does your present indisposition affect your sexual activity?" are preferable to "Do you engage in sex?" or "You don't still have sex, do you?" If the attitude of the counselor and the attitude of the counselee lead to requests for help to make sex more satisfying, counseling and technical advice are then in order (263, 370).

While thoughts about sex and sexual activity decline with many older persons, sexuality could play an important role for them, depending upon their health (60). Sex, self-esteem, and self-image are so closely related that Butler and Lewis regard sex education for older people as a realistic task for mental health specialists. There are people in this age group who need help in dealing with their personal feelings, their fears, and their misunderstanding of normal age changes so that they do not mistake these *physiologic* changes for loss of sexuality (61, 417). Then, again, there are men and women in this age bracket whose decline in sexuality is the result of a chronic inability to relate to other individuals in a cooperative, person-to-person relationship. Some men and women who attain their highest personal success within their careers are often thought by outsiders to have attained the best of both lives—professional and family. In reality, they may have invested so much of their energy in a "successful" career that upon retirement they find their skills for warm relationships relevant to normal sexuality may be undeveloped or even stunted. Without the accustomed adulation of subordinates who had surrounded them, without the competitive goals that absorbed so many of their growing years, without hobbies of a creative nature, some outwardly successful people find that retirement holds empty pages, in contrast to the new chapter in life that it holds for those who have developed a resiliency toward people and toward life.

Middle-age divorce is an increasing phenomenon in our society. So sex education may have to be widened to include marital counseling and pastoral counseling in order to prevent divorce or to help those involved in divorce readjust in terms of their sexuality needs (61). "Staying together until the children are grown" is a well-recognized phrase in our culture. Less well recognized are marital stresses among families that also have to cope with disability. Elliott, in counseling deaf couples, has found a most poignant situation. She points out how many marriages of deaf couples who have hearing children suffer considerable strain when these children leave the home, since the parents thereby lose a vital link with the hearing environment (121). As Joan Greenberg so perceptively states in her novel *In This Sign:* "When the Hearing Child leaves the house of the deaf, their mouths also are taken away from them and their ears are taken away and the child also, whom they love. For this, tears are not enough" (168). This area of family interdependence, which is even more acute in the presence of disability, is in great need of research. At present only empathetic concern can be offered.

Bandura cautions counselors when he observes, "Psychology cannot tell people how they ought to live their lives. It can, however, provide them with the means for effecting personal and social choices by assessing the consequences of alternative life-styles and institutional arrangements"(19). The disabled as well as their counselors should be aware that sexuality in later years exists in one form or another in all persons. This does not mean that sexuality must always express itself as the ability to have intercourse. As Berlin so graciously puts it, "For some, it expresses itself only in the need for continued closeness, affection and intimacy, in a continued intellectual interest in eroticism or in the need for some romance" (33).

DISABILITY'S IMPACT

THE IMPERTINENT QUESTION

The physiologic consequences of aging, by themselves, somewhat lessen the distinction between the able-bodied and the disabled since they share many of the same infirmities of age. They may also share some strengths. For some disabled persons (as for some able-bodied), aging brings self-acceptance wherein the individual is better prepared to look for wider perspectives and to accept new human contacts. This may be illustrated by "pen pal" requests received by a publication for a handicapped audience. Nothing in these spirited notes has been changed other than identifying cues:

—I am a 55-year-old woman who writes book reviews, sports reports and the disabled life stories for three disabled papers every month. I would like to correspond with a disabled man over 55.
—I'd like an intelligent male 50 to 55 years old, widower or single, to help me as I will help him. I am on crutches and in a wheelchair because of an accident. I'm 55

years old and I'm not a bad looker. I have a home, with a mortgage, three bedrooms, on level ground. I live alone and do all my housework and cooking.

Are these grown women nonplused by their disability? Should they be? Well, as Bronowski said, "Ask an impertinent question and you're on the way to a pertinent answer"(52). Whoever feels anything other than good wishes for the forthrightness and enterprise of these letter writers may share the stereotype attitude that led Butler and Lewis to observe, "The realization that people with chronic illnesses have sexual interests may be unexpected and even unwelcomed. It complicates the medical picture for doctors" (60). Perhaps it does, but the few studies reporting attitudes of the chronically ill and the physically disabled in this age bracket indicate that sexual interest and activity continue to be important to many of them.

There is one aspect of senior sexuality for which an impertinent question has not yet been formed, much less answered. It concerns the maintenance of sexual function in those who are *temporarily* disabled. Sexual communication is ruthlessly cut off between older couples who are affectionate and sexually active when one member is hospitalized or temporarily in a nursing home. All that is needed to prevent deterioration of the patient and the relationship is privacy which can and should be supplied (30, 78).

DETERMINERS OF SEXUAL ACTIVITY

Pfeiffer and Davis (as quoted by Griffith [159]) report in studies of the sexual functioning of older able-bodied men and women that the prime determiners of sexual activity for the older woman is enjoyment of sex during younger years *and* the availability of a socially acceptable partner. Therefore, they extrapolate that, if a woman enjoyed sex before a disability, she would seek interaction following disability. However, for both able and disabled in this age range, suitable partners may not be readily available in our beauty and youth oriented culture. The observations of Pfeiffer and Davis also confirm that sexuality is more than a sex act to a woman; it is the entire *repertoire of tender, loving gestures* that form a basis for a relationship. Therefore, they consider it essential to include these factors in future research in order to investigate the postdisability sexual functioning of women (172).

Sadoughi and colleagues mailed a questionnaire to 100 discharged patients, married, with a median age of 60, whose conditions included emphysema, arthritis, stroke, and amputations (366). Of the 55 replies, 78% reported a decline in the frequency of sexual activity following disability. Over half indicated that they had to make such changes in the pattern of their sexuality as changes in position, accepting a more passive role, masturbation by self or by partner, and oral techniques. Men, but not women, experienced a significant decrease in sexual interest following disability. Only 35% reported no change, while 7% found increased sexual interest. Some 36% indicated a desire for more satisfaction in their present sexual activity, and 43% expressed the belief that their spouses desired greater satisfaction.

Disability related physical limitations were the most frequently cited reasons for fear and for feelings of discomfort in carrying out sexual activity. The authors of this study conclude that, not only is there need to anticipate problems in predischarge counseling, but further exploration is also indicated for specific disability related psychosocial consequences of older people's sexual problems.

CARDIOVASCULAR INSULTS

The cardiovascular system is a good place to begin when considering the physical and psychosocial counseling aspects of some specific disability related sexual problems. Almost everyone has known some mature person with a heart condition, high blood pressure, a stroke, etc. However, the last thing that the general public, or many professionals, think about is the habitual sexuality pattern of that individual and whether the new physical insult will impact upon it. Occasionally people dig up the old rumor of the catastrophe that may occur to senior cardiovascular sufferers during intercourse. Actually, Labby finds that sudden death occurring during intercourse accounts for less than 1% of all sudden deaths. He agrees with other reports that claim *extra*marital intercourse is a stress factor in many of these sudden deaths—not intercourse per se (233).

QUESTIONS OF STRESS

Until recently, little was documented about the effects of sexual activity upon the aging, diseased, or damaged heart and circulatory system. Consequently, Wagner found that patients often act according to their limited knowledge, fears, opinions, or superstitutions. They may make unwarranted reductions in sexual activity, even to the point of abstinence, which Wagner believes may begin a cycle of behavior that could hamper full rehabilitation. For example, he cites that in some patients reduced sexual activity can lead to frustration and marital conflicts which not only impede recovery but often are associated with an increase in symptomatology (440). Butler and Lewis carry this perspective further by pointing out that potency may be affected psychologically because heart disease is not only frightening, but also tends to undermine confidence and physical capacities. However, for some people the anxiety and tensions caused by restricting sex may be greater than the actual physical risk (60, 61).

Opinions vary (234). Some physicians consider all patients with severe hypertension to be *at high risk* at any time, but especially at times of acute exertion. Others are less apprehensive about exertion per se, as might occur in sexual activity. In their overviews of the antihypertensive drugs, Labby and Page point out that sexual complications such as impotence and inhibited ejaculation which can be caused by the use and varied dosage of certain antihypertensive drugs are a more common phenomenon than cardiac risk associated with exertion (233, 312). In fact, Labby quotes Gifford as reporting not a single instance of cardiac or cerebral accident during sexual activity in his (drug controlled) hypertensive patients in more than 20 years.

When one reviews the literature on intercourse by hypertensive patients, what is meant by the "actual physical risk" is not that easily documented. As indicated in an excellent and concise editorial comment in a February 1976 issue of the British Medical Journal, advice must be tempered by realistic knowledge of normal physiologic stresses during intercourse and the capacity of the individual patient to work with his physician to determine his own stress range (76). The editorial also points out that research results of both Masters and Johnson, as well as the so called "sexercise test" where it was possible to monitor volunteers by electromagnetic tape in the privacy of their own bedroom, confirm that sexual intercourse of normal couples may cause transient tachycardia, hypertension, and hyperventilation in both sexes—but both heart rate and blood pressure fall rapidly to precoital levels after orgasm. Since electrocardiographic abnormalities were not observed in normal persons during intercourse, the question of how cardiac patients might fare was raised. Quoting a study of patients with ischemic heart disease, the following results were reported: Almost half were aware of rapid heart action and some angina pectoris—but this rarely forced termination of intercourse. Also, while electroencephalogram changes were common and heart rate averaged 120/min. for 10–15 sec, this suggested that the oxygen cost to the heart was little more than that incurred by mild exertion (76, 176).

In reviewing these same studies of Hallerstein and Friedman that were cited by the British editorial, Tobis concludes that, if the cardiac patient is capable of climbing one or two flights of stairs or walking a block briskly without difficulty or complaint, he is likely able to participate in the sex act (427). From a common sense approach, Wise suggests that a couple try mutual masturbation before intercourse. The cardiovascular demands of masturbation are less than intercourse. Frequently, a heart rate of 100–110 accompanies masturbation, and this can be done with a view to seeing how the patient feels, i.e., whether free of chest pains at this time (451).

COUNSELING BOTH PARTNERS

Counseling the wife, as well as the cardiac patient, may prevent her adding her anxieties to his. It may also make both of them more aware of the minimal physiologic costs of sexual activity and on the lookout for ways to reduce further this energy cost during intercourse, such as employing side by side or female-superior positioning (427). Another editorial—this one appearing in the Journal of the American Medical Association—also considered the problem of counseling the person recovering from a myocardial infarct (434). It reported on Stein's studies which supported Green's recommended program of physical exercise to enhance safety of sexual activity. Stein was able to attain a normalization of sexual function in 16 men between the ages of 46 and 54 who underwent a 16-week bicycle ergometer exercise by training

12–15 weeks after their last myocardial infarction (411). The complete editorial should be read, but the quality that is relative to counseling both members of a sexual partnership is delightfully expressed in Vaisrub's ending comment, "The act of sex is not a solo performance. A bicycle performance is hardly the complete answer to the anxieties of the lovelorn. It is no substitute for the leisurely ride on a *bicycle built for two*" (434).

CONTROVERSY OVER THE PILL

Most of the studies on patients recovering from cardiovascular insults relate to middle-aged *male* patients. In fact, Wagner remarks upon the well-known preponderance of cardiac disease among males. However, since women also have cardiac problems, he was surprised to find no published studies on cardiology concerning the sexual activities of females (440). Perhaps the most sensitive issue at present concerns the questioned relationship between the pill and possible cardiac complications in older women. In a bulletin to American doctors the Food and Drug Administration reported the results of two British studies that claim new evidence shows that increasing with age, women aged 30–44 who take the contraceptive pill are from 2.7 to 5.7 times more likely to have heart attacks than women who do not. Among women over 40, the likelihood of a fatal heart attack is four times as great among pill users as among non-pill users. It is claimed that the pill is synergistic in its effect. According to the Food and Drug Administration for instance, for women vulnerable to heart attack because they smoke, are overweight, or have diabetes, the use of the pill is claimed to combine with other factors in such a way that the total risk is much greater than the sum of the individual risks (455). There are, however, physicians who are critics of the actual research design of these British studies and who do not find the evidence clearcut. In fact, some of them claim that a comparison of risks must be made: is it riskier to take the pill or to avoid it when the death rate from pregnancy goes up with age? (149)

STROKE: A SEX THREAT?

Renshaw (346) points out that during the initial life-threatening aspects of stroke, a sexual history is impossible; during early recovery, sexuality still is not a high priority for patient, physician, or spouse. However, as hospital discharge approaches, physicians as well as patients and spouses may need to take stock of general knowledge about stroke victims and specific resolutions of new sexual difficulties. Renshaw cites three major points that the physician should remember to help a stroke patient adapt to physiologic change and subsequent psychologic concerns (346). *First,* unless the cerebral insult is very severe, the sexual response is usually spared, since it is presumably mediated through the limbic system and spinal cord. *Second,* partial erections, impotence, ejaculation delay, or retrograde ejaculation in men and decreased lubrication in women are *un*usual occurrences. *Third,* couples have worked out practical solutions to muscle weakness and unstable joints on the paralyzed side of the body; pillows, a handle on the headboard, a higher footboard, or simply alternative coital positions have solved mechanical difficulties. Others, fearing loss of sphincter control, empty the bladder before intercourse. While this abstracts the major points raised by Renshaw, the article itself should be read in full to do justice to the sensitive psychologic insights and suggestions for new research directions (346).

To conclude with responses from both male and female patients, an abstract of Leshner, Fine, and Goldman's study of "Sexual Activity in Older Stroke Patients" is quoted directly from the *Archives of Physical Medicine and Rehabilitation:*

Seventy-seven posthospitalized stroke patients (51 males and 26 females) between 50 and 70 years old, and their spouses, were given a structured in-depth sexual interview, along with the Marital Adjustment Schedule, the Tennessee Self Concept Test, and the Mini-Multi—a form of the Minnesota Multiphasic Personality Interview (MMPI). The interviews were administered by like-sexed interviewers. The sample was heterogeneous regarding race, religion, education and socioeconomic status. The interview questionnaire included the following areas: (a) biographical; (b) medical history; and (c) pre- and postmorbid sexual functioning (behavioral and cognitional). This paper will discuss illness-induced changes in behavioral and cognitive sexuality pre- to postonset. The majority of the subjects indicated a decline in the frequency of intercourse as a result of their CVA, while 45% stopped having intercourse completely. A variety of illness specific causes for the change in sexual behavior included difficulty in maneuvering, fear of making their condition worse and lack of feeling. Significant gender differences were indicated, the overall effect being that male patients were more affected sexually by their illness than female patients; and the male partner being more affected regardless of whether he was the patient or the spouse. For the professional who is responsible for treating stroke patients, the results indicate that he must be aware of the increase in sexual problems due to CVA, that the conflict will be greater in the male partner, and that early diagnosis and treatment of the sexual problem is possible and advisable. (245)

OTHER IMPACTS OF MIDDLESCENCE

Just as adolescence has its unique physical and emotional changes, so, too, does "middlescence." Obviously, they are different in character, but both are stress periods introducing a new status in life (61, 154). Unfortunately, the disabled are not excepted from these "rites of passage" prior to maturity. There is much written about able-bodied persons who at this age may still be willing to run downstairs but go upstairs at a slower pace, who pull out the first gray hairs and later highlight them in new beards or coiffures, who feel bereft as the last child leaves home to move far away but later travel widely on their own. Women may take menopause as a crisis or as a relief from fear of pregnancy and the nuisance of menstruation, and men may (erroneously) pin the fears of retirement and financial restrictions on a possible "male menopause" as they seek to hide depression. At this stage, depression, stress, and fatigue may strike a portion of heretofore unhampered individuals, as well as some of the disabled population. While Kaplan discusses the possible causes of sexual disinterest and dysfunction under these debilitating conditions, it suffices here to observe her counsel to "postpone sexual therapy to a time when the patient's psychophysiological state has improved to a point where he is more amenable to treatments" (220).

SURGERY AND VARIED OUTCOMES

The impact of physical disabilities on sexuality at middle age is a matter of some concern. When disease or injury is acute enough to require surgery, it is likely that at first both patient and physician are concerned with immediate danger or pain and then with the ultimate restorative values of the procedure. Eventually the impact of the operation upon the sexuality of the middle-aged patient is considered. Among serious conditions where physical disability is no longer accepted as an excuse to preemptorily dismiss sexuality in middle age are prostate surgery, radical surgery in the pelvic area, amputations, and colostomy. This respect for the residual sexuality is less attributable to the character of the disability than to the increasing interest of physicians in the "total" patient.

Prostate and Pelvic Repairs

Because of the generally known results, it is now possible for men undergoing prostate surgery to anticipate the character of their residual sexual function. Escamilla indicates that after a transurethral resection, which is the most frequently employed procedure, a man's sexual function usually returns, but ejaculation is retrograde into the bladder. Following extirpation of the prostate, the capacity for erection is lost (unless a penile implant is tried), but orgasm is still possible (130).

Radical surgery in the pelvic area may cause and contribute both to psychologic and physiologic sexual dysfunctions in the middle-aged person. Labby brings to our attention that, while surgery may remove a pathogenic process or may provide relief from disabling complications of a disease, a patient's expectations of having permanent sexual dysfunction may be so strongly reinforced that he or she may seem outwardly content to live out this expectation. At that point, Labby cautions that it requires an astute physician to sense the degree of psychogenic overlay and to help the patient return to satisfying sexual activity. Acceptable psychotherapy (233). takes careful timing since, as Kaplan notes, "when a person feels ill and debilitated or is in pain, he's not usually interested in pursuing erotic matters" (220).

Outlook for Amputees

In reviewing a basic national study of 12,000 new amputees, Mourad and Chiu observe that 60% of the group whose amputations were due to disease or chronic illness were above the age of 60 years (286). Since the majority of amputees who find their way to clinics are usually in an older age group, many physicians mistakenly feel that probing into their sex lives would be a waste of time and a source of irritation and embarrassment to them. However, Cummings recognizes that the older amputee does have specific sexual problems for which help is needed. He cites the obvious emotional trauma: the depression and mourning period, the distortion of body image, and the perception of self as not whole, as ugly, or as no longer feminine or masculine (93). In addition, associated changes such as phantom sensations, resultant difficulties in balance and in positioning may alter sexual performance on a purely physical basis. It is Cummings contention that members of the helping professions can guide the amputee in learning alternatives to physical obstacles and can promote supportive communication between partners.

Mourad and Chiu corroborate this outlook in their clinical experiences. They find that, when male patients begin to ambulate, having progressed successfully through postsurgical recovery and early prosthetic training, they start to feel the return of sexual arousal, morning erection, and libido, all associated with confidence in their sexuality. It is their impression that women who were married prior to the time of amputation continue to enjoy married life, and surprisingly enough, there is little incidence of marital difficulty among them after amputation (261). In discussing instances of amputee recovery and resumption of intercourse with a former or new partner, Mourad and Chiu refer to studies on older diabetic amputees which cite 40.2% of males are impotent and 35.2% of females have complete absence of orgasmic response. However, it is their contention that, among their patients, counseling encouraged the maintenance of healthy sexuality proportionate to normal age related expectancies. Problems quoted by their clients more often included psychologic barriers, such as "there was no actual attraction or love between them," than physiologic barriers for which no resolution was attained. In fact, the "attentive and cooperative spouse as the key to marital sexual readjustment" is the basis for their twofold counseling program of 1) full and early explanation of the anatomy and physiology of sex as related to amputation and 2) psychosocial support based on immediate management and future expectations.

Ability Goals for Ostomy

The United Ostomy Association is among the first of disability organizations to consider "ability goals" that include sexuality and sexual satisfaction. Their booklets candidly face up to the sexual hopes and realities of all the Association's members (385, 387). From these we learn that most colostomies are performed on persons over 40, and urinary ostomies because of cancer occur most often in the over 50 group. But do these facts lead to recommended celibacy? Far from it. This is an organization of people who have a people-oriented outlook. Where these conditions occur in men and women of middle age, childbearing no longer holds the importance of earlier years, but sexual pleasures continue as desirable. Only in extremely rare cases would the surgery be so extensive as to lessen a woman's capacity to enjoy sex. But men with urinary ostomies and radical colostomies are less fortunate. Those who had urinary ostomies in childhood usually perform sexually; however, they may be sterile. Men whose urinary surgery was directed against cancer may become impotent, while the sexual function of those with colostomies varies from full capacity for erection and orgasm to complete impotence (419). Faced with such wide variations in capacity as well as outlook, the Association promotes the same spirit as Calderone's message to ostomates, given at their 1971 convention, "The big question is how you resolve it in your particular situation. There are many ways of making love and achieving orgasm, and there are many ways of making love without orgasm and achieving satisfaction."

NEUROLOGIC DISORDERS

Central nervous system disabilities may interfere with sexual functions *directly* by altering one or more of the physical factors on which sexual activity is based or *indirectly* by the effect of medication, treatment, or emotional response to the onset of pathology. Global brain disease may result in sustained decline in cognitive, conative, affective, and perceptual functions. Behavioral decisions may be threatened, personality alterations may occur, and changes may be noted in the capacity to express or to receive affection. In some older patients, loss of social inhibitions and impairment of judgment may be manifested by uncontrolled sexual expression—or there may be a shift toward autoeroticism in response to inner or outer arousing stimuli. Sexual behaviors may have no concern for other's sensitivities or social acceptance. This is, of course, a very dependent patient (201).

In contrast, most of us are familiar with the basal ganglia disorder known as parkinsonism or paralysis agitans. Beginning in middle or old age, it affects the well-being and motility but not the intelligence or sensibility of its victims. The disorder is without effect on either the desire for or the capacity for sexual activity in younger persons, provided there is no severe orthopedic deformity. Therefore, any diminished responses among the majority of Parkinson victims are attributed to the stage of life at which this disorder appears, the time when both the intensity and frequency of sexual activity may have lessened. Other insults to well-being may also be present, such as depression, the loss of a parnter through illness or death, or a change of domicile that requires new and unwelcome adjustments. Interestingly enough, the original aphrodisiac effect that was attributed by some users to the L-dopa medication is more reasonably the result of recovered motility, relief of depression and return of a feeling of well-being (201).

SYSTEMIC PROBLEMS

Older subjects in Sadoughi's study of people with emphysema, arthritis, stroke, and amputation tended to indicate low levels of postdisability frequency, interest, and satisfaction in sexual activities (366). It does seem in keeping with traditional common sense that the physical stress of middle and older age plus the added stresses of a generalized debilitating condition should conspire against sexual interest and function. But untraditional common sense is growing, as the spotlight of research reveals heretofore unseen facets. For instance, Kaplan recognizes that "some diseases have damaging effects on sexual functioning by virtue of pathogenic mechanism which specifically injures the sex organs or their nervous or vascular supply. The disease may have endocrine effects on the sex centers of the brain or the process of the disease may diminish androgen or damage the genital organs directly" (220). Because Kaplan is aware of the actual physiologic impact of the disability, her counseling is wisely based on careful analysis of the *extent* of the debilitating condition, its impact on the individual's psychologic make-up, including sexuality, and whether or not the patient has a constructive grasp on the positive alternatives that are left.

Physicians too often assume that the emotional attention of a patient is concentrated exclusively on the primary disability. Naturally, in the face of pain and acute illness the amount of energy available for matters other than danger or discomfort is very slight, and the family may reinforce this main concern, even holding on to it beyond reasonable fact. However, in reality sexual energy and drive are abundant. While Labby concedes that their intensity is somewhat age related, nonetheless their effects overflow into every aspect of life. Therefore he believes that, in the course of routine medical care before any illness, the family physician should become the patient's ally and make himself thoroughly acquainted with the patient's general pattern of well-being, including the state of his sexual health. Therefore, when disease or illness do strike, the physician is prepared to assist the patient toward optimal functional recovery and rehabilitation. Should sexual dysfunction be associated with an illness, patients following Labby's procedures could help themselves to recover, ideally with "insight, knowledge, education and security provided by a wise physician who comprehends the total effect of illness" (233).

Although Labby's counsel is sound, our way of life at present conspires against it. In the first place, the person known as "the family physician" is receding from the American scene, replaced by overbusy specialists. On the positive side of the picture, however, interdisciplinary teams which include relevant specialists are appearing in all sections of the United States. They are giving their attention, not only to the individual and his specific needs, but to qualitative studies aimed at destroying destructive hearsay and replacing it with a horizon of alternatives.

Arthritis

A good illustration of how a team investigates a disability related problem of middle-aged people is the team effort of Temple University School of Medicine led by Fine, Leshner, and Goldman. Here is an abstract of their 1974 study on the "Sexual Effects of Arthritis."

A biracial sample of 40 female and 21 male rheumatoid arthritis patients, recruited from multidisciplinary rehabilitation facilities in a major metropolitan area, were administered a structured in-depth interview and a battery of psychological tests by a like-sexed interviewer. The mean age of the patient sample was 61.7 years. The sample was heterogenous with regard to religion, education, and socioeconomic status. The interview included the following areas: (1) biography; (2) activities of daily living (3) social functioning; (4) medical status; (5) sexual history; (6) premorbid sexual functioning at two time periods, mid-40s and immediately prior to disability onset; (7) postmorbid sexual functioning; and (8) sexual knowledge and attitudes. The interview focused on both behavior and cognitional expressions of sex, and included physical and psychological problem areas and disability-specific limitations. The psychological test batteries included a short form of the Minnesota Multiphasic Personality Interview, the Tennessee Self Concept Test, and the Marital Adjustment Schedule. Patients and their spouses were tested on two occasions separated by six months in order to assess the extent of variation in patterns of postmorbid sexual adaptation. The success of the patient's postmorbid sexual adaptation was, in turn, related to relevant biographic, medical, and sexual history factors. This investigation delineated the extent of disability-induced changes in sexual functioning, and highlighted the types of situations sought by arthritic patients and their spouses. The role of the physician as sexual counselor is apparent, although often disavowed. (137)

Diabetes

There are several reports that indicate a significantly higher incidence of secondary impotence in diabetics than in the general population. A practical rule of thumb is that impotence in diabetics correlates with an approximation of age (233). Roughly 20% of diabetic males are impotent in their 20s, 40% in their 40s, and 60% in their 60s (105). Other estimates indicate that some 35–50% of men over 45, who have insulin-necessary diabetes mellitus, have some sexual dysfunction which is ascribed by some investigators to a diffuse neuropathy that affects the bladder and parasympathetic system (120, 451). Impotence is often the first symptom of diabetes, and some success has been gained in reversing it by early, proper treatment (61). However, when impotence persists in well-controlled diabetics, it may be permanent. In fact, Ellenberg has used cystorometrograms to show the bladder dysfunction associated with diabetic impotence. So, in evaluating the sexual function of a diabetic male, it is necessary to check whether he has any trouble urinating, whether he can control dribbling, and what specifically is his ability to have erections (451). In addition, Wise points out how one has to be careful not to assume that impotence is of organic origin in all diabetics. He illustrates this by citing the case of a 45-year-old man with a 5-year history of diabetes who was controlled on oral medication but complained of inability to sustain an erection. Questioning revealed that this impotence occurred only during sex with his wife; he woke up some mornings with an erection, he had some wet dreams, and when he masturbated, he was able to ejaculate without any trouble—all of which pointed to a psychogenic cause of impotence in a drug controlled diabetic (451).

Diabetic women also have reported problems in sexual responses (53). Some 35% of 125 diabetic women under study at one clinic had sexual orgasmic dysfunction. This may be attributed to the effects of a generalized illness over a long period of time, since the longer the duration of any illness, the more sexual problems are reported. However, it is more likely to result from nervous system effects of the systemic illness (451). One finding relevant to women and diabetes is that [oral contraceptives may necessitate an increase in insulin doses but do not appear to be more hazardous than in nondiabetics (53).] Obviously, more research is needed on the sexuality of diabetic women—both from the physiologic and psychologic aspects.

Cancer

Over the past 25 years the reported incidence of cancer has increased materially. This is due to several factors: improved diagnostic methods, the increase in the total population, and the increase in the number of people living to old age. Fortunately, people are seeing their physicians for medical diagnosis at early ages when more can be done to prevent spreading of the problem to other parts of the body (65). Debilitating as cancer may be, one of its greatest threats is to the personality of the patient when surgery is done on the breast or uterus in women and on the prostate in men. Excision of such emotionally charged human organs has always precipitated a very meaningful psychosexual impact on both the patients and their sexual partners.

Mastectomy. Some of the physical results of mastectomy are loss of breast tissue, accompanying body deformity, initial limitations of arm movements, arm edema, and various sensory problems such as anesthesias and paresthesia. With today's procedures, postoperative care minimizes ensuing physical discomfort and can guarantee that 90% or more of patients will not have local recurrence, many will gain longevity of life, and some can look forward to breast reconstruction via plastic surgery (144).

The emotional impact after the loss of a breast is usually profound (449). Naturally, each person's reaction will differ, influenced by social and family attitudes as well as by each woman's personal and occupational experience. After mastectomy some women see themselves desexed and suffering from a disease which, in their fantasy, leads to a lonely death. Some fear that they will be sexually undesirable after the loss of a breast. Then again, the woman who feels herself mutilated and repulsive after mastectomy grieves for what is imagined an irreparable loss to her body image. While there is seemingly less psychologic stress experienced by some older women who live alone, even among senior citizens there are those who find this change incompatible with the body image to which they have grown accustomed.

Fortunately, many surgeons are unwilling to perform successful operations that are followed by the emotional death of their patients. As a result, increasing care is taken to counsel patients, their partners, and their family before as well as after the operations. Modern surgeons have taken the lead in recognizing the emotional impact of their procedures. As Ervin so cogently observes, "I consider obvious anxiety and tears, inability to concentrate for a brief period, and elements of panic all within normal limits. A bland, happy smile, withdrawal, distortion of reality, hostility, backward looking eyes are inappropriate and cause for particular concern" (129). Dietz counsels that no mastectomy patient should be left to handle her emotional burden alone, and no husband should be left with an empty feeling of not knowing how best to help his wife (107). In 1952, Renneker and Cutler equated mastectomy fears in the female with the castration complex in the male and, while Freeman considers this somewhat of an exaggeration, he finds it quite understandable to anyone who has seen these patients over the years (144).

To combat the psychologic trauma of mastectomy a very constructive team approach has been adopted by many hospitals, following the lead of Memorial Hospital in New York (107, 449). The surgeon and his nurse try to prepare both the patient and her family for the entire procedure, including admission procedures. At the time of hospitalization a short recording which covers basic information is made available. Then, a hospital team is assigned to help the patient learn methods of coping. This team consists of a social worker, nurse, physical therapist, and a volunteer from "Reach For Recovery" who comes from the local division of the American Cancer Society. The social worker can provide practical guidance and information on community services. Other team members join the social worker in helping the patient and her husband to bridge the initial postoperative shock and to face the ensuing attitudes and reactions to the body change as well as to the general illness. Many women are beset with misconceptions concerning the interrelationship between their condition and their sexuality. These are now the concerns of comprehensive rehabilitation.

What about the chances of a mastectomy patient who looks forward to finding a partner? When Ervin asked some of his patients about this, one woman replied that the first man who showed a serious interest in her never called again after she told him about her mastectomy. However, she subsequently met another man who responded with "What difference does that make!" Another woman who had never lacked for male companionship replied to Ervin's query as to whether the mastectomy caused any problems in relationships, "If there's love and tenderness, it doesn't matter. Otherwise who needs him?" (129)

Nowhere is the quality of mutual interest and collaboration in sex activity brought out more poignantly than in the case record of a cancer patient reported by Wise. This woman and her husband had taken her bilateral mastectomies in stride. They continued to have a fulfilling sex life. However, in a subsequent year, intercourse became progressively infrequent due to the interference of pain—the wife had an intolerably painful hip. Careful examination revealed terminal cancer with metastatic lesions all over her spine and hips. Radiation therapy only aggravated the pain during intercourse. They had been using the conservative woman-under position over the past 26 years but it now was accompanied by excessive pain. Alternative sexual options were discussed. Using a side position supported by pillows and adding mutual masturbation to their repertoire, this couple resumed full orgasmic response. The wife died some 6 weeks later, but her husband expressed gratitude for the pleasurable experiences they both shared until the end (451).

Prostatectomy. The prostate is a walnut-size gland in males that surrounds the neck of the bladder and the first part of the urethra. It produces a milky lubricating fluid which contributes to the ejaculation of sperm during sexual intercourse or masturbation. Prostrate problems have been blamed on both too much sex activity and too little. However, they are thought more likely to be connected with variations in hormone levels, since over half of older men may experience prostatitis and enlargement of this gland. Concomitant discomfort, urinary problems, and pain associated with prostate enlargements that are due to benign growths or to cancer may be relieved by surgery, if the condition has not been neglected beyond remedial help. Operations on the prostate after the age of 60 are quite common, although they may not have received the popular attention given to mastectomies.

Removal of the prostate for benign enlargement usually does not affect potency. Since the extent of cancer affects the extent of the operation, a similar blanket statement cannot be made in cases of malignant enlargement. In radical prostatectomy nerve and blood vessels involved in maintaining an erection may be damaged, and ejaculation may be retrograde into the bladder and will therefore not be visible. Patients should be informed of these possible changes and assured that they, in themselves, do not augur automatic impotence. The most frequent cause of impotence related to prostatectomy is psychologic.

The American Medical Association Commission on Human Sexuality states flatly that a surgeon

has a crucial role to play in preventing sexual problems in his patient: certain operations (*e.g.*, hysterectomy, prostatectomy and vasectomy) have spelled the end of sexual activity *simply because the patient was not informed* that the surgery would have no lasting organic effect on sexual ability (86).

It is a myth that most prostatectomies reduce libido and that subsequent interest and ability in sexuality vanish completely after age 60. Rather, some operations on some older men coincide with the time at which their interest or their partner's interest in intercourse abates. Furthermore, the failures that inevitably occur immediately after operation are met by anxiety to perform, which need not be permanent. Then again, some men psychologically associate the operation with castration, which is utterly misguided; even if the testes had been removed, hormone treatment could be given to compensate. So, in general, what the surgeon does to prepare his patient and what sources a man has to keep himself objectively informed will minimize the psychologic trauma (86, 359).

WHO SHALL COUNSEL THE MIDDLESCENT?

What lies behind the middle-aged or what lies ahead of them is less important for pursuing a meaningful life than what lies *within* them. Great fear and depression can result from misconceptions that accompany physical changes brought on by disability as well as by the aging process. These fears and misconceptions extend to concepts of sexuality and often penalize a partner, as well as the individual in question. People often have many mistaken ideas about what is good or normal sexual function for their age and for their physical condition. A woman may erroneously conclude that the loss of a breast or uterus will make her sexually undesirable. A man may experience impotence as an initial reaction to a change in himself or his partner and, erroneously, consider this a permanent situation. He may not be aware that the majority of normal men experience impotence from time to time as a consequence of anxiety, fatigue, alcohol, or other transient circumstances (65). Neither may be adequately informed by a competent physician about the relationship of their particular physical problem to their concept of satisfying sexual activity. Neither may be adequately informed about the sexual options that remain.

Where is this adequate information to come from? It has been stated that "the role of the physician as sexual counselor is apparent, though often disavowed" (137). Perhaps there would be fewer disavowals if the sentence were phrased, "The role of the physician can vary—some may be eminently qualified to serve as the patient's sexual counselor, others may serve as medical consultant to a team with an experienced counselor appointed at patient contact." Good patient contact counselors come from many different disciplines. Among physician–counselors are Emanuel Chigier (69), Theodore Cole (77), Ernest Griffith (171, 172), Helen Singer Kaplan (220), and Daniel Labby (233), to name but a few leaders in the field. Among nonphysician patient counselors who work in teams, there is George Hohmann (195, 355), Milton Diamond (104), Winefred Kempton (225), Silas Singh (395), Mary Romano (354), and Wanda Sadoughi (366). Fortunately, these lists would have to be much longer to include all the thoughtful and competent people who are applying their proficiencies and empathy to the sexual adjustment of individuals confronting disability.

IN CONCLUSION

Loren Eisely, anthropologist—educator—writer and compassionate advocate for man, has the following comment on the times in which we find ourselves:

The problems we face today are grave, one of the most serious being that each of us has little time to educate himself as to the nature of our civilization and technology.

What makes the situation especially difficult is that men are living on neither the same religious plane nor the same technological plane. Some are in the Stone Age; some are in an Atomic Age; and it is difficult for them to understand each other. (117)

One can reread this comment with the sexuality of able-bodied or disabled persons in mind. It reflects many of the dilemmas that arise between individuals as partners, between people with differing educational and religious outlooks, or between those who use sex as a solution and those who see responsible sexuality as one of the enriching components of a full life. Romano summarizes the dilemma between partners in her concept of sexuality as a

series of transactions between two people. For some people the purpose of the sexual transaction is procreation; for others it is a form of communication and can also be a kind of recreation. Sex can also be used as a means of obtaining power. Withholding it can be punishment; for example, a husband came home late from work without phoning and later that evening finds his wife "too tired" for intimacy. Sex is often a reward and equally often an apology, e.g., a way to make up after a fight. And, of course, sex is a way of making someone else happy, of reinforcing a love relationship by experiencing the closeness of two people in a sort of psychological and physiological oneness. Sexual transactions fulfill any and all of these purposes, not only for the able-bodied, but for the disabled as well. (354)

The many differences in the way men and women, individually and as couples, respond sexually are explained by Eisenberg and Rustad (119) as reflections of "a complex blend of social, psychological and physical influences." For this reason, they believe that open and honest communication between partners is essential. "The fact that sexual behavior is in part learned has another important implication. Provided an individual is sufficiently flexible and wants to learn, new attitudes and behaviors can be learned and old habits modified" (119). Bloom adds an important qualification to this which is applicable to all disabled couples, "With adequate information given by an informed counselor, the spinal cord patient's, and his partner's, willingness to experiment will provide the framework for a good sexual alliance" (41). When consideration is given to what constitutes an informed, mature counselor, it is useful to turn to an empathetic professional who has spent some 30 years accumulating information and counseling the able-bodied and disabled persons about sex. Hohmann states that

the most adequate counselor is one with warmth, gentleness and an effective personal interrelationship with patients. The counselor should know all about the neurological urology (and have access to competent sources concerning the physiologic impact of each disability [Ed]) and psychology of sex relationships before taking this on. The counselor should be relatively free of sex hangups; if not, he could exploit the patient with this feeling. The counselor must know something about typical male and female sex attributes in our society. (195, 196)

Disabled persons as well as workers in many rehabilitation disciplines must now take their isolated experiences and apply them to a developmental perspective of life within a multicultured society. Our future perspectives will depend upon the growing quality of clinical experience and research utilization. We shall have to learn to be compassionate with one another, since, as research unfolds new insights, it also leads to new problems to be faced. "But man has struggled through his problems in the past," Eisely reminds us. "As long as we are alive, as long as we are human, we will continue that struggle" (117).

EPILOGUE

Real maturity. . . . is the ability to look at oneself honestly and acknowledge the fact that there is a limitation in me. Here is a case where, because of some lack of experience or some personal incapacity, I cannot meet a situation; I cannot meet the need of someone whom I love dearly. . . . Either you must learn to allow someone else to meet the need, without bitterness or envy, and accept it; or somehow you must make yourself learn to meet it. . . . There is another ingredient of the maturing process that is almost as painful as accepting your own limitation and the knowledge of what you are unable to give. That is learning to accept what other people are unable to give. You must learn not to demand the impossible or to be upset when you do not get it.(Eleanor Roosevelt, in Lash, J.P.: Eleanor and Franklin, New York, W W Norton, 1971)

APPENDICES

APPENDIX A
SEX EDUCATION
CURRICULA FOR STUDENTS
IN REGULAR SCHOOLS

Unit Revision For Family Living Curriculum—Kindergarten to Grade 6, 1971. (#ED096548 CE002189). 57 p. Rochester City School District, NY. Available from ERIC Document and Reproductive Service Co., PO Box 190, Arlington, VA 22210.
Includes concepts of human sexuality at three levels: primary, early intermediate, and later intermediate.

Family Life Education—A Guide To Curriculum, 1967. 51 p. Kindergarten through Grade 12, Wetherfield, Connecticut. Available from ERIC Document and Reproductive Service Co., PO Box 190, Arlington, VA 22210.
Includes guides to sex education for teachers and counselors; covers emotional, physical, social growth and development.

Sex Education In Schools, 1969. National School Public Relations Association, Washington, DC.
Brief review of sex education programs in schools in various parts of the USA.

Family Life and Sex Education: Curriculum and Instruction. By Esther Schuly and Sally Williams. New York, Harcourt Brace & World, 1969.
Methods and materials for grades 1–12 based on Anaheim, California program.

Sex Education: Approach/Program/Resources for the Parish. Edited by G. Gilderhaus and E. M. Larsen. Minneapolis, Sacred Design Associates, Inc., 1968.
Useful resource for teachers and religious educators of upper elementary and high schoolers.

About Your Sexuality. By Derek Calderwood, Boston, Beacon Press, 1971. Program for junior high teenagers and adults, using audiovisual and group techniques to help individuals explore facts, feelings, attitudes, and values toward responsible decision making and appreciation for their own sexuality.

193

A Course Is Born. 45-minute 16mm film with sound, 1972. Available from Department Education and Social Concern, UUA, 25 Beacon Street, Boston, MA 02108

Describes development of "About Your Sexuality"; demonstrates youth and parents using course materials.

APPENDIX B
SEX EDUCATION
CURRICULA FOR
DISABLED GROUPS

Curriculum Guide in Sex Education for the TMR, 1973. (#ED109845—EC73243). By Kathy L. Stewart. 40 p. Available from ERIC Document and Reproductive Service Co., PO Box 190, Arlington, VA 22210
For teachers of trainable retarded, ages 12–21. Sex units: 1) body parts, gender, restroom signs, 2) living things, 3) reproduction, 4) growth, 5) Adolescence, menstruation, street language, 6) maturity—sexual feelings and birth control.

Development of a Sex Education Curriculum for a State Residential School for Deaf. Also The Deaf and Social Hygiene Guides, 1975. Available from Illinois School for Deaf, Jacksonville, IL 62650

Guide To Family Living and Sex Education. Available from Oregon State School for the Blind, 700 Church St. S.E., Salem, OR 97310

If I Have A Daughter—Sex Education Program For Teen-agers at Clarke Street School For The Deaf, Northampton, MA By A. S. Miller. Volta Review, 5(8):493–503, 1973
Discussion of the 16 years during which this program focused on teenage problems, using group techniques for boys and girls.

Planning and Implementation of Sex Education Program For Visually Handicapped Children in a Residential Setting. By Ruth Holmes. New Outlook for Blind 68(5):219–225, 1974
Discussion of program started in 1965 at Illinois Braille and Sight Saving School, Jacksonville, IL

Resource Guide in Sex Education for Mentally Retarded, 1971. 55 p. Available from American Association For Health, Physical Education and Recreation, Washington, DC. 20036
Prepared by a joint committee from SIECUS and AHPER this outlines a developmental approach to sexuality from infancy to adulthood.

SAR (Sexual Attitude Restructuring) 1976 Research. By H.E. Vandervoort, MD. Available from Human Sexuality Program, School of Medicine, University of California, San Francisco, CA

Educational process for staff and young adult disabled, using media to impart information and acceptance of sexuality as a natural and positive aspect of life.

Sex Education and Family Life for Visually Handicapped Children and Youth: A Resource Guide. By Irving Dickman et al. 1975. 86 p. Available from American Foundation For Blind, New York, NY 10011
Excellent guide for teachers, counselors, parents; provides a broad view and resources for family life and sex education.

Social and Sexual Development: Guide For Teachers of Handicapped. By S. Bernie Walden et al. 1971. 228 p. Available from Iowa State Dept. Public Instruction and Special Education, Curric Development Center, Iowa University, Iowa City, IA 52240
For teachers of educable mentally retarded; lesson plans at primary, intermediate, and advanced levels.

Advanced Family Life Education: Course developed by Human Sexuality Program, University of California Medical School, San Francisco, in conjunction with the special education and nursing staff of McAteer High School. Focuses on the emotional tasks of adolescence, the special problems of the disabled, as well as sexuality and disability. 1976

APPENDIX C
HORIZONS: NATIONAL
AND INTERNATIONAL

Global interest in the sexuality, sexual behavior, and sex-related problems of disabled persons is growing. In part, it reflects the rapidly changing social forces that may be equated with human liberation, as well as the increasing prominence given to sex in all communications media—from titillation to research. In the United States, the SIECUS reports were among the first materials available to the general public which included many references to current writings, audiovisual materials, and book reviews that related to the sexual activity disabled populations (391). Only within the past 5–10 years have national voluntary and governmental organizations sponsored study groups on sexuality of the disabled. The responsibilities of some of these groups included preparation of reports or monographs that proved useful to professionals in rehabilitation, as well as to the adult disabled themselves.

EXAMPLES OF AGENCY-SPONSORED PUBLICATIONS

A Resource Guide in Sex Education for the Mentally Retarded, sponsored by the American Association For Health, Physical Education and Recreation (349). In this handbook a national committee stressed the developmental aspects of sexuality with teaching cues for parents and adults in professional contact with the retarded. It is a reminder that any adult sexuality has as its base a psychosocial developmental growth pattern, as well as the sequelae of the disability factor.

Spinal Cord Injury, Hope Through Research, prepared by the Information Office, National Institute of Neurological Disease and Stroke (404). It covers an extensive base of published information on the subject of sexual function and dysfunction in subjects with spinal cord injury.

Sex, Courtship and the Single Ostomate, published by the United Ostomy Association (37). One of three pamphlets, it is reviewed by Calderone of SIECUS (63), who feels it is important since it draws our attention to and serves the special needs of a group of persons who live with artificial bowel openings in the abdomen. The United Ostomy Association has estimated that there are perhaps as many as one million such persons in the United States, a sizeable group. Calderone also pointed out that many young adults, whose health was at first debilitated because of the underlying condition that required the stoma, are restored to vigor following the operation, just at the time when their interest in dating and sex reaches a peak. *Sex, Courtship and the Single Ostomate* has been prepared especially for them, to help answer such usually unspoken questions as, "How do I explain the ostomy? Will my ostomy turn someone off? Will I be thought of as unwhole, or handicapped? Will it make me unfeminine or unmasculine?" Sections of the pamphlet have such headings as Lifestyles, Physical Sexual Incapabilities, Getting Started, Whom To Tell, How To Tell, When To Tell, Rejection And How To Handle It, How To Handle Acceptances, Preparation For Sex, Ostomating With Another Ostomate.

Sexual Rights and Responsibilities of the Mentally Retarded, proceedings of a conference sponsored by the American Association on Mental Deficiency (23). Burleson reviewed this for SIECUS (58) and from him we learn that this conference was one of the first efforts to come to grips with social attitudes and institutional policy relating to sexual rights of the retarded. Included are two provocative and entertaining presentations by Gordon, Director of Syracuse University's Institute for Family Research and Education, dealing with institutional attitudes about sexual behavior and communicating with youth about sex. Rosen, of the Elwyn Institute in Elwyn, Pennsylvania, offers a cogent theoretical model of psychosexual development of the retarded and explains the Institute's program and long-range research project on the adjustment to community life of Institute graduates. Goodman, ACSW, presents a sensitive analysis of parental dilemmas as they try to cope with the sexuality of their retarded son or daughter. Several programs at both the community and institutional levels that Burleson believes are well worth duplicating are also described in these proceedings. The bibliography and audiovisual resources listed in the appendix will prove helpful for those wishing to investigate the field further.

Sexuality and the Cerebral Palsy Project, a summary of research carried out in 1973–1974 under funding supplied by the United Cerebral Palsy Association's national office and the San Francisco affiliate (435). The study was carried out by the Human Sexuality Program of the University Of California Medical School in San Francisco. It encompassed aspects of individual counseling which indicated that listeners need patience to bridge the communications problems elicited by speech difficulties. It documented the interpersonal needs and stereotyped concepts of role expectations held by young cerebral palsied adults interviewed, and it organized pilot education programs for helping professionals as well as clients. In collaboration with the UCSF School of Medicine Cerebral Palsy Clinic, the study group produced a videotape, "Growing Up With Cerebral Palsy," wherein former clinic patients discuss problems encountered in childhood, youth, and now as adults. The project staff consulted with faculty at McAteer High School, San Francisco, and assisted in the development of a course, "Advanced Family Life Education for the Physically Disabled," which was offered to disabled high school students in the spring of 1974.

While discussing national publications, it would be a serious omission if *Rehabilitation Gazette* (341) and *Accent On Living* (5) were not mentioned. Both of these journals are written by and for the disabled. Both have a perspective which supplements the experience of professionals in the rehabilitation field. References will be made later in the appendix to items in various issues of these publications as those items relate to specific topics. Here, in order to give the flavor of each journal, two publications are noted:

Sexual Adjustment: A Guide for the Spinal Cord Injured, an *Accent* Special Publication (170). This guide is written by a vocational rehabilitation counselor whose husband became a C-5 quadriplegic as a result of an auto accident. They met while she was completing her rehabilitation counseling internship, and, as a couple, they have participated in several workshops at the Texas Institute of Rehabilitation and Research on sexuality.

Sex And The Disabled, a product of *Rehabilitation Gazette* (formerly known as *Toomey j Gazette*) (197). This warm, yet realistic, approach to feelings about sexuality is written by a practicing dermatologist who is a respiratory polio quadriplegic and who was among the first to speak out and for the sexual needs of disabled people.

WORKSHOPS AND STUDIES

At present such considerations of the sexuality of people with disabilities are limited by the availability of knowledgeable staff and funding. Here are examples of some thoughtful pioneering efforts by well-qualified teams around the United States.

Five 2-day workshops that focused on the *Sexuality of Adults with Spinal Cord Injuries,* were offered for rehabilitation professionals and spinal cord injured adults between December 1971 and October 1972 by the University of Minnesota's *Program in Human Sexuality* within the Department of Physical Medicine and Rehabilitation. The fifth workshop, jointly sponsored by the American Academy of Physical Medicine and Rehabilitation, included an optional third day on sexual counseling. Objectives of the workshops were to show the contact-care professional and the disabled participant how to face up to their own sexuality, the range of sexuality, and how to be more helpful to others. Sexual attitudes and attitude changes of attendees were evaluated and found to be similar to those measured in participants of other workshops involving medical and seminary students as well as community members. Subsequent workshops, curricula, and materials have been based on these findings and are useful references resources (4).

The development of a human sexuality program, directed toward the *Sexual Attitudes and Needs of Disabled Persons* was sponsored in 1974 by the Max and Anna Levison Foundation at Moss Rehabilitation Hospital in Philadelphia. An important element of this program was the 3-day workshops designed to train hospital staff to deal with the adult disabled's view of his own sexuality in the light of his changed body image, physiologic capabilities, and interpersonal resources (343).

Sexuality and Multiple Sclerosis was the topic of a seminar within the Patient Services Workshops at the 1974 annual conference in St. Louis, sponsored by the National Multiple Sclerosis Society (393). The presentation was handled with sensitivity and caution, guided by the realization that multiple sclerosis patients vary widely in their ability to handle emotionally laden materials and in their ethical and religious beliefs on this particular subject. (This is a most important point that is lacking in too many hastily conceived and superficially optimistic seminar efforts. [Ed] Discussion covered not only gross changes effected by the disease, but also the subtle alterations in apperceptiveness, responsiveness, sensitivity, mood, personality, and ability to transact in general. Recommendations were tempered by the wisdom of acquainting the disabled and the partner of the disabled with the remaining capabilities and the alternatives available in such cases, but leaving the ultimate choice and individualized solution to the final discretion of the people . . . "the most important criterion is whether the proposed behavior is satisfactory and acceptable to the patient and partner and whether it is going to help them achieve compatible sexual gratification. . . ."

INTERNATIONAL APPROACHES

On the international horizon several important conferences have laid the basis for serious study and exchange information. In 1969, the Swedish Central Committee for Rehabilitation held the first symposium on the sexual life of the disabled and the role of community and rehabilitation institutions in this aspect of adjustment to disability. The results of the symposium were published, and a bibliography of nearly 300 references on adult sexual function was completed for distribution. Meanwhile, ongoing studies in Germany to improve sex education programs for the disabled have been reported to Rehabilitation International, and the United Kingdom has contributed follow-up studies on the marriage problems of persons with cerebral palsy. In 1971 descriptions of research in progress on the sexuality of the disabled in Denmark, the Netherlands, and Sweden were presented at the First Congress of the International Cerebral Palsy Society at Arnheim, the Netherlands. More recently, in 1972 and 1976, International Symposia on Sex Education included seminars on sex and the handicapped, under the direction of Chigler of Tel Aviv, Israel. Fortunately, Rehabilitation International publishes the *International Rehabilitation Review* where notices and reports of these studies and conferences keep the interested clinician up-to-date on international activities (342).

The following summary of a unique program and research study initiated in the Netherlands in 1972 is quoted directly from the *International Rehabilitation Review* (348). It is titled "Activities of the Netherlands Committee on Sexual Problems of the Disabled."

The Committee was formed as a result of the awareness that rehabilitation could not be regarded as complete unless sexual problems were also taken into consideration.
Objectives
The following provisional objectives were formulated to take into account all the facts relating to sex and sexual activity among the disabled and to study means by which help can be given, including the exchange of information and views, to both the disabled and to those around them.
Inventory of Literature
Information was sought both at home and abroad, but it was found that little had been published on this subject. A start has been made on compiling documentation, which would ultimately provide a source of information for doctors, nurses, guardians, parents, partners, family members and the disabled. It is intended to publish notices concerning this documentation at some time in the future in the *Tydschrift voor Revalidatie.*
Scientific Study
Discerning an obvious need for a scientific socio-psychological study of the question, it was decided to entrust such a study to the Instituut voor Agologisch Onderzoek of the University of Amsterdam. The results of the two-year study, which will consist of interviews with disabled people conducted in discussion groups by the staff of the Instituut voor Voorlichtingskunde en Communicatie in Rotterdam, will be published.

The discussions will be based on a questionnaire, using interviewing techniques devised by sociologists. Questions will be divided into various categories; for example, practical and theoretical questions regarding relationships and sex, a number of questions on self-acceptance, and questions on ways in which behavior can be changed or improved. Observers will be present to assess the discussions and the value of the method applied. In addition, an assessment will be made of the effect of the entire study which may enhance the value of the report.

Through these activities, the Committee hopes to form a composite picture of the sexual problems of the disabled, in order to be able to provide help and information as effectively as possible.
Direct Help
Another aspect of the Committee's work involves direct help to disabled individuals and rehabilitation center patients and staff wishing to form discussion groups on sex. A training program has been developed for discussion group leaders and was first conducted in June, 1970. The Committee is also attempting to recruit and organize advisory teams composed of physicians, clergymen and social workers to provide guidance locally and regionally. The Committee is aware of the dangers inherent in this work, particularly the risk of disappointment when possibilities are suggested which will remain unattainable for some. In view of the great need, the Committee has consciously accepted the risk.

One of the most creative international approaches to the entire subject comes from Sweden. The January 1976 issue of *International Rehabilitation Review* contained a notice that "An international clearing-house on sexual and social intercourse has been established in Sweden." The information center will be operated as a project of the Social Commission of Rehabilitation International by the Swedish Central Committee for Rehabilitation, FACK, S–161 25 Bromma 1, Sweden.

This brief overview of recent national and international directions on behalf of the sexuality of the disabled is presented to set into Western cultural perspective the growing responses in this area and the major efforts which remain to be made.

APPENDIX D
RESOURCES
FOR MATERIALS:
SEX EDUCATION OF
THE DISABLED—
ORGANIZATIONS

American Association for Health, Physical Education, and Recreation (AHPER)
  1201 16th St. NW, Washington, DC 20036

American Association on Mental Deficiency
  5201 Connecticut Ave., N.W., Washington, DC 20015

American Association of Sex Educators and Counselors (AASEC)
  815 15th St., N.W., Washington, DC 20005

American Foundation for the Blind
  15 West 16 St., New York, NY 10011

American School Health Association
  515 East Main St., Kent, OH 44240

American Social Health Association
  1740 Broadway, New York, NY 10019

Association for Childhood Education International
  3615 Wisconsin Ave. NW, Washington, DC 20016

Child Study Association of America/Wel–Met Inc.
  50 Madison Ave., New York, NY 10010

Council for Exceptional Children (CEC)
  900 Jefferson Plaza, Route 1, Arlington, VA 22202

Educational Resources Information Center for Exceptional Children
  900 Jefferson Plaza, Route 1, Arlington, VA 22202

Eastern Association of Sex Therapists
  80 Barre St, Charleston SC 29401

Institute for Family Research and Education
  760 Ostrom Ave., Syracuse, NY 13210

National Association for Crippled Children and Adults—Easter Seal
    2023 W. Ogden Ave., Chicago, IL 60636
National Association for Retarded Citizens
    2709 Avenue E East, Arlington, TX 76010
National Clearinghouse for Mental Health Information, National Institutes of Health
    Bethesda, MD 20014
The National Council on Family Relations
    1219 University Ave., S.E., Minneapolis, MN 55414
National Foundation (Genetics)
    800 Second Avenue, New York, NY 10017
National Institutes of Health, Public Health Service, National Medical Audio-visual Center,
    Station K, Atlanta, GA 30324
Paralyzed Veterans of America
    7315 Wisconsin Ave., Washington, DC 20014
Planned Parenthood Federation Of America
    810 Seventh Ave., New York, NY 10019
Planned Parenthood of Southeastern Pennsylvania
    1402 Spruce St., Philadelphia, PA 19102
Rehabilitation International
    432 Park Ave. South, New York, NY 10016
School Health Education Study, Inc.
    1507 M St., N.W., Suite 800, Washington, DC 20036
United Cerebral Palsy Association, Inc.
    66 East 34 St., New York, NY 10016
United Ostomy Association
    1111 Wilshire Blvd., Los Angeles, CA 90017

ASSOCIATIONS FOR SPECIAL NEEDS

Association for Voluntary Sterilization
    708 Third Avenue, New York, NY 10017
Association for Study of Abortion
    120 West 57 Street, New York, NY 10019
CHOICE Religious Coalition for Abortion Rights
    Box 381, Scarsdale, NY 10583
Planned Parenthood
    810 Seventh Ave, New York, NY 10019
    Write for regional offices booklets.
Wickersham Voluntary Sterilization Service
    133 East 48 St., New York, NY 10022

American Public Health Association
   1015 Eighteenth St, N.W., Washington, DC 20036
   Write for VD information and resources.

AASK (Aid to Adoption of Special Kids) Association
   Box 11212, Oakland, CA 94611
   Adoption agency exclusively for adoption of children with special needs, due to disabling conditions.

APPENDIX E
RELATED SIECUS
PUBLICATIONS

SEX EDUCATION USEFUL FOR THE HANDICAPPED Available from Human Sciences Press, 72 Fifth Avenue, New York, New York 10011 (catalog on request). (Sold separately)

A. Study Guides
   Lester Kirkendall, PhD: Sex Education
   Alan Bell, PhD: Homosexuality
   Warren Johnson, EdD: Masturbation
   Lester Kirkendall, PhD: Sexuality and the Life Cycle
   John Gagnon, PhD; William Simon, PhD: Sexual Encounters between Adults and Children
B. Special Publications
   A Resource Guide for the Mentally Retarded—SIECUS and the American Alliance for Health, Physical Education and Recreation
   Developing Community Acceptance of Sex Education for the Mentally Retarded by Medora Bass
   A Bibliography of Resources in Sex Education for the Mentally Retarded

BOOK

Calderone, Mary S.: Sexuality and Human Values—The Personal Dimension of Sexual Experience. Foremost experts in medicine, social services and religion discuss sexual relations in the light of human values. One area of agreement among them is that sexual experience cannot be isolated from the context of human relationships.

THE HANDICAPPED AND SEXUAL HEALTH. SIECUS Report, 1976 Special Issue. Available from Institute for Family Research and Education, 760 Ostrom Avenue, Syracuse, New York 13210.

Contains articles by authorities in various fields of handicapping; a selective, annotated bibliography; audio-visual reviews of pertinent materials; resources to write for; book reviews of current materials.

APPENDIX F
AUDIOVISUAL RESOURCES

PRODUCERS AND DISTRIBUTORS: Development, Family Life,
Sexuality

1. ACI Films Inc.
   35 West 45 St., New York, NY 10036
2. American Foundation For The Blind
   15 West 16 St., New York, NY 10017
3. Audiovisual Aid Library, Dept. of Education and Social Concern,
   Unitarian–Universalist Association
   25 Beacon St., Boston, MA 02108
4. Calvin Productions
   1909 Buttonwood St., Philadelphia, PA 19130
5. Campbell Films
   Academy Ave., Saxtons River, VT 05154
6. Center for Marital and Sexual Studies
   5199 E. Pacific Coast Highway, Long Beach, CA 90804
7. Center for Mass Communication, Columbia University Press
   1125 Amsterdam Ave., New York, NY 10025
8. Centron Educational Films
   1621 West 9 St., Laurence, KA 66044
9. Churchill Films
   622 N. Robertson Blvd., Los Angeles, CA 90069
10. Concept Media
    1500 Adams Ave., Costa Mesa, CA 92626
11. Coronet Instructional Films
    65 E. South Water St., Chicago, IL 60601
12. Dept. of Physical Medicine and Rehabilitation
    University of Minnesota Hospitals
    Box 297 Mayo Memorial Bldg Minneapolis, MN 55455
13. Encyclopedia Britannica Films
    425 N. Michigan Ave., Chicago, IL 60611
14. Hallmark Films and Recordings
    1511 East North Ave., Baltimore, MD 21213
15. Hank Newenhouse Inc.
    1017 Longaker Rd., Northbrook, IL 60062

16. Harris Cty Center for Retarded
    3550 West Dallas, P.O. Box 13403 Houston, TX 77019
17. International Film Bureau
    322 S. Michigan Ave., Chicago, IL 60604
18. J. B. Lippincott & Co.
    Philadelphia, PA
19. John Wiley & Sons Inc., Customer Services
    1 Wiley Drive, Somerset, NJ 08873
20. J.P. Kennedy Foundation
    1701 E St. NW, Washington, DC 20003
21. McGraw Hill
    1221 Avenue of the Americas, New York, N.Y. 10020
22. Medical Arts Production
    414 Mason St., San Francisco, CA 94102
23. Multi-Media Resource Center
    540 Powell St., San Francisco, CA 94108
24. National Institutes of Health, Public Health Service, National Medical
    Audiovisual Center
    Station K, Atlanta, GA 30324
25. New Line Cinema
    121 University Place, New York, NY 10003
26. Perrenial Education Inc.
    1825 Willow Rd., Northfield, IL 60093
27. Planned Parenthood—Film Library
    267 West 27 St., New York, NY 10001
28. Planned Parenthood of Southeastern Pennsylvania
    1402 Spruce St., Philadelphia, PA 19102
29. Potomac Films
    4303 Elm, Chevy Chase, MD 20015
30. Program in Human Sexuality, Medical School, Research Bldg. East
    2630 University Ave., S.E., Minneapolis, MN 55414
31. Regional Resources Library Listing, Continuing Education Program,
    SUNY Buffalo
    27 Foster Annex, Buffalo, NY 14214
32. Stanfield House
    900 Euclid Ave., PO Box 3208, Santa Monica, CA 90403

ANATOMIC MODELS FOR THE BLIND

1. Cleveland Health Museum
   899 Euclid Ave., Cleveland, OH 44106
2. Denoyer Geppert
   5235 Ravenswood Ave., Chicago, IL 60640
3. DiMat Ltd.
   Kaul Bldg. Box 367, McLean, VA 22101

4. Hubbard Scientific Co.
   2855 Shermer Rd., Northbrook, IL 60062
5. Nystrom
   333 Elston Ave., Chicago, IL 60618

AUDIOVISUALS ABOUT DISABLED PERSONS (Code Number in parentheses refers to distributor list preceding.)

ABC of Sex Education for Trainable Persons. Film, 16 mm, sound, color. (14)

Attitudes Toward the Disabled. 1-hour Videotape, America '73 Series. Produced by Bruce Cohen for N-PACT, NET, and Ford Foundation, 1973.

Bertha. Film, 16 mm, sound, color. Explores decisions relating to implantation of IUD contraceptive for a retarded girl. (20)

Bringing It Up. Film, 16 mm, sound. Shows interviewing skills used with a hospitalized spinal cord injured male. (12)

Coital Positioning. Film, 16 mm, sound, color, 12 min. (6)

Coping in the Community. Film, 16 mm, sound, color, 30 min. Interviews with retarded adults on aspects of their sexuality in a community living situation. (16)

Don't Tell the Cripples about Sex. Film, 16 mm, sound, 30 min. Developed for counseling staff and multiply disabled young adults. Human Sexuality Program, School of Medicine, University of California, San Francisco.

Fertility Regulation for Persons with Learning Disability. Film, 16 mm, sound, color. (14)

Give It a Try. Film, 16 mm, sound. Sex counseling of a newly injured postdischarged quadriplegic man and his wife in a sexually dysfunctional and frustrating relationship. (12)

I Am Not What You See. Film, sound, color, 28 min. Produced by Canadian Broadcasting Corp., Toronto, Canada. Available from Rehabilitation International, NYC. Prize winning film at 1977 International Rehabilitation Film Festival. This is a powerful in-depth interview with Sandra Diamond, who was born with cerepral palsy. Though confined to a wheelchair and so severely physically disabled as to be unable to walk or dress herself, Miss Diamond speaks clearly, openly, and with intriguing perspective about her ambitions, her desires, her sexuality, and her moments of despair. She is a practicing psychologist working toward her PhD and an artist at communicating the meanings of humanness and the question of attitudes.

If Ever Two Were One. Film, 16 mm, sound, color, 14 min. Male partner in this film was injured in lower portion of his spine. Sensitively portrays oral and manual demonstrations of intimacy. Shows stuffing technique in which a flaccid penis is inserted and contained in a vagina. (23)

Just What Can You Do? Film, 16 mm, sound, color, 20 min. Spinal cord injured and their partners discuss the implications of their disabilities upon their sexual relationships and activities. (23)

Like Other People. Film, 16 mm, sound, 30 min. English film of cerebral palsied severely disabled young couples. Poignantly conveys the capacity of partners to surmount ordinary communication barriers. Raises questions of opportunities for love, marriage, and supportive environments in face of present day attitudes and realities. (28)

Love and Sex and Growing Up. By Eric and Corinne Johnson. LP record for blind children and disabled unable to hold a book. Ages 10–12. (18)

Love and Sex In Plain Language. By Eric Johnson. LP record for blind and disabled young adults. (18)

Materials and Resources for the Blind. Recorded materials, Braille, large print, and models for classroom use. (2)

Medical Conditions: Impact On Sexuality. 1 filmstrip and 1 audiotape casette. (10)

Mental Retardation and Sexuality. Filmstrip with record, 20 min. For inservice staff and parent education. (28)

On Being Sexual. Film, 16 mm, color, sound, 25 min. Parent workshop wherein problems of handling retarded adolescents are discussed and small groups of retarded teenagers and young adults are interviewed. Sol Gordon and Winifred Kempton bring in concepts of responsible sexuality and gaps in present sex education. (32)

Possibilities. Film, 16 mm, sound, color, 12 min. A spinal cord injured man, level C-5 and C-6, discusses impact of injury on his life. (23)

Sex Orientation slides. 34 cartoon 35-mm slides. Sex taboos in humorous vein, for young adult and staff groups. (23)

Sex Problems in Paraplegia. 90-min audiotape of a seminar chaired by Howard Rusk, MD at Institute of Rehabilitation Medicine, NYU Medical Center, NYC. (31)

Sex Subjects. 180 cartoon 35 mm slides. For staff and young adults. Topics include masturbation, penis size, female sexuality, the sexual response cycle, male and female sexuality. (23)

Surgical Conditions: Impact on Sexuality. 1 filmstrip and 1 audiotape casette. (10)

Touching. Film, 16 mm, sound, color, 16 min. A C-6 spinal cord injured man and his able-bodied partner explore satisfying sensory stimulation through pleasuring of the erogenous areas of their bodies when the male is unable to have an erection. (23)

Your Changing Body. Two casettes: One in "polite" language, the other with slang as a guided self-exploration for visually handicapped at ages 10–18. (26)

AUDIOVISUAL SUPPLEMENT

Produced for normal populations, but many are developmentally applicable.

Sex Education On Film—A Guide To Visual Aids and Programs. By Laura J. Singer and Judith Ruskin, Teachers College Press, Columbia University, New York, paperback 1971. Contents: 1) Family Relationships—The Influence of Mothering and Environment on Development; 2) Physical and Emotional Development; 3) The Creation Of Life; 4) Masculinity and Femininity; 5) Attitudes and Values; 6) Marriage; 7) Special Problems—VD, Prenatal Pregnancy, Family Planning; 8) Philosophy and Implementation of Sex Education—Sample Program in Sex Education for Parents and Teachers.

About Your Sexuality. by Derrick Calderwood. (For adolescents and young adults) Beacon Press, 25 Beacon St., Boston, MA 02108. Filmstrips: 1) Learning About Sex; 2) Breaking the Language Barrier; 3) Four Sequences; 4) Love Making; 5) Male and Female Anatomy. Records: 1) Learning about Sex; 2) The How-Not-To-Book; 3) Life Before Birth; 4) What Everyone Should Know About Birth.

Guide To Films: Planned Parenthood—World Population Film Library, 267 West 25 St., New York, NY 10001. Subject Index: 1) Abortion; 2) Birth Control; 3) Dating and Marriage; 4) Sex Education; 5) Staff Training/Counseling; 6) Sterilization.

Human Sexuality and Nursing Practice. Filmstrips and audiocasettes from Concept Media, 1500 Adams Ave., Costa Mesa, CA 92626. Subject Index: 1) Sexuality: A Nursing Concern; 2) Sexual Behavior: Nursing Reactions; 3) Medical Conditions: Impact on Sexuality; 4) Surgical Conditions: Impact on Sexuality; 5) Disabling and Deforming Conditions: Impact on Sexuality; 6) Viewpoint: The Nurse and Abortion; 7) Viewpoint: The Nurse and Homosexuality; 8) When the Topic is Sex. . . .

APPENDIX G
GENETIC COUNSELING
SERVICES AND RELATED
RESOURCES (USA)

ALABAMA*

Laboratory of Medical Genetics
University of Alabama Medical Center
Birmingham, AL
35294 Phone 205-934-4968

Pathology Department
The Children's Hospital
1601 Sixth Avenue South
Birmingham, AL
35233 Phone 205-933-4250

Department of Medical Genetics
2451 Fillingim Street
Mobile AL
36617

ALASKA

Public Health Service Genetics Clinics
University of Alaska
Box 95753
Fairbanks, AK
99701 Phone 907 979-7731

ARIZONA

Genetic Counseling Center
St. Joseph's Hospital and Medical Center
P.O. Box 2071
Phoenix, AZ
85001

Department of Zoology
Arizona State University
Tempe, AZ
85281

College of Medicine,
Obstetrics and Gynecology
University of Arizona
Tucson, AZ
85724

CALIFORNIA

Department of Zoology
University of California
Berkeley, CA
94720 Phone 415 642-2929

Department of Medical Genetics
City of Hope National Medical Center
1500 East Duarte Road
Duarte, CA
91010 Phone 359-8111 Ext. 220

Department of Developmental Cytogenetics
City of Hope National Medical Center
1500 East Duarte Road
Duarte, CA
91010 Phone 213 359-8111

Department of Pathology
Fresno Community Hospital
Box 1732
Fresno, CA
93715 Phone 209 233-0911

Medical Genetics & Dysmorphology Service
Valley Childrens Hospital/
Valley Medical Center
3151 North Millbrook
Fresno, CA
93703 Phone 209 221-2961 Ext 294

Genetic Counseling Clinic
Valley Children's Hospital
3151 North Millbrook
Fresno, CA
93703 Phone 209 227-2961

Department of Biology
California State University
at Fullerton
Fullerton, CA
92634 Phone 714 870-3610

*From Bergsma D, Lynch HT: International Directory of Genetic Services. The National Foundation-March of Dimes, 5th ed, 1977.

213

Department of Pediatrics
Southern California Permanente
Medical Group
1050 West Pacific Coast Highway
Harbor City, CA
90710 Phone 213 325–5111

Department of Pediatrics, Genetics Clinic
University of California at Irvine
Irvine, CA
92650 Ph 714 633–9393 Ex. 150

Medical Genetics Unit
University of California, School of Medicine
La Jolla, CA
92039 Phone 714 452–4307

Biochemical Genetics Laboratory
University of California,
School of Medicine
La Jolla, CA
92037

Neurosciences Department
University of California, School of Medicine
La Jolla, CA
92093 Phone 714 452–3376

Departments of Community Medicine and
    Pediatrics
University of California at San Diego
P.O. Box 109 San Diego County Public
Health Clinics
La Jolla, CA
92037 Ph 714 453–2000 Ex. 1792

Dept. of Pediatrics, Genetics, Birth Defects
& Chromosome Service
Loma Linda University Medical Center
Loma Linda CA
92354

Division of Medical Genetics
Childrens Hospital of Los Angeles
4650 Sunset Blvd.
Los Angeles CA
90054 Ph 213 663–3341 Ex. 2603

Department of Pediatrics and Psychiatry
University of California, Center for the
Health Sciences
760 Westwood Plaza
Los Angeles, CA
90024 Phone 213 825–0109

Division of Medical Genetics
Children's Hospital of Los Angeles
4650 Sunset Boulevard
Los Angeles, CA
90054 Ph 213 663–3341 Ex. 2603

L.A. County-USC Medical Center
Genetics Birth Defects Center
1200 North State Street
Los Angeles, CA
90033 Phone 213 226–3816

L.A. County-USC Medical Center
Genetics Birth Defect Center

1129 N State Street 10–30 General Lab.
Bldg.
Los Angeles, CA
90003

L.A. County-USC Medical Center
Genetics Birth Defects Center
1129 N State Street 16–30 General Lab.
Bldg.
Los Angeles, CA
90003

Department of Psychiatry, U.C.L.A.
760 Westwood Plaza
Los Angeles, CA
90024

Department of Medical Genetics
Fertility, Gynecology & Endocrinology
Medical Clinic, Inc.
12301 Wilshire Blvd., Suite 415
Los Angeles, CA
90025 Phone 213 820–3723

Department of Pathology
Hospital of the Good Samaritan
616 S. Witmer Street
Los Angeles, CA
90017

L.A. County-USC Medical Center
Genetics Birth Defects Center
1129 N State Street 16–39 General Lab.
Bldg.
Los Angeles, CA
90003

Departments of Medicine and Pediatrics
UCLA School of Medicine
760 Westwood Place
Los Angeles, CA
90024 Phone 213 825–5720

Department of Cytogenetics,
Room 16–607
USC-LAC Medical Center
1200 North State Street
Los Angeles, CA
90033 Phone 213 226–4606

Department of Pediatrics
University of Southern California Medical
School
1200 North State Street
Los Angeles, CA
90033

Departments of Pediatrics and Genetics
Kaiser Foundation Hospital
280 West Macarthur Boulevard
Oakland, CA
94611 Phone 415 645–5816

Medical Genetics
Medical Center
Children's Hospital
Oakland, CA
94609 Phone 415 654–5600

Department of Pediatrics
Kaiser-Permanente Medical Center
13652 Cantara Street
Pangrama City, CA
91402 Phone 213 781–2361

Sacramento Medical Center
2315 Stockton Boulevard
Sacramento, CA
95817

Mercy Hospital and Medical Center Clinic
4077 Fifth Avenue
San Diego, CA
92103 Phone 714 298–4141

Mercy Hospital & Medical Center Clinic
4077 Fifth Avenue
San Diego, CA
92103 Phone 714 298–4141

Birth Defects Center
Children's Health Center
8001 Frost Street
San Diego, CA
92123 Phone 714 277–5808

San Diego County
University Hospital
P.O. Box 3548
San Diego, CA
92103 Ph 714 277–5808 Ex. 203 or 209

Child Development Center
San Diego Center for Developmental
Disabilities
8001 Frost Street
San Diego, CA
92123 Phone 565–1511 Ext. 209

Department of Pediatrics
University of California
San Francisco, CA
94143

Department of Pediatrics
University of California
San Francisco CA
94143 Phone 415 666–2101

Pediatrics Clinic
Kaiser Hospital
900 Killy Boulevard
Santa Clara, CA
95051

St. John's Hospital
1328 22nd Street
Santa Monica, CA
90404 Phone 829–5511 Ext. 745

Genetic Counseling Clinic
Stanford University
School of Medicine
Stanford, CA
94305 Phone 415 497–5198

Department of Pediatrics
Birth Defects Center
Stanford University Medical Center

Stanford, CA
94305 Phone 415 497–6858

Division of Medical Genetics
Harbor General Hospital
1000 West Carson Street
Torrance, CA
90509 Phone 213 328–2380

Ventura County Health Department
Genetic Counseling Center
Ventura, CA
93001

Ventura Community Health Dept.
Genetic Counseling Center
Ventura, CA
93001

COLORADO

Department of Human Genetics
University of Colorado
1100 Fourteenth Street
Denver, CO
80202 Phone 303 674–5727

Department of Biology
University of Northern Colorado
Greeley, CO
80631

CONNECTICUT

Department of Human Genetics
Connecticut Twin Registry
79 Elm Street
Hartford, CT
06115

Departments of Human Genetics
Yale Medical School
New Haven, CT
06520 Phone 203 436–3654

Genetics Clinic
Newington Children's Hospital
Newington, CT
06111

DELAWARE

Department of Pediatrics
Wilmington Medical Center
P.O. Box 1668
Wilmington, DE
20007

DISTRICT OF COLUMBIA

University Affiliated Center for Child
Development
Georgetown University
Medical Center
3900 Reservoir Road, N.W.
Washington DC
20306 Phone 202 676–4096

Armed Forces Institute of
Pathology

Washington, DC
20306 Phone 202 576–2950

Dept. of Obstetrics and Gynecology
The George Washington
University Clinic
2150 Penn Avenue, N.W.
Washington, DC
20037 Phone 202 676–4096

Department of Pediatrics
Howard University College of Medicine
Division of Medical Genetics
Washington, DC
20001 Phone 202 797–1766

Division of Clinical Genetics and Birth
Defects
University Affiliated Program for Child
Development
3800 Reservoir Road, N.W.
Georgetown University Hospital
Washington, DC
20007 Phone 625–7676

FLORIDA

Birth Defects Center
J. Hillis Miller Health Center
Gainesville, FL
32610 Phone 904 392–2958

Mailman Center
University of Miami
School of Medicine
Miami, FL
33152

GEORGIA

Department of Psychiatry
Georgia Mental Health Institute
Emory University
Atlanta, GA
30306 Phone 404 894–5951

Division of Perinatal Pathology
Emory University School of Medicine
80 Butler Street, S.E.
Atlanta, GA
30303 Ph 404 659–1212 Ex. 4051

Department of Pathology
St. Joseph's Hospital
265 Ivy Street, N.E.
Atlanta, GA
30303

Department of Pediatrics, Birth Defects
Center
Medical College of Georgia, Eugene
Talmadge Memorial Hospital
1459 Gwinnet Street
Augusta, GA
30902 Ph 404 724–7111 Ex. 8423

Department of Pediatrics
Medical College of Georgia, Birth Defects
Center

Augusta, GA
30902

Department of Obstetrics and Gynecology
Medical College of Georgia
Augusta, GA
30902

Central State Hospital
Milledgeville, GA
31061 Ph 808 531–3511 EX. 164

HAWAII

Department of Birth Defects
Kauikeolani Children's Hospital,
University of Hawaii-Dept of Pedia
Honolulu, HI
96817 Phone 531–3511 Ext. 164

Population Genetics Laboratory
University of Hawaii
2411 Dole Street
Honolulu, HI
96822

IDAHO

Mental Retardation Program
Idaho State School and Hospital
Box 47
Nampa, ID
83651

ILLINOIS

Peoria School of Medicine
University of Illinois College of
Medicine
123SW Glendale Avenue
Peoria, IL
61605

Amniocentesis Service
Michael Reese Hospital and Medical
Center
530 East 31st Street
Chicago, IL
60616 Phone 312 791–2261 Ext. 411

Department of Obstetrics—Gynecology
Prentice Womens Hospital and Maternity
Center
333 E. Superior Street, Suite 464
Chicago, IL
60611

Department of Obstetrics
and Gynecology
University of Chicago
5841 South Maryland Avenue
Chicago IL
60637 Phone 312 947–5310

Department of Pediatrics
University of Chicago
950 East 59 St.
Chicago, IL
60637 Phone 312 947–6211

Department of Psychology and Social
Sciences
College of Health Sciences
Rush Presbyterian St. Lukes's Medical
Center
Chicago IL
60612 Phone 312 942–6652

Department of Pediatrics
University of Illinois Medical Center
Chicago, IL
60612 Phone 312 996–6714

Department of Genetics
Children's Memorial Hospital
Chicago, IL
60614 Phone 312 348–4040

Division of Medical Genetics
Michael Reese Medical Center
29th Street and Ellis Avenue
Chicago, IL
60616 Phone 312 791–3844

Department of Pediatrics
University of Illinois Hospital
840 S Woods St
Chicago, IL
60612 Phone 312 996–6711

Illinois State Pediatric Institute
1640 West Roosevelt Road
Chicago, IL
60608

Department of Pediatrics Genetics and
Human Development Section
Rush Medical School,
Rush-Presbyterian St. Luke's Medic
Chicago, IL
60612

Genetic Counseling Service
Allied Agencies Center
320 East Armstrong Avenue
Peoria, Il
61603 Phone 309 673–6481

Center For Genetics
University Of Illinois Medical Center
Chicago Il
60612 Phone 996–4970

Genetics Counseling Service
School Of Basic Medical Sciences
University Of Illinois
Urbana, Il
61801 Phone 217 333–8172

INDIANA

Department Of Medical Genetics
Indiana University Medical School
Indianapolis, In
46207

IOWA

Department Of Pediatrics
University Hospital

Iowa City, Ia
52240 Phone 319 356–2674

KANSAS

Department Of Medicine
Kansas University Medical Center
Kansas City, Ks
66103 Phone 913 236–5252

The Lattimore-Fink Laboratories, Inc.
Medical Arts Building, West
West 10th Street
Topeka, Ks
66604

KENTUCKY

Department Of Community Medicine
University Of Kentucky Medical Center
Lexington, Ky
40506

Child Evaluation Center
University of Louisville
Medical School
540 South Preston Street
Louisville, Ky
40202 Phone 558–5331

LOUISIANA

Department Of Medicine, Section Of
Genetics
Louisville State University Medical Center
1542 Tulane Avenue
New Orleans, La
70112 Phone 504 527–5033

Department Of Pathology
Tulane University School Of Medicine
1430 Tulane Avenue
New Orleans, La
70112

Department Of Anatomy
Tulane University
New Orleans, La
70112

Department Of Pediatrics
Tulane University School Of Medicine
1430 Tulane Avenue
New Orleans, La
70112

Dept. Of Pediatrics Heritable Disease
Center
L.S.U. School Of Medicine
1542 Tulane Avenue
New Orleans, La
70112 Phone 504 527–8233

Department Of Pediatrics
L.S.U. School Of Medicine In
Shreveport-Birth Defects Center
P.O. Box 3932
Shreveport, La
71130 Phone 318 635–6495

Department Of Pediatrics
L.S.U. School Of Medicine In Shreveport,
Birth Defects Center
P.O. Box 3932
Shreveport, La
71130 Phone 207 667–5311

MAINE

Department Of Pediatrics
Eastern Maine Medical Center
489 State Street
Bangor, Me
04401 Phone 207 947–3711

Genetic Counseling Center
50 Union Street
Ellsworth, Me
04605

General Couns. Clinic
Maine Medical Center
Portland, Me
04102

Birth Defects Clinic
Maine Medical Center
22 Branhall Street
Portland, Me
04101

MARYLAND

Dept. Of Obstetrics And Gynecology
University Of Maryland Hospital
Baltimore, Md
21201 Phone 301 528–5964

Department Of Medicine, Division Of
Medical Genetics, Chromosome Lab
The Johns Hopkins Hospital University
School of Medicine
601 North Broadway
Baltimore, Md
21205 Phone 301 955–3461

Department Of Medicine, The Moore Clinic
The Johns Hopkins Hospital University
School Of Medicine
601 North Broadway
Baltimore, Md
21215 Ph 301 367–7800 Ex. 8630

Department Of Pediatrics
University Of Maryland Hospital
Baltimore, Md
21201 Phone 301 528–6669

Human Genetics Laboratory
John F. Kennedy Institute
707 North Broadway
Baltimore, Md
21205 Phone 301 955–4173

Natl. Institute Of Neurological &
Communication Disorders & Stroke
National Institutes Of Health
Bethesda, Md
20014 Phone 301 496–5821

MASSACHUSETTS

Blood Grouping Laboratory
Center For Blood Research
800 Huntington Ave.
Boston, Ma
02115

Blood Grouping Laboratory
Center For Blood Research
800 Huntington Avenue
Boston Ma
02115

Department Of Dermatology, Cutaneous
Genetics Unit
Massachusetts General Hospital
32 Fruit Street
Boston, Ma
02114 Phone 617 726–3993

Department Of Pediatrics, Children's
Service Genetics Unit
Harvard Medical School
Massachusetts General Hospital
Boston, Ma
02114 Phone 617 726–3826

Boston Hospital For Women
221 Longwood Avenue
Boston, Ma
02115

Center For Genetic Counseling And Birth
Defect Evaluation
Tufts—New England Medical Center
171 Harrison Avenue
Boston, Ma
02111

Clinical Genetics Division
Children's Hospital Medical Center
Boston, Ma
02115 Phone 617 734–6000 Ext. 35

Department Of Pediatrics
Massachusetts General Hospital
Boston, Ma
02114 Phone 617 893–4909

Birth Defect Evaluation Center And Cleft
Palate Center
Tufts-New England Medical Center Hospital
171 Harrison Ave.
Boston, Ma
02111 Phone 617 956–5456

Birth Defect Evaluation Center
Tufts-New England Medical Center
171 Harrison Avenue
Boston Ma
02111 Phone 956–5461

E.P. Joslin Research Laboratory
170 Pilgrim Road
Boston, Ma
02215

Channing Laboratory
Boston City Hospital

Boston, Ma
02118 Phone 617 424–4757
Heredity Of Deafness Division
Dept. Research And Clin. Services
The Clarke School For The Deaf
Northampton, Ma
01060

MICHIGAN

Department Of Human Genetics
University Of Michigan
Ann Arbor, Mi
48108 Phone 313 763–2532

Departments Of Gynecology And
Obstetrics, Birth Defects Center
University Of Detroit
Detroit Mi
48221 Phone 313 342–1000

Birth Defects Center, Department
Gynecology And Obstetrics
Wayne State University School Of Medicine
275 East Hancock
Detroit, Mi
48201

Department Of Pediatrics
Henry Ford Hospital
2799 West Grand Boulevard
Detroit, Mi
48202 Phone 313 876–3121

Pediatric Neuro-Muscular Disease Clinic
Blodgett Memorial Hospital
1810 Wealthy S.E.
Grand Rapids, Mi
49506 Phone 616 454–5951

Butterworth Hospital
Grand Rapids, Mi
49503

Department Of Zoology
Michigan State University
Lansing, Mi
48901 Phone 517 353–4520

Department Of Mental Health
Lapeer State Home And Training School
Lapeer, Mi
48446 Phone 313 664–2951

Department Of Anatomic Pathology
William Beaumont Hospital
Royal Oak, Mi
48072 Ph 313 549–7006 Ex. 701

MINNESOTA

Cytogenetic Laboratory And Genetic Clinic
School Of Dentistry And Health Science
Center
University Of Minnesota
Minneapolis, Mn
55455

Department Of Pediatrics
University Of Minnesota Hospital

Box 231, Mayo
Minneapolis, Mn
55455 Phone 612 373–4529

Human Genetics Clinic
University Of Minnesota Hospital
Minneapolis, Mn
55455

Dight Institute For Human
Genetics
University Of Minnesota
Minneapolis, Mn
55455

Human Genetics Unit
Minnesota Department Of Health
Minneapolis, Mn
55440 Phone 612 378–1150 Ext. 26

Medical Genetics Division
Department Of Laboratory Medicine And
Pathology
University Of Minnesota Hospital
Minneapolis, Mn
55415 Phone 376–3309

Genetics Consulting Service
Mayo Clinic
200 1st Street, S.W.
Rochester, Mn
55901 Phone 507 282–2511

MISSISSIPPI

Human Genetics Service
Keesler Usaf Medical Center
Biloxi, Ms
39534 Phone 601 377–6546

Department Of Preventive Medicine
University Of Mississippi
Medical Center
2500 North State Street
Jackson, Ms
39216 Phone 601 362–4411

MISSOURI

Neurology Department
Children's Mercy Hospital
Kansas City, Mo
64108 Phone 816 471–0626

Chile Development Clinic
University of Missouri School
of Medicine Children's Mercy Hospital
24th at Gillham Road
Kansas City, Mo
64108 Ph 813 471–0626 Ex. 429

Genetic Counseling Center
Children's Mercy Hospital
24th at Gillham Road
Kansas City, Mo
64108 Phone 816 471–0626 Ext 460

Cardinal Glennon Hospital
1465 South Grand Boulevard

St. Louis, Mo
63104 Phone 314 865–4000

Department of Pediatrics and Medicine,
Division of Medical Genetics
Washington University Medical School
4550 Scott Avenue
St. Louis, Mo
63110 Phone 314 367–6880 Ext. 35

Department of Cytogenetics
Saint Mary's Health Center
6420 Clayton Road
St. Louis, Mo
63110 Phone 314 644–3000

MONTANA

Shodair Genetic and Birth
Defects Unit
840 Helena Ave.
Helena, Mt
59601

NEBRASKA

University of Nebraska Medical Center
42nd and Dewey Avenue
Omaha, Ne
68105 Phone 402 541–4570

Department of Preventive Medicine
Creighton University School of Medicine
2500 California Street
Omaha, Ne
68178 Phone 402 449–2942

Center for Genetic Evaluation
Children's Memorial Hospital
44th and Dewey
Omaha, Ne
68105 Phone 402 553–5400

University of Nebraska Medical Center
42nd and Dewey Avenue
Omaha Ne
68105 Phone 402 541–4570

NEW HAMPSHIRE

Department of Maternal and Child Health
Dartmouth-Hitchcock Medical Center
Hanover, NH
03755 Phone 603 646–2734

NEW JERSEY

Dept. Biological Science
Rutgers, The State University
35 Bishop Street
New Brunswick NJ
08903 Phone 201 932–9579

Department of Pediatrics
New Jersey Medical School
100 Bergen Street
Newark, NJ
07103 Phone 201 456–4499

Hoffman-La Roche, Inc.

Nutley, NJ
07110 Phone 201 235–2884

NEW MEXICO

Dept. of Pediatrics
Univeristy of New Mexico School of
Medicine
Albuquerque, NM
87106 Phone 505 277–4361

Dept. of Obstetrics & Gynecology
University of New Mexico School of
Medicine
Albuquerque, NM
87106 Phone 505 277–4051

NEW YORK

Division of Genetics, Department of
Pediatrics
College of Physicians and Surgeons,
Columbia University
630 W. 168 Street
New York, NY
10032 Phone 212 694–3901

Division of Hematology
Jewish Hospital of Brooklyn
555 Prospect Place
Brooklyn, NY
11238 Phone 240–1211

Pediatric Service
Maimonides Medical Center
Brooklyn, NY
11219 Phone 212 853–1200

Department of Pediatrics
Downstate Medical Center
450 Clarkson Avenue
Brooklyn, NY
11203

Birth Defects Center-Ophingolipiosses
Isaac Albert Research Inst., Kingsbroom
Jewish Med. Center
80 East 49th Street
Brooklyn, NY
11203 Ph 212 756–9710 Ex. 2628

Department of Pediatrics
Brookdale Hospital Medical Center
Linden Boulevard at Brookdale Plaza
Brooklyn, NY
11212 Phone 212 240–5883

Department of Obstetrics and Gynecology
Downstate Medical Center-Suny
450 Clarkson Avenue
Brooklyn, NY
11203 Phone 212 270–2072

Pediatrics Service
Coney Island Hospital
Ocean & Shore Parkways
Brooklyn, NY
11235 Phone 212 743–4100

Dept. of Obstetrics & Gynecology

State University of New York, Downstate
Medical Center
450 Clarkson Avenue
Brooklyn, NY
11203 Phone 212 270–2066

Isaac Albert Research Institute
Kingsbrook Jewish Medical Center
Rutland Road and East 49th Street
Brooklyn, NY
11203 Ph 212 756–9700
Ext 2601/2602

Department of Pediatrics
Jewish Hospital and Medical Center of
Brooklyn
Greenpoint Affiliation
Brooklyn, NY
11211 Ph 212 387–3010 Ex. 301, 412

Medical Genetics Unit Department of
Medicine
Buffalo General Hospital
100 High Street
Buffalo, NY
14203 Phone 716 845–6467

Division of Human Genetics Dept. of
Pediatrics
State University of New York at Buffalo
Children's Hospital
Buffalo, NY
14222 Phone 716 878–7530

Clinical Services Division
Creedmore Institute
Station 60
Jamaica, NY
11427 Phone 212 464–7500

Division of Genetics
North Shore University Hospital
Cornell University College of Medicine
Manhasset L.I., NY
11030 Phone 516 562–2175

Division of Genetics
North Shore University Hospital
Cornell University College of Medicine
Manhasset L.I., NY
11030 Phone 516 562–2175

Columbia-Presbyterian Med. Center
BH-South 202
630 W. 168th St.
New York, NY
10032

Division of Human Genetics
NY Hospital—Cornell University Medical
Center
525 East 68th Street
New York, NY
10021

Department of Pediatrics
NY Medical College—Flower and Fifth
Avenue Hospital
5th Avenue at 106 Street

New York, NY
10029

Rubella Project Pediatric Service
The Roosevelt Hospital
428 West 59th St.
New York NY
10019 Phone 212 554–6801

Developmental Disabilities Center Pediatric
Service
The Roosevelt Hospital
428 W 59th St.
New York NY
10019 Phone 212 554–6565

Department of Pathology
New York Medical College-Metro.
Hospital
97 Street and First Avenue
New York, NY
10029 Ph 360–6454/PL 3–3055

The New York Blood Center
310 East 67th Street
New York, NY
10021 Phone 212 879–7470

Department of Pediatrics
Mt. Sinai School of Medicine
New York NY
10029 Phone 212 876–1000 Ext. 82

Medical Genetics
88th Israel Medical Center
10 Nathan Perlman Place
New York NY
10003 Ph 212 673–3000 Ex 2998/4187

Department of Genetics
Albert Einstein College of Medicine
1300 Morris Park Avenue
New York, NY
10461 Phone 212 430–2451

Medical Genetics
Long Island Jewish Hospital
Hillside Medical Center
New Hyde Park NY
11040 Phone 212 470–2175

Department of Pediatrics, Division of
Pediatric Hematology
The New York Hospital—Cornell Medical
Center
525 East 68th Street
New York, NY
10021

Genetic Counseling Program
Albert Einstein College of Medicine
Bronx Municipal Hospital Center
New York NY
10461 Phone 212 430–2501

Department of Medical Genetics
New York State Psychiatric Institute
722 West 168 Street
New York, NY

10032 Ph 212 568–4000 Ex. 267

Albert Einstein College of Medicine
Eastchester Road and Morris
Park Avenue
New York NY
10461

Presbyterian Hospital
New York, NY
10032 Phone 212 694–6460

Department of Pediatrics
Babies Hospital
3975 Broadway
New York, NY
10032 Phone 212 679–3200 Ext. 36

Dept. of Pathology
NY University Medical Center
550 First Avenue
New York, NY
10016 Ph 212 or 9–3200 Ex. 3677

Division of Human Genetics at NY U School
of Medicine
550 First Avenue
New York, NY
10016 Ph 212 or 9–3200 Ex. 2931

Division of Genetics
University of Rochester Medical Centre
Rochester NY
14642 Phone 716 275–3461

Division of Genetics
University of Rochester Medical Center
Rochester NY
14642 Phone 716 275–3461

Division of Genetics
University of Rochester Medical Center
Rochester NY
14642 Phone 716 275–3461

NY State Department of Mental Retardation
1050 Forest Hill Road
Staten Island, NY
10314

NY State Department of Mental Retardation
Institute for Research in Mental Retardation
1050 Forest Hill Road
Staten Island, NY
10314

Department of Pediatrics
Upstate Medical Center Hospital
Syracuse, NY
13210

Laboratory of Cytogenetics, Department of
Pediatrics
State University Hospital, Upstate Medical
Center
750 East Adams Street
Syracuse NY
13210

Cytogenetics Laboratory
Letchworth Village

Thiells, NY
10984 Ph 914 947–3487/914 947–1000 Ex.
444

Westchester County Medical Center
Grasslands Hospital
Valhalla, NY
10595 Phone 914-LY2–8500

Department of Pediatrics and
Genetics
M.R. Institute of NY Medical College
Valhalla, NY
10595 Phone 914 347–5353

NORTH CAROLINA

Department of Biostatistics
University of North Carolina, School of
Public Health
Chapel Hill, NC
27514 Phone 919 966–1197

Department of Pediatrics
Charlotte Memorial Hospital
P.O. Box 2554
Charlotte, NC
28201

Department of Obstetrics and Gynecology
Duke Medical Center
Box 3274
Durham, NC
27706

Medical Genetics Section, Department of
Pediatrics
Bowman Gray School of Medicine
Wake Forest University
Winston-Salem, NC
27103

Moses H. Cone Memorial Hospital
1200 North Elm Street
Greensboro, NC
27405 Phone 919 397–4073

Duke University Medical Center
Box 3062
Durham, NC
27710 Phone 919 684–4137

OHIO

Department of Pediatrics
Childrens Hospital Research Foundation
Cincinnati, OH
45229

Department of Anatomy
Case Western Reserve University
Cleveland, OH
44106

Department of Pediatrics
Case Western Reserve Medical School
Cleveland Metropolitan General Hospital
Cleveland, OH
44109 Phone 216 398–6000

Department of Biology

Case Western Reserve University
Cleveland, OH
44106 Phone 216 368–3700

Department of Pediatrics
Children's Hospital
Columbus, Oh
43205 Phone 614 253–8841

Seaple Diagnostic Inc.
P.O. Box 2440
Columbus, Oh
43216 Phone 614 224–5633

Medical Genetics Section
Department of Pathology
Kettering, Medical Center
Kettering, Oh
45429 Phone 298–4331 Ext. 439

Cytogenetics Laboratory
Mt. Vernon State Institute
Mount Vernon, Oh
43050 Phone 614 397–1010

OKLAHOMA

Department of Pediatrics
University of Oklahoma Children's Hospital
P.O. Box 26901
Oklahoma City, Ok
73190 Phone 405 271–5509

Children's Medical Center
5300 E. Skelly Drive
Tulsa, Ok
74135

OREGON

Crippled Child Division, Genetics Clinic
Rogue Valley Memorial Hospital
2825 Barnett Road
Medford, Or
7501 Phone 503 773–6281 Ext. 18

Genetics Clinic—Crippled Child Division
University of Oregon Medical School
Portland, Or
97201 Phone 503 225–8344

PENNSYLVANIA

Department of Biology
California State College
California, Pa
15419 Phone 412 938–4204

Department of Pathology
Geisinger Medical Center
Danville, Pa
17815 Phone 717 784–4660 Ext 333

M.S. Hershey Medical Center, Department
of Pharmacology
Pennsylvania State University, College of
Medicine
Hershey, Pa
17033

Department of Obstetrics and Gynecology

Temple University Health Sciences Center
3401 N. Broad St.
Philadelphia, Pa
19140

Division of Genetics
Jefferson Medical College
1025 Walnut Street
Philadelphia, Pa
19107 Phone 215 829–6955

Department of Human Genetics
University of Pennsylvania School of
Medicine
Philadelphia, Pa
19174 Ph 215 662–3232/662–3227

Dept. of Obstetrics—Gynecology and
Pediatrics
University of Pittsburgh, Magee-Womens
Hospital
Halmet Street and Forbes Avenue
Pittsburgh, Pa
15213

Childrens Hospital
Pittsburgh, Pa
15213 Ph 412 681–7700 Ex. 561

Department of Obstetrics and Gynecology
Magee-Womens Hospital
Pittsburgh, Pa
15213

SOUTH CAROLINA

South Carolina Department of Mental
Health
William S. Hall Psychiatric Institute
P.O. Box 119
Columbia, SC
29202

Section of Clinical Genetics, Dept. of Oral
Medicine
Medical University of South Carolina
80 Barre Street
Charleston, SC
28401 Phone 803 792–2489

Vince Moseley Diagnostic and Evaluation
Clinic
Coastal Center
Charleston, SC
29401

Genetics Laboratory
William S. Hall Psychiatric Institute
Columbia SC
37916

Greenwood Genetic Center
1020 Spring St. at Ellenberg
Greenwood, SC
29646

SOUTH DAKOTA

Department of Pathology
Medical Genetics Program Developmental

Disabilities Evaluation
University of South Dakota Medical School
Julian Hall 209
Vermillion SD
57069 Ph 675 624–8313

TENNESSEE

Birth Defects Evaluation Center
University of Tennessee Memorial Research
Center and Hospital
1924 Alcoa Highway
Knoxville, Tn
37916 Phone 615 971–3184

Department of Pediatrics
University of Tennessee
Center for the Health Sciences
Memphis, Tn
38163 Ph 901 528–6595/528–6492

Department of Medicine
Vanderbilt Hospital
Nashville, Tn
37203

Department of Pediatrics
Meharry Medical College
Nashville, Tn
37208 Phone 256–3631

Medical Genetics Section
Department of Pediatrics
Meharry Medical College
Nashville, Tn
37208 Phone 615 327–6399

TEXAS

Department of Pediatrics
University of Texas, Southwestern Medical
School
5323 Harry Hines Boulevard
Dallas, Tx
75235 Ph 216 637–3820 Ext. 214

Division of Medical Genetics, Internal
Medicine Department
University of Texas, Southwestern Medical
School at Dallas
5323 Harry Hines Boulevard
Dallas, Tx
75235

Cytogenetics Laboratory
Genetics Screening and Counseling Center
404 W. Oak
Denton, Tx
76201 Phone 817 383–3232

Genetic Screening and Counseling Center
404 W Oak
Denton Tx
76201 Phone 817 383–3561

Department of Pediatrics and Human
Genetics
University of Texas Medical Branch
Galveston, Tx

77550

Birth Defects Center
Texas Childrens Hospital, Baylor College of
Medicine
Houston, Tx
77030 Phone 713 521–3261

Section of Medical Genetics
Baylor College of Medicine
Houston, Tx
77025 Phone 713 529–4951 Ext 420

Department of Biology
M.D. Anderson Hospital
Houston, Tx
77025

Department of Pediatrics, Division of
Genetics
University of Texas Medical School
Texas Medical Center
Houston, Tx
77025 Phone 713 527–4555

Department of Pediatrics
Texas Tech University School of Medicine
Box 4569
Lubbock, Tx
79409

Departments of Genetics and Pediatrics
Texas Tech University School of Medicine
and Lubbock State School
P.O. Box 4569
Lubbock, Tx
79409 Ph 806 742–5116/742–5117

Newborn Nurseries
St. Joseph Hospital
1919 La Branch
Houston, Tx
77002

Genetic Service
Wilford Hall USAF Medical Center
Lackland AFB, Hospital
San Antonio, Tx
78236 Phone 512 536–3584

Department of Pediatrics, Section of
Genetics and Cytogenetics
University of Texas Medical School at San
Antonio
7703 Floyd Curl Drive
San Antonio, Tx
78229 Phone 512 696–6251

Department of Anatomy
University of Texas Health Science Center
7703 Floyd Curl Drive
San Antonio, Tx
78284 Phone 512 696–6535

Genetic Service
Wilford Hall USAF Medical Center
Brooks AFB, Box 35313
San Antonio, Tx
78235 Phone 512 536–3584

UTAH

Department of Internal Medicine College of Medicine
University of Utah
50 N. Medical Drive
Salt Lake City Ut
84112 Phone 581-7761

Department of Pediatric Neurology
University of Utah College of Medicine
50 North Medical Drive
Salt Lake City, Ut
84132 Phone 581-7877

VERMONT

Department of Pediatrics Mary Fletcher Unit
University of Vermont Medical Center Hospital
Burlington, Vt
05401 Ph 802 656-2272/656-2296

VIRGINIA

Chromosome Research Laboratory
University of Virginia Medical School
Charlottesville, Va
22901

Genetic Unit
University of Virginia School of Medicine
Charlottesville Va
22901

Division of Medical Genetics
University of Virginia School of Medicine
Charlottesville, Va
22901 Phone 804 924-2201

Department of Pathology
Depaul Hospital
Norfolk, Va
23505

Department of Genetics
Cytogenetics Laboratory
Box 33, MCV Station
Richmond, Va
23219

Department of Human Genetics
Medical College of Virginia
Box 330 MCU Station
Richmond Va
23298 Phone 804 355-0754

Department of Pediatrics
Medical College of Virginia
Richmond, Va
23219

WASHINGTON

Birth Defects Study and Counseling Program
Health Services Div.—Dept. of Social and Health Services
1704 N.E. 150th St.

Seattle Wa
98155 Phone 206 545-6783

Department of Medicine
University of Washington
Seattle Wa
98195 Phone 206 543-1705

Department of Pediatrics
Dysmorphology Unit
University of Washington, Medical School
Seattle, Wa
98195 Phone 206 543-6685

Department of Pediatrics
Mary Bridge Children's Health Center
Tacoma, Wa
98405

WEST VIRGINIA

Department of Medical Genetics
West Virginia University Medical Center
Morgantown WV
26506 Ph 304 293-4451/293-2524

WISCONSIN

Immunobiology Research Center
1150 University Avenue
Madison, Wi
53706

Department of Medical Genetics
University of Wisconsin Medical School
Madison, Wi
53706

Department of Medical Genetics
University of Wisconsin Medical School
Madison, Wi
53706

Department of Pediatrics
University of Wisconsin Medical School
Madison, Wi
53706

Central Wisconsin Colony and Training School
317 Knutson Drive
Madison, Wi
53704

Department of Medical Genetics
University of Wisconsin Medical School
Madison, Wi
53706

USA, COMMONWEALTH OF PUERTO RICO

Pediatric Endocrinology and Medical Genetics Section
Mayaguez Medical Center
P.O. Box 1868
Mayaquez, Puerto Rico
00708 Ph 809 832-8656 EXT 1723

Cancer Center
University of Puerto Rico

San Juan, Puerto Rico
Section de Genetica Medica Departmento
de Pediatria

Hospital Universitario de Ninos
Recinto de Ciencias Medicas, ORP G. P. O.
Apariado 5067
San Juan, Puerto Rico
00936

APPENDIX H
CATHOLIC CODE ON SEX*

A new study of sexuality commissioned by the Catholic Theological Society of America advises Catholics not to rely solely on biblical injunctions or church codes as guides to sexual behavior but to make their own judgments about sexual morality.

The society is the main professional organization of Catholic theologians in Canada and the United States. It is not part of the Catholic hierarchy, but its members play an influential role as teachers of priests and interpreters of doctrine.

A sexual act is to be judged moral, the study counsels, if it is "self-liberating, other-enriching, honest, faithful, socially responsible, life-serving and joyous." No act is to be considered intrinsically evil: "It is the whole action including circumstances and intention that constitues the basis for ethical judgment."

The result, some Catholics say, is not necessarily a permissive view of sex. When the proposed tests of morality are applied, said John Kirvin, who edited the study for the publisher, Paulist Press, "you would be hard-pressed to conclude that adultery is morally justified."

Entitled "Human Sexuality: New Directions in American Catholic Thought," the study discusses such topics as contraception, extramarital sex, masturbation, sterilization, child-free marriage and homosexuality without condemning any as wrong under all circumstances.

This contrasts with the position of the Catholic bishops of the United States. Last November they approved, by a vote of 172 to 25, a pastoral letter upholding the church's traditional and absolute prohibition against divorce, artificial birth control, abortion, extramarital and premarital sex and homosexual acts.

*The New York Times, May 29, 1977

APPENDIX I
SOME COUNSELING PRECAUTIONS*

In counseling with cord injured individuals regarding their sexual lives, several cautions should be kept in mind by the counselor regardless of the profession or discipline he represents. A few of these are the following:

1. *Don't get people into trouble with their God or their morality.* Many men have strong moral and religious convictions about various types of sexual activity. For example, certain Catholic priests would consider any kind of sexual activity other than genital–genital contact as a type of masturbation and therefore a sin to be atoned for in the confessional. To urge people to abandon such beliefs without an understanding of their importance in the individual's psychic economy is dangerous and may produce severe reactions of depression, anxiety, suspiciousness and guilt. Before undertaking counseling, the skillful counselor should explore carefully the patient's religious and moral convictions and work within that context, or work together with the patient and the theologian to modify those religious or moral concepts.

2. *Don't hang your morality on the patient.* Not only do patients have certain scruples, inhibitions, and religious convictions, but so do counselors. The counselor should be well aware of his own biases and convictions, and he should not impose them on the patient. Although he is free to live his own life as he pleases, he should not attempt to persuade the patient to his sense of morality. It cannot be emphasized too strongly that sexuality is an extremely sensitive issue with people whose sexual existence has been severely threatened. They must be treated with great gentleness and understanding.

3. *Don't force the patient to talk about sex.* The timing of discussions is of utmost importance. If an adequate interpersonal relationship has been developed with the patient, he will introduce the subject at the time he feels a sufficiently pressing need. In interactions with the patient, one should make it clear that sexuality is an open topic. The counselor should then wait until the patient takes the lead in initiating the discussion.

*Hohman GW: Considerations in management of psychosexual readjustment in the cord injured male. Rehabil Psychol 19(2): 50–58, 1972. (From Rehabilitation Psychology 19(2): 50–58, 1972. Copyright © 1972 Rehabilitation Psychology. Reprinted by permission)

Group presentations are more difficult than individual discussions and forcing the patient to attend such groups is fraught with danger.

4. *Don't threaten the patient with your sexuality.* Male counselors, especially those who may harbor some lingering doubts about their own sexual adequacy, may brag about their sexual exploits in the presence of the patient, thus building the counselor's own faltering ego at the expense of the already injured patient. Likewise, women may sometimes behave in an excessively seductive manner around cord injured patients, confident that their seductive attempts will not be accepted. Contemporary mythology portraying all paraplegics as completely dysfunctional in sexual interest or ability should not be fostered by the counselor. With inordinate frequency, for example, a neighbor may offer jocularly to the cord injured person to "take care of your homework." Such problems must be dealt with by the counselor, and he cannot do so if he shares the mythology.

5. *Don't make sex an all-or-none experience.* In discussing sexuality, the wise counselor will keep in mind that sex has many meanings. If a patient does not have, and with the best prognosis will not get, genital sexual functioning, he should not be told to "forget about sex; your sex life is over," as has happened in some cord injury centers. Rather, the patient should be encouraged to explore whatever relationships are open to him.

6. *Don't assume that once sexuality has been discussed, it is forever resolved for that patient.* Sexuality must be a topic continually open to discussion between patients and staff. Injured men, like anyone else, experience changes in their psychosexual situations. New issues, new experiences, new inclinations and new desires may arise with which the patient may need some help.

7. *Don't assume that there is only one way to convey sexual information.* Too often the assumption is made that adequate information can be communicated only by a formal presentation, followed by discussion. "Latrine talk," with one patient sharing experiences with another, is quite as effective in conveying sexual information among the cord injured as it is among the population at large. One cannot over-estimate the efficacy of informal communication among patients, in producing effective attitudes and adjustments. Much information also can be conveyed and the general implications of the paraplegic's sexual situation can be introduced in a jocular or kidding environment. Perhaps the method that is most effective is the guidance of a counselor who fills the role of a gentle friend.

8. *Don't expect too much from spouses in their ability to change roles.* Much of the care that must be proffered by the spouse, especially to the severely disabled quadriplegic man, may have the effect of destroying libidinous interest. For example, many wives have told us it is nearly impossible to routinely provide bowel care, feeding, nursing for their husbands and still retain an interest in, and image of, their husbands as sexual objects. If such tends to be the case, the wise counselor will try to

preserve the sexual aspect of the relationship by encouraging the use of outside resources, such as visiting nurses, and part-time attendants, in doing these unesthetic chores.

9. *Don't forget that all relationships and, in particular, that most intense of relationships, marriage, is a matter of compromise.* The important things to urge upon any cord injured patient and his spouse are attitudes and feelings of mutual trust, willingness to discuss each other's needs, and a sincere search for how they may mutually satisfy each other. The sexual relationships of cord injured men can be as effective a bulwark to marriage and family life as for the non-injured person, if they grow out of a deep feeling of mutual respect, love, tenderness and concern.

APPENDIX J
SEXUAL FUNCTION IN
PHYSICAL DISABILITY*†

OBJECTIVES:

1. To understand the sexual attitudes and behavior of paraplegics and quad-riplegics;
2. to learn in what ways the paraplegic and quadriplegic has problems in expressing his sexuality;
3. to develop methods to solve sexual problems caused by spinal cord injury;
4. to seek ways to make health care professionals aware that they must take the initiative in discussing sexuality as equals with their patients.

METHODOLOGY:

1. Paraplegic and quadriplegic adults at the Sister Kenney Institute and other hospitals throughout the country are given an opportunity to enter the project. Prior to entering, individuals fill out a research questionnaire designed to provide information on sexual attitudes and behaviors.
2. Participants enter an intensive two day course of desensitization, demyth-ologization, and resensitization in human sexual behavior, preferably with their partners. The course seeks to increase participants' understanding of their own sexual behavior, and to provide a comfortable and safe set-ting for discussion of feelings about human sexuality. Slides, films, lectures, and group discussions among the participants are used. Well adjusted and experienced paraplegics and quadriplegics and their partners are in-volved in experience showing.
3. Following exposure to this material, participants are again questioned about sexual attitudes and behavior. The two questionnaires are com-pared to provide information relative to the stated objectives.

*University of Minnesota Rehabilitation Research and Training Center project. Research Directory of the Rehabilitation Research and Training Centers, Fiscal Year 1975. Rehabilitation Services Administration, Office of Human Development, US–DHEW, Washington, DC 20201
†Principal Investigator: Theodore M. Cole

PROGRESS AND FINDINGS:

1. Physically disabled college students found this methodology personally beneficial.
2. The National Paraplegia Foundation co-sponsored a subscription of a number of participants who provided 65 positive evaluations of the usefulness of this methodology to physically disabled adults and their partners.
3. Requests for advice, research findings, and audiovisual material was received last year from approximately 50 health care facilities in the U.S. Numerous inquiries were also received from foreign countries.
4. Last year 95 questionnaires were mailed to spinal injured adults and their partners who participated in this research project; 70% returned their questionnaires. Tabulation shows that of that number 95% reported they were glad to have participated in the project, 82% reported that involvement in the project was personally beneficial to them, and 89% stated that they could recommend involvement in a similar project to other people with disabilities similar to their own.

APPLICABILITY:

Persons with spinal cord injury are becoming less content to lead lives affected by the myths commonly believed by many medical personnel and others in society. These myths deny them a satisfactory sex life, a respectable self-image, and the expectation of being treated like other people who have a need for emotional and sexual expression. By increasing understanding of sexual attitudes on the part of both patients and rehabilitation personnel, this project will help paraplegics and quadriplegics to develop a more satisfactory sex life and more successful personal adjustment.

APPENDIX K
RELEVANT BIBLIOGRAPHIES

A Bibliography of Affective Materials for Adolescent Years. By J. Bolen. 1973. Instructional Materials Center for Special Education, University of Southern California, Los Angeles, CA

A Bibliography of Resources in Sex Education for the Mentally Retarded. SIECUS, 1973. Available from Behavioral Publications, Inc. 72 Fifth Ave., New York, NY 10011

A Guide To Sexuality Handbooks. Prepared by Youth and Student Affairs, Planned Parenthood Federation of America, 810 Seventh Ave., New York, NY 10019

A Selection of Public Affairs Pamphlets. Public Affairs Committee, Inc., 381 Park Avenue South, New York, N.Y. 10016

Family Life and Child Development–A Selected Annotated Bibliography— cumulative through 1975. Child Study Press, Child Study Association of America/Well-Met Inc., New York, NY

Growth Patterns and Sex Education—Preschool to Adulthood, 1972. American School Health Association, Kent, OH

Sex and the Spinal Cord Injured; A Selected Bibliography. By P.L.Lasser, 1973. Paralyzed Veterans of America, Inc., 7315 Wisconsin Ave., Washington, DC 20014

Sex Education and Family Living. In Educator's Guide To Free Health, Physical Education and Recreation, 1968. Educator's Progress Service, Randolph, WI

Sexuality and The Cerebral Palsied. (In preparation) Human Sexuality Program, University of California Medical School, San Francisco, CA

Sexuality of the Mentally Retarded—Resource Bibliography. By Judy Hall, PhD, 1976. Center for Developmental and Learning Disorders, University of Alabama, Birmingham, AL

Special Education Publication On Sexuality. Ed-U-Press, University of Syracuse, 760 Ostrom Ave., Syracuse, NY 13210

VD Curriculum Materials. In Changing Education. Spring 1973, p. 31

Age of majority, and ages at which state legislation, court action or attorneys general opinions have specifically affirmed the right of individuals to consent for medical care in general, for contraceptive services, for examination and treatment of pregnancy and VD, and for abortion; as of December 31, 1975 (X = any age)*

STATE	AGE OF MAJORITY	MAY CONSENT FOR MEDICAL CARE IN GENERAL			MAY CONSENT FOR:			
		NO LIMITATION	IF MARRIED (M) OR EMANCIPATED (E)	IN EMERGENCY	CONTRACEPTION	PREGNANCY CONNECTED CARE	VD CARE	ABORTION
Ala.	19	14	E[9], M	X	14	X	X	14
Alaska	19, MF	19	E[6,7,8]	X[5,28]	X	X	X	18
Ariz.	18	18	E, M	X[10]	18	18	X	18
Ark.	18	X[2,4]	E, M	X	X[2,4,12]	X[14]	X	18
Calif.	18	18	15E[6], M	X	X[3]	X	12	X
Colo.	18[1]	18	15E[6], M	18	X[2]	18	X	X
Conn.	18	18	E, M	18	18	18	X[18]	18
Del.	18	18	E, M	18	12[11]	12	12	18
Fla.	18	18	E, M	X	X[20]	18	X	X
Ga.	18	18[3]	M[3]	X	XF[3]	X	X	X
Hawaii	18	18	18	18	18	14[27]	14[27]	14[27]
Idaho	18	18	18	18	X[4]	18	14	18
Ill.	18[1]	18	M[7]	X	X[15]	X	12	X[24]
Ind.	18	18	E, M	X	18	18	X	X[24]
Iowa	18, M	18	E, M	X	18[12]	18	X	18
Kans.	18	X[4], 16[5]	18	16	X[4]	X	X	X[4]
Ky.	18	18	E, M[8]	X	X[3]	X	X	X
La.	18, M	X[21,3]	M	X	18[12]	X[3]	X	X
Maine	18	18	E	X	X[23]	18	X	18
Md.	18	18	M[8]	X	X[3]	X	X	X
Mass.	18	18	E[3,6], M[8]	X	18	X	X[19]	X
Mich.	18	X[4]	E, M	X	X[4,12]	X[4]	X	X[4]
Minn.	18	18	E[6], M[8]	X	X[13]	X	X	X[29]
Miss.	21	X[4]	E, M	X	X[16]	X	X	X[4]
Mo.	18[1]	21	E, M[8]	X	21	X[14]	X	18

(continued)

Age of majority, and ages at which state legislation, court action or attorneys general opinions have specifically affirmed the right of individuals to consent for medical care in general, for contraceptive services, for examination and treatment of pregnancy and VD, and for abortion; as of December 31, 1975 (X = any age)*

STATE	AGE OF MAJORITY	MAY CONSENT FOR MEDICAL CARE IN GENERAL			MAY CONSENT FOR:			
		NO LIMITATION	IF MARRIED (M) OR EMANCIPATED (E)	IN EMERGENCY	CONTRACEPTION	PREGNANCY CONNECTED CARE	VD CARE	ABORTION
Mont.	18	X[23,3,14]	E[3,14] M[7,3,14]	X	18	X[14]	X	18[27]
Nebr.	19, M	19	M	19	19	19	X	X[24]
Nev.	18	18	E[3,4,14] M[3,4,14]	X[3,4,14]	18	16	X	18
N. H.	18	X[4]	E, M	X[4]	X[4]	X[4]	14	X[4]
N. J.	18	18	E, M[7]	18	18	X	X	X
N. Mex.	18	18	E, M	X[10]	18[12]	X[17]	X	18
N. Y.	18	18	E, M[8]	X	X	X[4]	X	X[4,25]
N. C.	18	18	E, M	X	18	18	X	18
N. Dak.	18	18	E, M	18	18	18	14	18
Ohio	18	X[4]	18	X[4]	X[12,4]	X[4]	X	18
Okla.	18	X[23,3,14]	E[3,14] M[8,3,14]	X	18[12]	X[3,14]	X	18
Oreg.	18[1], M	15	M	15	15[14]	15[14]	12	18
Pa.	21	18	E[9], M	X	X[26]	X	X	X
R. I.	18	18	E	16, M	18	18	X	18
S. C.	18	16[22]	E, M	X	16	16	X	16
S. Dak.	18	18	E, M	18	18	18	X	18
Tenn.	18	18	18	18	X[3]	18	X	18
Tex.	18	18	16E, M	X	18	X	X	X
Utah	18, M	18	M	X	X	X	X	X[27]
Vt.	18	18	E, M	18	18	18	12	18
Va.	18	18[3]	E	18	X[3,14]	X[14]	X	18
Wash.	18	18	E	18	18	18	14	X
W. Va.	18	18	18	X	18[12]	18	X	18
Wis.	18	18	E, M	18	18	18	X	18
Wyo.	19	19	19	19	19[12]	19	X	19
D. C.	18	18[3]	E, M[3]	X	X[3]	X[3]	X	X
Total								
At 18	45	35	6	13	21	18	0	24
<18		12	44	36	27	31	51	26

*The fact that no affirmative legislation, court decision or attorney general's opinion has been found in a particular state does not mean that some or even all categories of minors below the ages shown in the table do not have the right to obtain some or all medical services on their own consent.

(Paul EW, Pilpel H, Wechsler N: Family Planning Perspectives 8(1):16–22, 1976. Reprinted with permission.)

(continued)

Note: Because of reporting lags, the table probably does not include all applicable legislation, cases and attorneys general opinions for 1975. M = Married; F = Female; E = Emancipated

1. For purposes of signing contracts.

2. Excluding voluntary sterilization if under 18 and unmarried.

3. Excluding voluntary sterilization.

4. If mature enough to understand the nature and consequences of the treatment. See discussion in text of the "mature minor doctrine."

5. If parent not immediately available.

6. Emancipated defined as living apart from parents and managing own financial affairs.

7. And/or pregnant.

8. Or parent.

9. Emancipated defined as a high school graduate, a parent or pregnant.

10. If no parent available, others may consent in loco parentis.

11. If sexually active.

12. Comprehensive family planning law permits (or does not exclude) services to minors without parental consent.

13. Unless parent has previously notified treating agency of objection.

14. Excluding abortion.

15. If referred by clergyman, physician or Planned Parenthood or if "failure to provide such services would create a serious health hazard."

(continued)

16. If referred by clergyman, physician, family planning clinic, school or institution of higher learning or any state or local government agency.

17. Examination only.

18. In public health agencies, public or private hospitals or clinics.

19. In publicly maintained facilities.

20. If married or pregnant or "may suffer, in the opinion of the physician, probable health hazards if such services are not provided." Surgical services excluded.

21. If minor "is or believes himself to be afflicted with an illness or disease."

22. Except for operation essential to health or life.

23. If physician finds probable health hazard.

24. Parental consent requirement temporarily enjoined by court.

25. In New York City, municipal hospitals perform abortions on minors without parental consent if married, emancipated or at least 17 years old or if seeking parental consent would endanger the physical or mental health of the patient.

26. Minors are being served under a state law which permits doctors to serve minors of any age if delay in treatment "would increase the risk to the minor's life or health."

27. Parent notification, but not consent, is required, where possible.

28. If parent refuses to grant or withhold consent.

29. County Attorney stated that legislature did not intend to include abortion as pregnancy-related treatment.

APPENDIX M
"RIGHTS" AND RIGHTS

The rights of the retarded to live as normal a life as possible is bringing up for serious discussion their rights to live together, to marry, and to have children. Along with these rights go the reciprocal obligations of being responsible for their own actions. A retarded individual who does not know the relationship between having sex and having a baby cannot be responsible for his or her sexual behavior. The right to have a baby is a complex problem which must be studied from the point of view of the rights of the handicapped individual, the rights of the potential child, the rights of the parents who wish to do the best thing for their handicapped child, and the rights of the community which may become responsible for the care and support of the baby. To resolve these sometimes conflicting rights will require the best thinking of those in the field of ethics, medicine, law psychology, sociology, social work and family planning.*

The incursion into the powers of the family by the state, here as in other places, is often cast in the noble language of rights. What is really at issue in many arguments about "fetal rights," "infant's rights," and so on, is in reality the relocation of delegated autonomy and power from one institution—the family—to another—the state. Too often, the kind of government intervention we have been seeing in these difficult cases, where right and wrong are too finely balanced for comfort or confidence in any decision, represents arrogance rather than compassion.†

BASIC RIGHTS: SEX INFORMATION, EXPRESSION AND BIRTH CONTROL SERVICES§

1. People with special needs, as all people, should have free access to information on sexuality and birth control.
2. Masturbation is a normal expression of sex no matter how frequently it is done and at what age. It becomes a compulsive, punitive, self-destructive behavior largely as a result of guilt, suppression and punishment (and absence of other self-fulfilling alternatives [Ed]).

*Bass, MS: Sex Education For the Handicapped. The Family Coordinator, January 1974, p27
†Gaylin W: Case Study in Bioethics. Hasting's Center Report 6(2):15, 1976
§Gordon S: Sexual Rights For the People Who Happen To Be Handicapped. Monograph. Notes From the Center #6, Center on Human Policy, Syracuse University, Syracuse, NY, 1974

3. All direct sexual behavior involving the genitals should be in privacy. Recognizing that institutions and hospitals for the retarded, mentally ill and delinquent are not built or developed to ensure privacy, the definition of what constitutes privacy in an institution must be very liberal—bathrooms, one's own bed, the bushes, basement are private domains.
4. Anytime a physically mature girl and boy have sexual relations, they risk pregnancy.
5. Unless they are clear about wanting to have a baby, and the responsibility that goes with child rearing, both the male and female should use birth control. (Staff should not condition girls of any age to believe that every woman wants and must have babies in order to be "normal.") Birth control services and genetic counseling should be available to all disabled adults.
6. Unless you are, say 18, society feels you should not have intercourse. After this, you decide for yourself—providing you use birth control.
7. Adults should not be permitted to use children sexually.
8. In the final analysis, sexual behavior between consenting adults (regardless of mental age) and whether it is homo or hetero should be no one else's business—providing there is little risk of bringing an unwanted child into this world.

The following additional factors need to be considered:

1. We need greater acceptance of abortion as a safe, legal alternative to bringing an unwanted child into this world.
2. Voluntary sterilization can be a desirable protection for some individuals who can function perfectly well in a marriage if there are no children.

APPENDIX N
SEX EDUCATION OF
THE DEAF-BLIND
A SURVEY REPORT—1975

A SURVEY REPORT—1975*†

A questionnaire was dispatched to each of the 205 agencies responsible for the education of deaf-blind children in the United States as listed in Directory of Regional Centers and Educational Programs Providing Services to Deaf/Blind Children and Youth in the United States. Of 121 responses (day schools 58, residences 51, both 12): 10 had a program of Sex Education: 9 replied that there programs started at the following ages: pre-school 1; three 2; five and above 1; six 1; eight 2; ten 1; and eleven to twelve 1. Of two responses to necessary level of communication: one stated first grade reading level and basic communication skills, while the other stated receptive language only is needed. Of the ten who had a sex education program:

Three used a prepared curriculum, one used a prepared curriculum in part, one used its own curriculum and two replied, "no" (perhaps intending they developed a local curriculum).

Two sites treated Sex Education as an independent program and eight included it as a unit in a broader program.

Four utilized available standard instructional materials, one did in part and four did not.

One setting utilized locally prepared materials "in toto" and eight did in part.

Five used graphic materials, three did not.

Six programs incorporated three dimensional models, four used two dimensional models and four utilized break-apart models. One stated use of the human body itself.

All ten programs incorporated both anatomical and physiological aspects of human sexual function.

Eight sites included the psychosocial aspects of human sexual behavior and one did not.

*Mimeo, avaliable from AAHPER
†Written by Carl J Davis

Eight incorporated Family Life Education in their program and one did not.

Four of the sites had special qualifications for teaching Sex Education and five did not.

There were 111 day schools and residential settings without sex education who were concerned with the following aspects of relating Sex Education to the deaf-blind child. In order of frequency:

1. The children functioned at a level that was too low to consider the provision of such a program at the present time and/or in the future.
2. The lack of communication skills militated against such a program.
3. The need for such a program is felt necessary but help is needed to provide such a program.
4. Some settings felt that the problem was being met by teaching body awareness.
5. Others questioned the need to provide to the profoundly retarded anything beyond teaching personal hygiene.
6. An ambiguous comment referred to confining teaching to "human sensuality."
7. Several responses from a certain state stated that "Sex Education" was illegal in that geo-political entity.
8. Another commenter stated that "sexual modesty was practiced even with our two year olds."
9. Many comments were seeking suggestions as to how to provide a program of Sex Education for their students no matter what their level of functioning and their level of communication.

APPENDIX O
SEX EDUCATION FOR MEMBERS OF HELPING PROFESSIONS WHO WORK WITH DISABLED POPULATIONS

SELECTED RESOURCES

Training for Medical Students
1. As volunteers to work in sex education programs in Washington, DC, as a part of their psychiatry clerkship
2. Planned Parenthood of Metropolitan Washington in conjunction with Howard University Medical School

Seminars for Health Professionals
  Write: Dorothea Glass, MD
          Director Rehabilitation
          Moss Rehabilitation Hospital
          12 St and Tabor Rd
          Philadelphia, PA 19141

          Theodore Cole, MD, and Sandra Cole
          Physical Disability Project
          Program in Human Sexuality
          U of Minnesota Medical School
          2630 University Ave.
          Minneapolis, MN 55414

Seminars for Educators Working with Disabled School Children
  Write: Sol Gordon, PhD
          Institute For Family Research and Education
          Syracuse University
          760 Ostrum Ave.
          Syracuse, NY 13210

Seminars for the Treatment of Sexual Dysfunctions

Write: Helen S Kaplan, MD, PhD
        Department of Psychiatry
        Cornell University Medical College
        525 East 68 St.
        New York, NY 10021

APPENDIX P
DISABILITY STATISTICS

NATIONAL

In 1975 there were approximately the following number of severely handicapped persons in the United States:

Noninstitutionalized Population   8,280,000
    Under age 18 (180,000)
    18–64 (4,200,000)
    65 and over (3,900,000)
Institutionalized   <u>1,787,000</u>

TOTAL   10,067,000

Resource: Comprehensive Needs Study for DHEW, 1976, Urban Institute, Washington, DC

INTERNATIONAL

In the Decade of Rehabilitation, 1970–1980, there are
    More than 450,000,000 who have physical or mental impairments which lead to significant disability
    More than 300,000,000 disabled persons who cannot obtain adequate help.

Resource: International Rehabilitation Review 2, 1976, Rehabilitation International, New York, NY 10016

APPENDIX Q
WHITE HOUSE
CONFERENCE ON
HANDICAPPED INDIVIDUALS

2500 People, 3500 Issues*
MAY 23–27, 1977, WASHINGTON, D.C.

CONFERENCE SIGHTS AND SOUNDS

—a wide-eyed bartender passes a drink to an agile prosthetic arm
—a two-year old proudly "pushes" her father in an electric wheelchair
—the sound of 100 hands talking
—bored guide dogs patiently nose through crutches and wheelchairs
—a pundit calls the President's speech the "Magna Carter"
—signs announce special meetings for "non white" delegates, for disabled women, for "dissidents"
—a dance troupe of mentally retarded children nervously eye the brightly lighted stage

*Reprinted from International Rehabilitation Review, February 1977, p 3

APPENDIX R
AMERICAN ACADEMY FOR CEREBRAL PALSY AND DEVELOPMENTAL MEDICINE ANNUAL MEETING: PROGRAM NOTES

ABSTRACT 39. SEXUALITY AND MENTAL RETARDATION*

Mentally retarded individuals are sexual beings; they need sex education to understand their sexuality, accept themselves, increase self esteem, protective reasons, and to adopt a positive preception of their own individual sexuality where possible. Many mentally handicapped individuals need sex education because they possess characteristics that make it difficult to acquire knowledge. There are various methods of instructions that can be used to educate the retarded in human sexuality. The methods of instruction that can be used for nonhandicapped can be used for the retarded. The techniques would include such items as vocabulary, the Scarborough approach to teaching handicapped students, classroom discussion where appropriate, use of visual aids, techniques for young children, *i.e.*, modeling clay, dolls and models, puppets, drawing, audio-visual materials, posters, teaching by means of social and recreational activity, dramatic play, *i.e.*, role playing, pantomine, improvisation, and other teaching methods applied to sex education; *i.e.*, personal adjustment training, behavior modification. Three case histories will illustrate the techniques involved in teaching sex education to severe and profoundly retarded adults in a residential program.

ABSTRACT 40. SEXUALITY OF THE DEVELOPMENTALLY DISABLED CHILD†

*J. P. Stowell, Pinehill Rehabilitation Center, Philadelphia, Pennsylvania
†Jessie K. M. Easton, M.D. Department of Physical Medicine and Rehabilitation, University of Minnesota, Minneapolis, Minnesota

The developmentally disabled child tends to be treated as an asexual being by parents, teachers, and society in general. The reasons for this are related to general social and vocational expectations.

Development of sexual identity is important if the disabled child is to function satisfactorily as an adult. The most influential factors in the development are the family and school as they provide needed models, information, and experience.

Parents, teachers, therapists, and all involved in the care and training of the disabled child can help or hinder, and all need support, education, and encouragement to treat the disabled child as a potential adult.

ABSTRACT 41. SEXUALITY AND THE DEVELOPMENTALLY DISABLED: CONSIDERATIONS FOR THE HEALTH CARE PROFESSIONAL*

The health care professional may be faced with a variety of sexual concerns and problems of the developmentally disabled child and the child's family. Fruitful interaction may be difficult for all concerned. Meaningful assistance can be provided, however, if the professional is equipped with information, practiced in skills and prepared in attitudes to work with this very personal subject. Often, however, the professional feels deskilled and will avoid the subject because of concerns about appropriateness, information and discomfort. We recommend that sexuality be supportively dealt with as a normal health issue, free from judgmentalism and guilt. Recognition of sexual concerns can lead to appropriate intervention or referral. The professional should initiate discussions which lead to a broad understanding of sexuality in the context of comfort, relationships and competence. However, the professional must prepare in the areas of medical, psychological, social and interpersonal aspects of sexuality. He or she must become trained and practiced in the necessary skills and be prepared for the possibility of initial resistance and disapproval by fellow staff members and sometimes by the family which may wish to protect the child from a risky yet rewarding aspect of adult life.

ABSTRACT 42. SOCIAL AND SEXUAL PROBLEMS OF THE ADOLESCENT AND YOUNG ADULT WITH CEREBRAL PALSY†

Many people with congenital physical disabilities have sexual as well as social and vocational problems. This session will deal with some of these

*Theodore M. Cole, M.D., Sandra S. Cole, B.A. University of Michigan Medical Center, Ann Arbor, Michigan
†Thomas E. Strax, M.D. Moss Rehabilitation Hospital, Philadelphia, Pennsylvania

problems and how they developed. The development of an adult appears as a succession of periods. Each of these extends a previous period, reconstructs on a new level, and then surpasses it. Occasionally, there is an arrest in the maturation process. This is much more common with the disabled individual. There are four major developmental tasks an adolescent must accomplish. He must consolidate his identity, achieve independence from his parents, establish new love objects outside the family, and find a vocation. The actual time period varies from culture to culture, modified by socioeconomic factors within the culture. Achieving these four major developmental tasks during a period of biological stress is extremely difficult for the disabled individual. Methods of handling stress and how the disabled is limited as to the number of outlets available, will be discussed. If the disabled is going to exist in society, he must be integrated early. His social and vocational problems of integration will be discussed in this paper.

REFERENCES

1. Abernathy V: Sexual knowledge, attitudes and practices of young female psychiatric patients. Arch Gen Psychiatry 30(2):180–182, 1974
2. Abortion (editorial): Lancet 7725(2):646–647, 1971
3. Abortion. In Hastings Center Bibliography 1976–1977. Hastings-on-Hudson, NY, Institute Of Society, Ethics and The Life Sciences, pp 62–65
4. Academy/Congress Abstract. Arch Phys Med Rehabil 54(12:582, 1973
5. Accent On Living. (Ed): Raymond Cheever, PO Box 700, Gillum & High Drive, Bloomington, IL 61701
6. Adams A: Information Memorandum, RSA–111–76–109, August 16, 1976, p 3
7. Adolescent health, sex and fertility. Am J Public Health 61(4):
   (a) Brunswick AF: adolescent health, sex and fertility, pp 711–729
   (b) Gabrielson IW et al.: Adolescent attitudes toward abortion, pp 730–738
   (c) Arnold CB, Cogswell BR: A condom distribution program for adolescents—findings of a fertility study, pp 739–750
   (d) Appel W, Royton AB: Teenage births, pp 751–757
8. Alcoholic Babies. Column, US News & World Report, May 17, 1976
9. American Psychological Association: Statement regarding homosexuality. Am Psychol. 30(6):633, 1975
10. Amniocentesis: safe, accurate (abstr). Child Today 5(1): 28, 1976
11. Amniotics gets the green light. Column, Med World News 16(22):17–19, 1975
12. Anderson CM: Early brain injury and behavior. J Am Med Wom Assoc 11(4):113–119, 1956
13. Anderson TP, Cole TM: Sexual counseling of the physically disabled. Postgrad Med 58(7): 117–123, 1975
14. Arnoff FN: Social consequences of policy toward mental illness. Science 188:1277–1281, 1975
15. Asher JD: Abortion counseling. Am J Public Health 62(5):686–688, 1972
16. Association For Study of Abortion: The Supreme Court Decision—New Legal Facts—New Medical Facts. Booklets, 1975, available from Association, 120 W 57 St., New York, NY, 10019
17. Attitudes Toward The Disabled, 1–hour videotape, America 73 series, produced by Bruce Cohen for N-Pact, NET & Ford Foundation, 1973
18. Balester RJ: Sex education, fact and fantasy. J Spec Ed 5(4):355–357, 1971
19. Bandura A: Behavior theories and the models of man. Am Psychol 29(12):859–870, 1974
20. Banham-Bridges KM: Emotional development in early infancy. Child Dev 3:340, 1932
21. Barnett SA: Animals to man. In Ethology and Development, Clinics in Developmental Medicine. London, W Heineman, 1973, p 104
22. Bass M: Sex education for the handicapped. The Family Coordinator, vol. 16, January 1974, pp 27–33
23. Bass MS (ed): Sexual Rights and Responsibilities of the Mentally Retarded, 1973, p 155. Available from the editor at 216 Glen Road, Ardmore, PA 19003
24. Battle CV: Disruptions in the socialization of a young, severely handicapped child. Rehabil Lit 35(5):130–140, 1974
25. Beach FA: Human sexuality and evolution. In Montagna W, Sadler W: Reproductive Behavior. New York, Plenum Press, 1974
26. Beach FA (ed): Human Sexuality in Four Perspectives. Baltimore, Johns Hopkins Press, 1977
27. Beaumont G: Sexual side effects of drugs. J Sex Med 1(5):10–12, 1974
28. Beels CC: Whatever happened to father? The New York Times Magazine, August 25, 1974, pp 10–12, 52–68

29. Bell RW: Mom's reaction to colicky infant has parallel in animal world. Today's Child 21(9):4, 1973
30. Bengston VL: Sex in nursing homes. Med Aspects Human Sexuality 9(7):6–7, 1975
31. Beric B, Kupresanin M: Vacuum aspiration for legal abortion as an outpatient up to the 12th week of pregnancy. Lancet 7725(2):619–621, 1971
32. Berkman AH: Sexuality—a human condition. J Rehabil 41(1):13–15, 37, 1975
33. Berlin H: Effects of human sexuality on well-being from birth to aging. Med Aspects Hum Sexuality 10(7)10–27, July 1976
35. Bidgood FE: Sexuality and the Handicapped. SIECUS Report, Vol II No. 3, January 1974
36. Bidgood FE: A study of sex education programs for visually handicapped persons. New Outlook 65(12):318–323, 1971. (Reprinted by American Foundation For The Blind, New York, NY)
37. Binder DP: Sex, Courtship and the Single Ostomate. Booklet 1973, United Ostomy Association Inc., 1111 Wilshire Blvd, Los Angeles CA 90017
38. Birth Control. Chicago, American Medical Association Booklet, 1975
39. Block JM, Kester NC: Role of Rehabilitation in the Management Of Multiple Sclerosis. Reprint from Modern Treatment 7(5), 1970. (Available from National Multiple Sclerosis Society, New York, NY 10010)
40. Blom GE: Some considerations about the neglect of sex education in special education. J Spec Ed 5(4):359–361, 1971
41. Bloom DS: The sexual aspects of physical disability. Am Arch Rehabil Ther 22:32–39, 1974
42. Blum G, Farly A, Guthals H: The concept of body image and remediating of a body image disorder. J Learning Dis 3(9)440–447, 1970
43. Bogdanovic S: Prenatal detection of Down's syndrome. JOGN Nursing 4(11–12):35–38, 1975
44. Booth CW: Amniocentesis—a tool for prenatal detection of fetal abnormality. Pediat Bull (Lutheran General Hospital, Park Ridge, IL) 2(4):4–13, Summer 1976
45. Boys: the disadvantaged sex in early childhood. Today's Child 22(5):3, 1974
46. Branch D: Report from discussion group in Conference On Marriage and the Handicapped. Third International '62 Club Conference, Reading, England, July 1969, p 29. (Available from Spastics Society, London, England)
47. Breaking The Language Barrier. 35 mm film strip, Teacher Training Aids, 27 Harvey Drive, Summit, NJ 07901
48. Brenton M: Sex and the mentally handicapped. Physician's World (10):35–38, 1974
49. Brenton M: Mainstreaming the handicapped. Today's Ed, March-April 1974, p 20
50. Broderick CB, Bernard J (eds): The Individual, Sex and Society. A SIECUS Handbook For Teachers and Counselors. Baltimore, Johns Hopkins Press, 1969
51. Bromwick RM: Focus on maternal behavior in infant intervention. Am J Orthopsychiatry 46(3):439–446, 1976
52. Bronowski J: The Ascent Of Man. Boston, Little, Brown, 1974
53. Brooks MH: Effect of diabetes on female sexual response. Med Aspects Human Sexuality 11(2):63–64, 1977
54. Brooks PA: Masturbation. SIECUS Reprint, 1975
55. Brown S: My Left Foot. New York, Simon & Schuster, 1955
56. Browning E, Brown H: In Bartlett's Familiar Quotation New York, Permabooks, 1953, p 41, section r
57. Bundy K: What You Should Know About Paraplegia. No. SRS-RSA-119-70, booklet, 12 pp, 1970. (For sale Supt of Documents, GPO, Washington DC 20202)
58. Burleson D: Review of MR Report. SIECUS Report, vol 4, January 1974, pp 5–6
59. Burt RA: Legal restrictions on sexual and familial relations of mental retardates—old laws, new guises. In LaVeck GD, De La Cruz GD (eds): Human Sexuality and The Mentally Retarded. New York, Bruner/Mazel, 1973
60. Butler RN, Lewis MI: Aging And Mental Health—Positive Psychosocial Approaches. St. Louis, CV Mosby, 1973, pp 99–105
61. Butler RN, Lewis MI: Sex After Sixty: A Guide For Men and Women For Their Later Years. New York, Harper & Row, 1976
62. Byon SW: Ages, stages and naturalization of human development. Am Psych 23(6):419–428, 1968
63. Calderone M: Review of Ostomy Booklet. SIECUS Report, January 1974, pp 5–6
64. California Recognizes Sexuality of The Retarded. SIECUS Report, January 1974, p 3
65. Cancer Guide For Practical Nurses. Booklet, 1970. American Cancer Society, New York, NY 10017
66. Caplan G: Elements of a comprehensive Community Health Program for Adolescents In

Caplan G, Lebovici S: Adolescence-Psychosocial Perspectives, New York & London, Basic Books, 1969
67. Carlson E: Born That Way. New York, John Day, 1941
68. Chess S, Thomas A, Cameron M: Temperament—its significance for early school learning. NYU Ed Q 7(3):24–29, Spring 1976
69. Chigier E: Sexual Adjustment Of The Handicapped. Sydney, Australia, Proceedings Preview of Twelfth World Congress of Rehabilitation International, 1972, pp 224–227
70. The Child Abuse Factor. Column, Crusader, Fall 1976, p 6. UCPA, New York, NY 10016
71. Children of the severely injured. Commun J Human Res 8(2):242–249, Spring 1973
72. Child Study Association of America: What To Tell Your Child About Sex. New York, Pocket Books, 1974
73. CHOICE: Religious Coalition For Abortion Rights. Newsletter, March 1976. Box 381, Scarsdale NY 10583
74. Cohen R, Rudin C: How schools can fight the VD menace. Changing Ed 4: 29–31, Spring 1973
75. Coital Positioning, film, 12 min, 16 mm, sound, color. Center for Marital and Sexual Studies, 5199 E Pacific Coast Highway, Long Beach CA 90804
76. Coitus and Coronaries: Editorial. Br Med 1(2):414, 1976
77. Cole TM: Sexual function in physical disability (abstr). In Research Directory of Rehabilitation Research and Training Centers, 1975, p 52. RSA, Office of Human Development, DHEW, Washington DC 20002
78. Cole TM: Sexuality and physical disabilities. Arch Sex Behav 4(4):389–403, 1975
79. Cole TM: Spinal cord injury patients and sexual dysfunction. Arch Phys Med Rehabil 56(1):11–12, 1975
80. Cole TM: The physician's role in working with the sexuality of the elderly. In Kelly JT, Weir J (eds): Perspectives On Human Aging. Minneapolis, Craftsman Press, 1976
81. Cole TM, Chilgren R, Rosenberg P: A new program of sex education and counseling for spinal cord injured adults and health care professionals. Paraplegia 11:111–124, 1973
82. Cole TM, Cole SS: The handicapped and sexual health. SIECUS Report 4(5):1–2, 9–10, May 1976
83. Comarr AE: Sexual response of paraplegic women. Med Aspects Human Sexuality 10(2):-124–128, February 1976
84. Comarr AE, Grinderson BB: Sexual function in traumatic paraplegia and quadriplegia. Am J Nursing 75(2):250–255, February 1975
85. Commager HS: Comment made during interview with Bill Moyer, Channel 13–TV, May 21, 1974
86. Committee On Human Sexuality: Human Sexuality. Chicago, American Medical Association, Monograph, 1973, 299 pp
87. Cook R: The Biological Basis of Pediatric Practice. New York, McGraw Hill, 1968
88. Cook R: Sex education program service model for the multihandicapped adult. Rehabil Lit 35(9):264–287, 1974
89. Cooper I: The Victim Is Always The Same. New York, Harper & Row, 1972
90. Cornwell M: Early Years. London, Disabled Living Foundation, 1975. (Reviewed in Rehabil World, Spring 1977, p 42)
91. Cox M: Sex and secularization. In The Secular City. New York, Macmillan, 1966
92. Crises In Child Mental Health: Challenge for the 1970s. New York, Harper & Row, 1970, pp 315, 316, 327, 352
93. Cummings V: Amputees and sexual dysfunction. Arch Phys Med Rehabil 56(1):12–13, 1975
94. Daily EF: Contraceptive methods prior to hospital discharge. Am J Public Health 60(6):-965, 1970
95. Dansak DA: Sexual relations of the psychiatrically ill. Med Aspects Hum Sexuality 11(3)-53–54, 1977
96. David HP: Abortion—public health concern—needed psychosocial research. Am J Public Health 61(3):510–515, 1971
97. David HP, Smith JD, Friedman E: Family planning services for persons handicapped by mental retardation. Am J Public Health 66(11):1053–1057, 1976. See also, Hastings REPORT 7(2); 43, 1977
98. Davidson A: Deprived, Exhibited. New York Times, January 7, 1976
99. Deacon J: Tongue Tied. London National Association of Mentally Handicapped Children, 1974. Book from which "Joey" English film was made—shown on NOVA, Public Broadcasting System

100. Deafness Research & Training Center: Deafness Census—Summary. NYU Ed Q, Winter 1975, p 32
101. Denhoff E: Cerebral Palsy—The Preschool Years. Springfield, IL, C Thomas, 1967
102. De Rapp R: Sex Energy. New York, Delta Books, 1969, pp 131, 236
103. Developmental Psychology Today. Del Mar, CA, CRM Books, 1971 p 346
104. Diamond M: Sexuality and the handicapped. Rehabil Lit 35(2):34, 1974
105. Diamond M: Quiz Item #5—Diabetes Mellitus. Med Aspects Hum Sexuality 10(11):89, 1976
106. Dickman IR: Sex Education for Disabled Persons. Public Affairs Pamphlet No. 531, Public Affairs Committee Inc, New York, 1975
107. Dietz HJ: COMMENTARY. In Ervin CJ: Psychologic adjustment to mastectomy. Med Aspects Hum Sexuality 7(2):65, 1973
108. Dito WR, Patrick CW, Shelly JS: Amniocentesis—general discussions. In Clinical Pathological Correlations in Amniotic Fluid. American Society of Clinical Pathologists in cooperation with Division of Educational Media Services, Chicago, 1975
109. Donovan P: Sterilizing the poor and incompetent—who needs protection from whom? The Hastings Center REPORT 6(5):7–8, October, 1976
110. Drug Related Assault To The Fetal Nervous System. Research Grant to Virginia Tennyson MD, 1975, United Cerebral Palsy Assoc, Research & Education Foundation, New York, NY 10016
111. Duberman M: The Gay Sergeant. New York Times, November 9, 1975, p 16, 58–62
112. Durall EM: Why Wait Till Marriage. New York, Association Press, 1968
113. Eckert RG (ed): Sex education. In Deutsch A. Fishman H (ed): Encyclopedia of Mental Health. New York, Franklin Watts, 1963, pp 1842–1845
114. Edgerton RB, Dingman RF: Good reasons for bad supervision; dating in a hospital for mentally retarded. Psychiatr Q: 2, 1964
115. Education For Parenthood. Fathering Instinct. Pamphlets, Joint Project of Office of Education & Office Of Child Development. Washington DC, DHEW, GPO 1973-0–494–522
116. Effects of childhood experience can be reversed by later events. Today's Child 18(9):7, 1970
117. Eisely L: The Night Country. New York, Charles Scribner & Sons, 1971
118. Eisely L: Quotation. In Saturday Review/World, December 14, 1974, p 71
119. Eisenberg MG, Rustad LC: Sex And Spinal Cord Injured—Some Questions And Answers. Booklet, March 1975, VA Hospital, Cleveland OH. (Available from Supt Documents, USGPO #051–00081–1)
120. Ellenberg M: Impotence in diabetes—a neurologic rather than an endocrinologic problem. Med Aspects Hum Sexuality 7(4):12–20, 1973
121. Elliott H: Marriage counseling with deaf clients. J Rehabil Deaf 8(2):29–36, 1974
122. Enby G: Let There Be Love—Sex and the Handicapped. New York, Taplinger Publishing, 1975
123. English RW: Correlates of stigma toward physically disabled persons. Rehab Res Prac Rev 2:4, Fall 1971
124. Engstrand JL: Psychosocial adjustment of spinal man and the multidisciplinary approach to patient care. Rehabil Nurs J 1(1):5–7, 1975
125. Enis CA, Catarizolo M: Sex education in the residential school for the blind. Ed of Visual Handicap 4(2):61–64, 1972
126. Erikson E: Childhood Society. New York, WW Norton, 1950
127. Erikson E: Identity and The Life Cycle. New York, University Press, 1959
128. Erikson EH: Identity—Youth and Crisis. New York, WW Norton, 1968
129. Ervin CJ: Psychologic adjustment to mastectomy. Med Aspects Hum Sexuality 7(2) 42–61, 65, 1973
130. Escamilla RF: Physical diseases which cause disturbances of sexual development and function. Med Aspects Hum Sexuality 9(11):47–48, 1975
131. Fairer sex active movers in student power movement. Today's Child 18(3):3, 1970
132. Fairservis WA: Costumes of the east. Natural History, November 1971, p 31
133. Fatherhood. 22 articles. The Family Coordinator, October 1976. Published by National Council On Family Relations, 1219 University Ave, SE, Minneapolis, MN 55400
134. Feldman, JM: Effects of TB on sexual functioning. Medical Aspects Hum Sexuality 11(5)-29–30, May 1977
135. Felstein I: Diabetes and sexual disabilities. Br J Sex Med 3(1):35–37, 1976
136. Fertility Regulation For Persons With Learning Disabilities. 16mm film, color, sound, 18 min. Available from Education Division, Hallmark Films and Recordings, 1511 East North Ave, Baltimore, MD 21213

137. Fine HL, Leschner M, Goldman A: Sexual effects of arthritis. Arch Phys Med Rehabil 55(12):570, 1974
138. Flavell JH, Hill JP: Developmental psychology. Annu Rev Psychology 20:1969
139. Fleming JD, Maxey D: The drive of the pure researcher—pursuit of intellectual orgasm —A conversation with Frank Beach. Psych Today 8(3):69–75, 1975
140. Ford CS, Beach F: Patterns of Sexual Behavior. New York, Perennial Library, Harper & Row, 1951
141. Forum—Sexual Rights and Wrongs. Time Magazine: December 9, 1974, p 76
142. Forum—Sexual Rights and Wrongs. Time Magazine: December 9, 1974, p 86
143. Fosfor J, Nelson M: Endemiology of drugs taken by pregnant women—drugs that may affect the fetus adversely. Clin Pharmacol Therapeut 14 (4, Part 2):632–642, July–August 1973. Also quoted in Ferguson, Lennox, Thomas: Drugs And Pregnancy—Research Issue, November 1974, p 147. Report, National Institute On Drug Abuse, Rockville, MD 20850
144. Freeman BS: COMMENTARY. In Ervin CJ:Psythologic adjustment to mastectomy. Med Aspects Hum Sexuality 7(2):65, 1973
145. Freeman RD: Psychiatric problems of adolescents with cerebral palsy. Devel Med Child Neurol 12:64–70, 1970
146. Friedman RC, Richart RM, VandeWiehle RL (eds): Sex Differences in Behavior. New York, John Wiley & Sons, 1974
147. Friends Around The World. Rehabil Gazette 16:24–25, 1973
148. Gadpaille WJ: Research into physiology of maleness and femaleness. Arch Gen Psychiatry 26(3):193–205, 1972
149. Gallagher D: Is your contraceptive safe for you? Redbook, May 1976, pp 91, 140–145
150. Galloway D: Sightless father/soundless daughter. The Independent 3(1)15–16, Fall 1975. Published by Center For Independent Living, Berkeley CA
151. Gebhard P (Institute for Sex Research, Bloomington IN 47401, Hooker E (UCLA)
152. Genetic Counseling. Programs For The Handicapped, November 28, 1975, p 2, 3. DHEW Office For Handicapped Individuals, Washington DC 20201
153. Ghatit AZ, Hanson RW: Outcome of marriage existing at the time of a male's spinal cord injury. J Chronic Dis 28:383–388, 1975
154. Gilman AE, Gordon AR: Sexual behavior in the blind. Med Aspects Hum Sexuality 7(6):-48–61, 1973
155. Girls given less loafing time than boys. Today's Child 22(5):8, 1974
156. Goodman RL: Family planning programs for the mentally retarded in institution and community. In LaVeck GD, De La Cruz FF: Human Sexuality and The Mentally Retarded. New York, Bruner/Mazel, 1973
157. Gordon S: Facts About Sex For Exceptional Youth. New York, Charles Brown, 1969
158. Gordon S: Sex ed in special education. J Spec Ed 5(4):380, Winter 1971
159. Gordon S: Facts About VD For Today's Youth. New York, John Day, 1973
160. Gordon S: On Being The Parent Of A Handicapped Youth. Booklet, 1973, New York Association For Brain-Injured Children
161. Gordon S: Sex Rights For People Who Happen To Be Handicapped. Monograph No. 6, Jan, 1974. Center on Human Policy, Syracuse University, Syracuse, NY
162. Gordon S: Sex education—love, sex and marriage for people who have disabilities. Except Parent 6 (6):18–21, 1976
163. Gordon S: Why sex education is important for people with disabilities. Except Parent 7(3)41–44, June 1977
164. Gordon S, Dickman IR: Sex Education—The Parent's Role. Public Affairs Pamphlet #549. Public Affairs Committee Inc. NYC July 1977
165. Gould RE: What We Don't Know About Homosexuality. New York Times Magazine, February 24, 1974, p 73
166. Gould RE: Sexual Diversity: Reply to Letters To The Editor. New York Times Magazine, March 17, 1974, p 73
167. Green MR: Safety of prolonged coitus for elderly. In Answers To Questions. Med Aspects Hum Sexuality 10(7):6, 7, 1976
168. Greenberg J: In This Sign. New York, Holt, Rinehart & Winston, 1970
169. Greengross W: Entitled To Love—The Sexual Needs of the Handicapped. London, Malaby Press, 1976. (Reviewed in Rehabel World, Spring 1977, p 43
170. Gregory MF: Sexual Adjustment—A Guide For The Spinal Cord Injured. Accent Special Publication 1974, Accent On Living Inc, PO Box 726, Bloomington IL 61701
171. Griffith ER, Tomko MA, Timms RJ: Sexual function in spinal cord patients—a review. Arch Phys Med Rehabil 54(12):539–543, 1973

172. Griffith ER, Trieschman R, Hohmann G, Cole T, Tobis J, Cummings V: Sexual dysfunctions associated with physical disabilities. Arch Phys Med Rehabil 56(1):8–21, 1975
173. Group For Advancement of Psychiatry, Committee of The College Student: Sex and the College Student. Report #60, New York, 1965
174. Guttman L, Walsh JJ: Prostigmine assessment test of fertility in spinal man. Paraplegia 9:39–51, 1971
175. Hall JE, Morris HL, Barker AR: Sexual knowledge and attitudes of mentally retarded adolescents. Am J Ment Defic 77(6):706–709, 1973
176. Hallerstein HK, Friedman EH: Sexual activity of the postcoronary patient. Arch Intern Med 125:987–999, 1970
177. Hamilton E: Sex Before Marriage. New York, Meredith Press, 1969
178. Hamson JL, Hamson JG: The ontogenesis of sexual behavior in man. In Young WC (ed): Sex and Internal Secretions, vol 2. Baltimore, Williams & Wilkins, 1961
179. Hanson J, Smith D: The Fetal Hydantoin Syndrome. Program Notes. American Academy for Cerebral Palsy, Annual Meeting, Sept 1975 1975, New Orleans, LA.
180. Harasymiv SJ, Horne MD, Lewis SC: A longitudinal study of disability group acceptance. Rehabil Lit 37(4):98–99, 1976
181. Hardukewych D: Gas-Liquid Chromatographic Analysis Laboratory. Michigan C/P Topics, United Cerebral Palsy Association of Michigan, Flint, MI, 1975
182. Hargreaves W (ed): Marriage and the Handicapped. Presentations at Third International '62 Club Conference. Reading University, Reading, England, July 1969, p 17–60. (Available from Spastics Society, London, England)
183. Harlow HF: Learning To Love. New York, Jason Aronsen, 1974
184. Harlow HF, Harlow MK, Suomi SJ: From thought to therapy—lesson from a primate laboratory. Am Sci 59(5):538–549, 1971
185. Harrington D: Sex, the family and the future. Community News, March 1975, p 4, Community Church, NYC 10016
186. Hartman WE, Fithian MA: Treatment of Sexual Dysfunction—A Bio Psychosocial Approach. Long Beach, CA, Center for Marital Studies, 1972
187. Hathaway K: The Little Locksmith quote from p 6, New York, Coward McCan, 1942. In Barker R, Wright B, Gonick 19: Adjustment To Physical Handicap. New York, Social Science Research Council, 1953, p 7
188. Havighurst RJ: Developmental Tasks and Education, 2nd ed. New York, Langman's Green, 1952
189. Held JP, Cole TM et al.: Sexual attitude reassessment workshops: effect on spinal cord injured adults, their partners and rehab professionals. Arch Phys Med Rehabil 56(1):-14–18, 1975
190. Helsingak K, Schellen AM, Verkuyla A: Not Made Of Stone—The Sexual Problems of Handicapped People. Springfield, IL, Thomas, 1974
191. Hill A: Some guidelines for sex education of the deaf child. Volta Review 73(2):120–125, 1971
192. Hix K: Sex attitudes and Counseling—A Laboratory Seminar in Human Sexuality of Physically Disabled Adults. Program in Human Sexuality at University of Minnesota, Medical School, Minneapolis, Mn, 1977
193. Hoffman ML, Hoffman LW: Review of Child Development Research. New York, Russell Sage Foundation, 1974
193a. Hofmann A: Adolescence Sex and Education. NYU Quarterly 8(4)7–14, Summer 1977
194. Hohmann GW: Considerations in management of psychosexual readjustment in cord-injured males. Rehabil Psychol 19:50–58, 1972
195. Hohmann GW: Sex and the spinal cord injured male. Accent On Living 18(2):23–25, Spring 1973
196. Hohmann GW: The insider-outsider position and the maintenance of hope. Rehabil Psychol 22(2):136–141, 1975
197. Holbert D: Sex and the Disabled. Toomey J Gazette 10:14–15, 1967
198. Holder AR: Rights of the retarded. The Hastings Center REPORT 6(4):4, August, 1976
199. Holmes RV: The planning and implementation of a sex education program for severely handicapped children in a residential setting. New Outlook For Blind 68(5):219–225, 1974
200. Hopkins MT: Patterns of self destruction among orthopedically disabled. Rehabil Res Pract Rev 3(1):7, Winter 1971

201. Horenstein S: Sexual dysfunction in neurological disease. Med Aspects Hum Sexuality 10(4):7–11, 18–30, 1976
202. Human genetic centers. Child Today 3:29, 1974
203. Human Genetic Centers—Program For The Handicapped. Pamphlet, May 15, 1975, pp 6, 7. Office For Handicapped, DHEW, Washington DC 20201
204. Ilkley R, Hall M: Psychosocial aspects of abortion. Bull WHO 53(1):83–106, 1976
205. Illinois School for the Deaf: The development of a sex education curriculum for a state residential school for the deaf and social Hygiene guides, 1975. Jacksonville, IL 62650
205a. IMPACT Newsbriefs. Vol 1, No. 2, February 1977. Published by Institute for Family Research and Education, Syracuse, NY
206. Innes B: I was afraid to come to college but then I met a guy in a wheelchair. Accent On Living 20(2):42–43, Fall 1975
207. Is Sexual Activity Vital To Good Health? Harper's Bazaar, October 1974, pp 38, 54
208. Jacobson GF, Strickler M, Morley WE: Generic and individual approaches to crisis intervention. Am J Public Health 58(2):338–343, 1968
209. Johnson WR: Sex education of mentally retarded children. Sexology, Jan, 1967 (reprinted by SIECUS)
210. Johnson WR: Masturbation. In Broderick CB, Bernard J (eds): The Individual, Sex and Society. Baltimore, Johns Hopkins Press, 1970
211. Johnson WR: Human Sexual Behavior and Sex Education. Philadelphia, Lea & Febiger, 1973
212. Jones KL, Shainberg LW, Byer CO: Sex and People. New York, Harper & Row, 1977
213. Ju KS, Park IJ et al.: Prenatal sex determination by observation of the X-Chromatin and the Y-Chromatin of exfoliated amniotic fluid cells. Obstet Gynecol 47(3):287–290, 1976
214. Kahn E: The impact of our relationship. J Rehabil Med 4:14–17, 1972
215. Kahn JV: Moral and cognitive development of the mild and moderate retarded. Am J Ment Def 81(3):209–214, 1976. See also, Hastings REPORT 7(2):43, 1977
216. Kalma SA: Sex education within biology classes for hospitalized disturbed adolescents. Except Child 42(8):451–455, 1976
217. Kanton L: A disabled partner in a marriage. Accent On Living 19(5):24–31, Summer 1975
218. Kapor S: Three phases of abortion process and influence on women's mental health. Am J Public Health 62(7):906–907, 1972
219. Kaplan D, Mearig J: A community support system for a family coping with chronic illness. Rehabil Lit 38(3):79–82, 1977
220. Kaplan HS: The effects of illness on sexuality. In The New Sex Therapy—Active Treatment Of Sexual Dysfunction. New York, Bruner/Mazel, 1974, pp 75–85
221. Kaplan HS: The New Sex Therapy—Active Treatment of Sexual Dysfunction. New York, Brunner Mazel, 1974
222. Kaplan HS: The Illustrated Manual of Sex Therapy. New York, New York Times Book Co, 1975
223. Karper MI, Lipke LA: Sex education as a part of an agency's four week workshop for visually impaired youngsters. New Outlook For Blind 68(6):260–267, 1974
224. Kempton W: Sex education—a cooperative effort of parent and teacher. Except Child 41(8):531–535 1975
225. Kempton W: Sex Education for Persons With Disabilities That Hinder Learning—A Teacher's Guide. North Seituite, MA, Duxbury Press, 1975
226. Kempton W et al.: Love, Sex and Birth Control For The Mentally Retarded—A Guide For Parents. Booklet, 1973, Planned Parenthood Association of SE Pennsylvania, Philadelphia, PA 19107
228. Keniston K: Review of sex and the college student. Am J Orthopsychiatry 37(1):157–158, 1967
229. Kimura D: The asymmetry of the brain. Sci Am 228(3):70–75, 1973
230. Kirkendall LA: Sexuality and The Life Cycle. Booklet, SIECUS Study Guide No. 8, July 1974. (Distributed by Behavioral Publications, New York NY 10011
231. Kistner RW: When contraceptive effect of the pill starts. Med Aspects Hum Sexuality 10(11):142–143, 1976
232. Kohlberg L: Stage and sequence cognitive developmental approach to socialization. In Developmental Psychology Today. DelMar CA, CRM Books, 1971
233. Labby DH: Sexual concomitants of disease and illness. Postgrad Med 58(1):103–111, 1975
234. Labby DH: Sexual ability of stroke patients. In Answers To Questions. Med Aspects Hum Sexuality 10(7):6, 7, 1976

235. Landesman R, Saxena BB:Results of the first 1000 radioreceptorassays for the determination of human chorionic gonadotropin: a new rapid, reliable and sensitive pregnancy test. Fertil Steril 27(4):357–368, 1976

236. Landis C, Bolles MM: Personality and sexuality of physically handicapped women. In Barker RG, Wright BA, Gonick HR: Adjustment to Physical Handicap and Illness. New York, Social Science Research Council, Bulletin 55, 1973

237. Langmuir CJ: Varieties of coital positions: advantages and disadvantages. Med Aspects Hum Sexuality 10(6):129–139, 1976

238. Larshan B: Personal communication, 1968

239. Laurie G: Housing and Home Services for the Disabled. Guidelines: 7 Experiences in Independent Living. Hagerstown, MD, Harper & Row, 1977

240. LaVeck GD, De La Cruz FF: Contraception for the medically retarded—current methods and future prospects. In De La Cruz FF, LaVeck GD: Human Sexuality and the Mentally Retarded. New York, Bruner/Mazel, 1973

241. Lear M: Are we trying to solve too many problems with sex? Woman's Day, May 1975, pp 61, 62, 129, 130

242. Lebell RR: Genetic decision-making and parental responsibility. Linacre Q 43(4):280–291, 1976. (2825 N Mayfair Rd, Milwaukee WI 53222) See also, Hastings REPORT 7(2):43, 1977

243. Leff DH: Boy or girl—now choice, not chance. Med World News 16(26):45–56, Dec 1, 1975

244. Lerner M: Quotation. In May R: Antidotes For The New Puritanism. Saturday Rev, March 26, 1966, p 19

245. Leschner M, Fine H, Goldman A: Sexual activity in older stroke patients (abstr). Arch Phys Med Rehabil 55(12):578, 1974

246. LeShan E: The need for privacy. Woman's Day, May 1975, pp 12, 134–135

247. Liddick B: Can Love Find A Way? Los Angeles Times News Service. In Providence Sunday Journal, July 6, 1975, p E–3

248. Like Other People. 16mm film, sound, color, 37 min. (Available from Perrenial Education Inc, 1825 Willow Road, Northfield IL 60093)

249. Living Lines (Letters to ed): Accent On Living 19(2): 11, Spring 1974

250. Loewit K et al.: Determination of foetal sex from maternal excretion in early pregnancy (abstr). Dtsch Med Wochenschr 99:1656–57, 16 August, 1974

251. Loring J: Sex, Marriage and the Handicapped. New York, Proceedings 12th World Congress, Rehabilitation International, 1973

252. Lovitt R: Sexual adjustment of spinal cord injury patients. Rehabil Res Pract Rev 1(3):-25–29, Summer 1970

253. Luebking S: Getting there is half the fun—the sexually active quad. The Independent 3(4):20–21, Spring 1977

254. Maccoby EE, Jacklin CN: Psychology Of Sex Differences. Stanford, CA, Stanford University Press, 1975

255. Maddock J: Sex education for the exceptional person—a rationale. Except Child 41(1):-273–278, 1974

256. Deleted in revision

257. March of Dimes study find defective child tries marriage ties. Today's Child 18:4 1970

258. Marmor J: Letter from the President of the American Psychiatric Association to the Editor of the New York Times, August 29, 1975

259. Mattison J: Marriage and mental handicap. In De La Cruz FF, LaVeck GD (eds): Human Sexuality and the Mentally Retarded. New York, Brunner/Mazel, 1973

260. Marriage & Parenting: Issues for people with disabilities & their parents. Special Section in The Exceptional Parent 7(2) April 1977; 7(3)6–10, June 1977

261. Deleted in revision

262. May R: Antidotes For The New Puritanism. Sat Rev Lit, March 26, 1966, pp 19–43

263. Mayerson EW: Putting The Ill At Ease. New York, Harper & Row, 1976

264. McBride AB: The Growth and Development of Mothers. New York, Harper & Row, 1973

265. McGrath N, McGrath C: Why have a baby? The New York Times Magazine, May 25, 1975, pp 10–12

266. Medinick MT, Weissman HJ: The psychology of women-selected topics. In Rosenzweig MT, Porter LW (eds): Ann Rev of Psychol, Vol 26. 1975

267. Meirowsky AM: The management of the paraplegic patient. J Tenn State Med 47:431–435, 1954

268. Menolaseino FJ: Sexual problems of the mentally retarded. Sexual Behavior, November 1972 (Reprinted by SIECUS)

269. Meyen EL, Carr DL: A social attitude approach in sex education for educable mentally retarded. Inservice Training Materials For Teachers of Educable Mentally Retarded, Session III. Iowa State Dept of Public Instruction, Special Ed Curriculum, 1967
270. Michelmore S: Sexual Reproduction. Garden City, NY, The Natural History Press, 1964
271. Milkovich L, van den Berg BJ: Effects of prenatal meprobamate and chlordiazepoxide on embryonic and fetal development. N Engl J Med 291(24):1268–1271, 1974
272. Minde K, Hackett JD, Kellou D, Silver S: How they grow up—41 physically handicapped children and their families (abstr). Rehabil Psychol: 187, 1972
273. Molloy L, Director, National Arts and the Handicapped Information Service. Quoted in New York Times, This Week In Review, Sunday, Feb 13, 1977
274. Money J: Psychosexual development in man. In Deutsch H, Frohman H: Encyclopedia of Mental Health, Vol V. New York, Franklin Watts, 1963
275. Money J: Special sexual education and cultural anthropology—innovative programs. J Spec Ed 5(4):369–377, Winter 1971
276. Money J: Interview. APA Monitor, June 1976, pp 9–11
277. Money J: Comment. WNET, New York, January 28, 1977
278. Money J, Early JT: Reviews of the literature—the psychology of sex differences. Am J Orthopsychiatry 45(8):893–894, 1975
279. Money J, Ehbarat AA: Man and Woman, Boy and Girl. Baltimore, Johns Hopkins University Press, 1972
280. Montagu A: The Direction of Human Development. New York, Harper 1955
281. Mooney T, Cole TM, Chilgren R: Sexual Options For Paraplegics and Quadriplegics. Boston, Little, Brown, 1975
282. Morgan E, Hohmann GW: Psychosocial rehabilitation in VA spinal cord injury centers. Rehabil Psychol 21(1):3–34, 1974
283. Morgan MR: Marriage and the Handicapped. Presentation at Third International '62 Club Conference. Reading University, Reading, England, July, 1969 (Available from Spastics Society, London, England)
284. Morgenstern M: Sexual Behavior And Education Of The Retarded. Paper presented at Second International Symposium On Mental Retardation. Madrid, Spain, March, 1969
285. Morgenstern M: Sex Education For The Retarded? PCMR Message, August 1969, pp 10–12. Issued by President's Committee for Mental Retardation, Washington DC
286. Mourad M, Chiu WS: Marital sexual adjustment of amputees. Med Aspects Hum Sexuality 8(2):47–52, 1974
287. Movius M: Voluntary Childlessness—the ultimate liberation. Family Coordination 25(1):-57–63, January 1976
288. Mussen P, Conger J, Kagan J: Child Development and Personality. New York, Harper & Row, 1963
289. Mussen P, Rosenzweig MT (eds): Annual Review of Psychology, Vol 23. Palo Alto, CA, Annual Reviews Inc,
290. Muthard J, Hutchinson J: The Cerebral Palsied—Their Education and Employment. Monograph 1968, University of Florida, Gainesville FL
291. Myers JK: Consequences and programs of disability. In Sussman M (ed): Sociology and Rehabilitation. New York, American Sociology Association, 1965
292. Myers R: Retarded Newlyweds Seek New Life. The Washington Post No. 259, Section A, pp 1 & 16, Sunday, August 21, 1977
293. Myerson L: Physical disability as a social problem. J Soc Issues, Fall 1968
294. Mysak E: Principles of a Reflex Therapy Approach to Cerebral Palsy. New York, Teachers College Press, Columbia University Bureau of Publications, 1963
295. Nathanson B: Ambulatory abortion—experience with 26,000 cases. N Engl J Med 286(8):-403–407, 1972
296. National Center For Family Planning Services: State Of The States—Birth Control For Minors. Monograph, DHEW Pub No. (HSM) 73–16003, April, 1973
297. National Research Council Study For Controlled Genetic Screening. PCMR Message, August 1975, p 3, 4. Issued by President's Committee for Mental Retardation, Washington DC
298. New MI, Levine LS: Congenital adrenal hyperplasia. In Human Genetics, Vol 4. New York, Plenum Press, 1974
299. Nigro G: Sexuality and the Handicapped. Paper presented at Fifth Annual Short Course in Pediatric Rehabilitation, Institute of Rehabilitation Medicine, New York, November 1973

300. Nigro G: Recreation and adult education. Rehabil Lit 35(9):268–271, 1 1974
301. Nigro G: Sexuality in the handicapped; some observations on human needs & attitudes Rehab Lit 36(7)202–205, 1975
302. Nigro G: Some Observations On Personal Relationships and Sexual Relationships Among Lifelong Disabled Americans. Speech presented at Seminar on Motivation Of Life For Severely Disabled Persons. Arheim Netherlands, September 1975
303. Nordquist I: Life Together—The Situation Of The Handicapped. Olofssons Boktryckeri, AB, Stockholm, 1972
304. Nordquist I: Sex, Handicapped Individuals and Their Environment. In Proceedings Preview of the Twelfth World Congress, Sydney, Australia, 1972. Rehabilitation International, New York NY
305. Nordquist I: Sexual Problems of Physically Disabled Adolescents. Presented at International Symposium on the Disabled Adolescent, Tel Aviv, Israel, June 1973
306. Novak M: The family out of favor. Harpers, April 1976
307. Deleted in revision
308. O'Malley J et al.: Impairment of human drug metabolism by contraceptive steroids. Clin Pharmacol Ther 13:552, 1972
309. Oregon State School for the Blind: A Guide To Family Living and Sex Education, 1974 Oregon State School For Blind, 700 Church St SE, Salem, OR 97310
310. Deleted in revision
311. Ounsted C, Taylor D: Gender Differences. Baltimore, Williams & Wilkins, 1972, pp 241–262
312. Page LB: Advising hypertensive patients about sex. Med Aspects Hum Sexuality 9(1):-103–114, 1975
313. Parcel GS, Money J, Bronfenbrenner U: Caution: gender identity a sensitive area. Today's Child 24(7):5, 1976
314. Parent Infant Program. Booklet, United Cerebral Palsy of New York City, 1976, 21 pp
315. Parks W: Community Study of Adolescents with Cerebral Palsy in Franklin County, Ohio. Report for Ohio State Dept Health & Education and United Cerebral Palsy of Ohio, 1966
316. Pashayan HM: The basic concepts of medical genetics. J Speech Hear Disord 40(2):-147–163, 1974
317. Pattula A: Puberty For The Girl Who Is Retarded. Booklet, National Association For Retarded Children, New York, NY, 1969
318. Paul E: Legal Issues In Family Life Education and Family Planning For The Mentally Retarded. Remarks made by the author at Naomi Gray Regional Workshop on "Family Life Education and Family Planning For The Mentally Retarded." NY, April 9, 1975 (Mimeograph)
319. Paul E, Pilpel H, Wechsler H: Pregnancy, teenagers and the law, 1976. Fam Plann Perspect 8(1):16–21, 1976
319a. Paul EW: Danforth & Bellotti—A breakthrough for adolescents. Family Plan Pop Rep 6(1) 3–5, 1977
320. Pearce JE, Newton S: The Conditions of Human Growth. New York, Citadel Press, 1963, p 112
321. Peck JR, Stephens WB: Marriage of young adult male retardates. Am J Ment Defic 60(6):818–827, 1965
322. Perese DM, Prezio JA, Perese EP: Sexual dysfunction caused by injuries to the cervical spinal cord without paralysis. Spine 1(3):149–154, 1976
323. Perske R, Perske M: Sexual development. In New Directions For Parents Of Persons Who Are Retarded. Nashville, Abington Press, 1973
324. Personal communication received by Robinault at United Cerebral Palsy Association National Headquarters, New York, NY, 1969
325. Petts M, Branch BN: Legal abortion in the USA—a preliminary assessment. Lancet 7725(2):651–653, 1971
326. The Pill: Column. Herald Statesman, Westchester, NY Jan 19, 1977
327. Plionis BM: Adolescent pregnancy—review of the literature. Social Work 20(4): 302–307, 1975
328. Poling DA: Socio-sexual Distance and the Disabled. Paper presented at Workshop on Sexuality and the Disabled: Community Attitudes and Responsibilities, Toronto, Canada, June 17, 1974. (Copies available UCP–NYC, 122 E 23 St, NY 10010)
329. Pomeroy W: Sexual myths of the 1970's. Med Aspects Hum Sexuality 11(1)62–74, 1977

330. Porteus J, Hullinger JL: A Survey of Severely Disabled In Iowa—Client and Counselor Perceptions Of Vocational Deterrants And Rehabilitation Needs. RSA Grant No. 065-14-605, May–June, 1975, p 11

331. Powledge TM: Amniontics Shown Safe and Effective—from Experimental Procedure To Accepted Practice. Hastings Center REPORT Institute of Society, Ethics and Life Services 6(1):6–7, 1976

332. Pregnancy and Abortion in Adolescence—Report of a WHO Meeting. World Health Organization Technical Report Series #583. WHO, Geneva, 1975

333. Preliminary Abortion Study (Mgt Sanger Clinic). In RV Inventory: A Survey of Current Research, Community Council of Greater New York, 1975

334. Price J: Is he avoiding you? Accent On Living: 16–20, Winter 1976

335. Quinn JM: Do animals have belly buttons? Child Today 5(5):2–9, 1976

336. Race AR, Leecraft J, Crist T: The Sex Scene—Understanding Sexuality. New York, Harper & Row, 1975

337. Rafael B: The Parent Infant Program at United Cerebral Palsy of New York City. Booklet, 1976, 20 pp mimeo. (Available UCP-NYC, 122 E 23 St, NY 10010)

338. Rathbun L: Letter to the editor. Accent On Living 19(4):11–12, Spring 1975

339. Rebuck H: Sex Education—Dating, Courtship and Marriage. Speech prepared for United Cerebral Palsy of Pennsylvania, 1968, Eastern State School & Hospital, Trevose, Pa

340. Reed D: Sex and the Aging. Lecture presented at Human Sexuality Seminar, Moss Rehabilitation Hospital, Philadelphia, PA, April 1975

341. Rehabilitation Gazette, (Eds): Gini Laurie, Joseph Laurie, 4502 Maryland Ave, St Louis, MO 63108

342. Rehabilitation International, 432 Park Ave South, NY 10010. International Rehabilitation Review issued 6 times a year. (Eds): Norman Acton, Susan Hammerman, Barbara Duncan

343. Rehabilitation notes. J Rehabil 40(5):5, 1974

344. Reich M, Harshman H: Sex education for handicapped children: reality or repression? J Spec Educ 5(4):373–378, Winter 1971

345. Reif A: Erich Fromm. Hum Behav:17–23, April 1975

346. Renshaw DC: Sexual problems in stroke patients. Med Aspects Hum Sex 9(12):68–74, Dec 1975

347. Report to the President—Mental Retardation: Century of Decision. President's Committee on Mental Retardation, March 1976, Washington DC 20201

348. Research referral service. Int Rehabil Rev 23(1):22, 1972

349. A Resource Guide in Sex Education for the Mentally Retarded. Booklet, American Association for Health, Physical Education & Recreation in collaboration with SEICUS, AAH-PER Publications, Washington DC, 1971

350. Rhodes P: Psychosexual problems of chronic handicapping disease. Med J Aust 2:688–692, October 30, 1976

351. Richards BA: Medical aspects of coital positions. Br J Sex Med 3(1):30–34, 1976

352. Riesman D: Sex and secularization. In Cox H: The Secular City. New York, MacMillan, 1966

353. Rise Of The Singles—Forty Million Free Spenders. US News & World Report, October 7, 1974

354. Romano MD: Sexuality and the disabled female. Accent On Living 18(3):27–35, Winter 1973

355. Romano MD: Sex and the handicapped. Nurs Care:18–20, July 1977

356. Romano M, Lassiter R: Sexual counseling with the spinal cord injured. Arch Phys Med Rehabil 53(12):568–575, 1972

357. Rosen M: Conditioning appropriate heterosexual behavior in mentally and socially handicapped populations. Reprint, pp 173–177, available from Psychology Dept, Elwyn Institute, Elwyn, PA 19063

358. Rosenthal D: Genetic Theory and Abnormal Behavior, New York, McGraw-Hill, 1970

359. Rubin I: Sexual Life After Sixty. New York, Basic Books, 1965

360. Rusk H: Sex problems in paraplegia—round table. Med Aspects Hum Sexuality 1(4):46–50, 1967

361. Rusk H: Sex problems in Paraplegia. (tape casette) Available from Institute for Rehabilitation Medicine, New York University Medical Center, NY 10016

362. Rutter M:Normal psychosexual development. In Chess S, Thomas A(eds):Annual Progress in Child Psychiatry and Child Development. New York, Brunner/Mazel, 1972

363. Ryder NB, Westoff CF: Reproduction In The United States, 1965. Monograph, Princeton University Press, 1971
364. Ryder NB, Westoff CF: The Contraceptive Revolution. Monograph, Princeton University Press, 1977
365. Ryor J: Mainstreaming. Today's Education 65(2):5, 1976
366. Sadoughi W, Leshner M, Fine H: Sexual adjustment in a chronically ill and physically disabled population—a pilot study. Arch Phys Med Rehabil 51(7):311–317, 1971
367. Sagarin E: The Anatomy of Dirty Words. Paperback Library, 1969
368. Saghir MT, Robins E: Male and Female Homosexuality. Baltimore, Williams & Wilkins, 1973
369. Sanctuary J: Facing Up To Contraceptive Education. Speech at University of Connecticut, Storrs, CT, July 16, 1970 (SIECUS Reprint)
370. Sander F: Aspects of sexual counseling with the aged. Soc Casework 57(8):504–510, 1976
371. Sandowski CL: Sexuality and the paraplegic. Rehabil Lit 37(11–12):322–327, 1976
372. Sarlin MB, Altshuler KZ: Group psychotherapy with deaf adolescents in a school setting. Int J Group Psychother 18(3):337–344, 1968
373. Satir V: People Making. Palo Alto, CA, Science & Behavior Books, 1972
374. Schaie KW, Gribbin K: Adult development and aging. Annu Rev Psychol 26:65–98, 1975
375. Scheer RM: Human Growth, Social Hygiene and Sex Education Class For Male Rehabilitation Candidates. Report HIP Project, Austin State School, TX, 1967 (mimeo)
376. Scheer RM et al.: Community Preparedness for Retardates. Booklet, Austin State School, TX, 1969
377. Schein JD, Delk MT: The Deaf Population. Silver Springs MD, National Association of Deaf of the USA, 1974
378. Scholl GT: The psychosocial effects of blindness: implications for program planning in sex education. New Outlook For Blind 68(5):201–209, 1974
379. Schontz F: The Psychologic Aspects of Physical Illness & Disability. New York, McMillan 1975
380. Schwarz B: Sex offenders and their rehabilitation—a study based on the literature. Rehabil Res Pract Rev 41(1):19–22, Winter 1972
381. Secker L: Sex education and mental handicap. Spec Ed 62(1):27–29, 1973
382. Secret of sex solved by saliva. Today's Child 19(8):1, 1971
383. Service J: Glamour on wheels. Rehabil Gazette 14:9–10, 1971
384. Sex And The Male Ostomate. Booklet, 1975. United Ostomy Association, 1111 Wilshire Blvd, Los Angeles, CA 90017
385. Sex, Courtship and The Single Ostomate. Booklet, 1973, United Ostomy Association, Los Angeles, CA
386. Sex Education For The Visually Handicapped In Schools and Agencies—Selected Papers. Booklet, American Foundation For The Blind, NY, 1975
387. Sex, Pregnancy, and the Female Ostomate. Booklet, 1975, United Ostomy Association Los Angeles CA
388. Sexually Transmitted Diseases—A Challenge To Health Education. Int J Health Educ [Suppl] 18(3):1–17, 1975
389. Shaw CR, Wright CH: The married mentally defective, a follow-up study. Lancet 30:- 273–274, 1960
390. Sherrington C: Man On His Nature. Garden City, NY Doubleday & Co, 1951, p 285
391. SIECUS Reports. SIECUS publications available from Human Sciences Press, Behavioral Publications Inc, 72 Fifth Ave, New York, NY 10011
392. Silverman M, Lazlo I, Cramer J: Deviant preschool children—the contribution of constitutional predisposition and parental crisis. Am J Orthopsychiatry 37(3):331–335, 1967
393. Simmons JQ: Sexuality and MS Report of St Louis Conference 1974. National Multiple Sclerosis Society, 257 Park Ave South, New York, NY 10010
394. Singer I: The Goals Of Human Sexuality. New York, WW Norton & Co, 1973, p 157
395. Singh SP, Wagner T: Sex and self—the spinal cord injured. Rehabil Lit 36(1):2–10, 1975
396. Smith BH: Multiple sclerosis and sexual dysfunction. Med Aspects Hum Sexuality 10(1):- 103–104, 1976
397. Smith BM: Competence and adaptation. Am J Occup Ther 28(1):11–15, 1974
398. Smith J, Bullough B: Sexuality & the severely disabled. Am J Nurs 75 (12):2194–2197, 1975
399. Sociologist prophecies. Today's Child 16(8):7, 1967
400. Sociologists see sexuality entering play area. Column, Todays' Child, October, 1973 p 6
401. Sorensen RC: The Sorensen Review—A Response. SIECUS Report, January 1974, p 11

402. Sorrel PM, Sorrel LJ: A sex counseling service for college students. Am J Public Health 61(7):1341–1345, 1971
403. Sparberg M: The birth control pill. In Sex, Courtship and the Single Ostomate. Pamphlet, 1973, p 18, United Ostomy Association, Los Angeles, CA
404. Spinal Cord Injury, Hope Through Research. Publication #1747, National Institutes of Health, Bethesda, MD (Reprinted 1970)
405. Spira R: Artificial insemination after intrathecal injection of neostigmine in paraplegia. Lancet 1:670–671, 1976
406. Spock B: Baby & Child Care. New York, Pocket Books, 1962
407. Stamper E, Ardmore J: My problem and how I solved it—born deaf. Good Housekeeping 182(4):28, 34–39, April, 1976
408. Statistical Abstracts of US, 1973. Social & Economic Statistical Administration, Bureau of Census, US Dept Commerce, Washington, DC, 20002
409. Statistics. National Foundation, PO Box 2000, White Plains, NY 10602
410. Stauffer D: Proud father. Rehabil Gazette 14:18, 1971
411. Stein RA: Effects of exercise on heart rate during coitus in the post-myocardial infarction patient. Circulation (Suppl) 51(2):116, 1975
412. Stewart TD: Coping Behavior and Moratorium Following Spinal Cord Injury. 1976, publication pending (Psychiatrist VA Boston, personal communication)
413. Stewart TD, Gerson SN: Penile prosthesis—psychological factors. Urology 7(4):400–402, 1976
414. Stoller RJ et al.: A symposium—Should homosexuality be in the APA nomenclature? Am J Psychiatr 130 (11):1207–1216, 1973
415. Stone G: Program Planning—The Embryonic Stage. Paper presented March 23, 1970 at American Personnel & Guidance Association Convention, New Orleans. (Available from APGA, Washington DC)
416. Stone I: Man is his own Pigmalian . . . quote. Washington Weekly Reader, 1975
416a. Stowell G: Sexuality and Mental Retardation, Paper presented at Academy for Cerebral Palsy & Developmental Medicine. Annual Meeting, Atlanta, Oct 9, 1977
416b. Strax TE: Social and Sexual Problems of the Adolescent and Young Adult with Cerebral Palsy. Paper presented at Academy for Cerebral Palsy and Developmental Medicine. Annual Meeting, Atlanta, Oct 9, 1977
417. Strickler M: Crisis intervention and the climacteric man. Soc Casework: 85–89, February 1975
418. A Survey of Medicine and Medical Practice for the Rehabilitation Counselor. US-HEW-VRA, Washington DC, 1966, p 48
419. Sutherland AM, Orbach CE: The psychological impact of cancer and cancer surgery. Cancer 5(5):857–872, 1952
420. Swinyard C: Genetic Counseling In Rehabilitation. Proceedings of Twelfth World Congress, Rehabilitation International, Sydney, Australia 1972, pp 640–651
421. Swinyard C: A Follow-up Study Of Nine Hundred Patients With Cerebral Palsy—Based On data acquired by the late Meyer A Perlstein, MD. Report, Academy For Cerebral Palsy, Annual Conference, New Orleans, September, 1975
422. Tanner JM, Taylor GR: Growth, Life Science Library. New York, Times Inc, 1965, p 80
423. Taussig LM: Psychosexual and psychosocial aspects of Cystic Fibrosis. Med Aspects Hum Sexuality 10(2):101–102, 1976
424. Teal J, Athelson G: Sexuality and spinal cord injury—some psychosocial considerations. Arch Phys Med Rehabil 56(6):264–268, 1975
425. They Have Guts—They're Patient. Column, New York Times Resort and Travel Section, Sunday, February 23, 1975
426. To Be A Friend. 10 mm film, sound & color, 13½ min. Billy Budd Films, 235 E 57 St, NY
427. Tobis JS: Cardiovascular patients and sexual dysfunction. Arch Phys Med Rehabil 56(1):-11–12, 1975
428. Torbett DS: A humanistic and futuristic approach to sex education for blind children. New Outlook for Blind 68(5):210–215, 1974
429. Trend of married couples not to have children—and why. Mike Wallace Reports, WNET, May 12, 1974
430. Trieschmann RB: Sex, sex acts and sexuality. Arch Phys Med Rehabil 56(1):899, 1975
431. Trimble J (ed): 5000 Adult Words and Phrases. , Brandon House, 1966
432. Turnbull A, Woodford FP (eds): Prevention of Handicap Through Antenatal Care. New

York, American Elsevier, 1976 (Originally published in Amsterdam, Netherlands by Associated Scientific Publishers, 1976)
433. US Finds Epidemic of Child Abuse Rate. New York Times, Nov 30, 1975
434. Vaisrub S: Risk factors and risque humor (editorial). JAMA 235(8): 847, 1976
435. Vandervoort H, Geiger RC, Knight SE: Sexuality and Cerebral Palsy, Research Project 1973–74. Final Report, United Cerebral Palsy Association, New York, NY
436. Veatch RM: Value—Freedom in Science Technology—A Study of the Importance of Religious Ethics, and other Socio Cultural Factors in Selected Medical Decisions Regarding Birth Control. Missoula, MT, Scholars Press, 1976 See also, Hastings REPORT 7(2):43, 1977
437. VIEWPOINTS: Why do unmarried women fail to use contraception? Med Aspects Hum Sexuality 7(5):154–168, 1973
438. Vincent CE (ed): Human Sexuality In Medicine and Practice. Springfield, IL, C C Thomas, 1968
439. Vogel HD: A follow-up study of former student-patients at the Crippled Children's Hospital and School, Sioux Falls, SD. Rehabil Lit 36(9):270–272, 1975
440. Wagner N: The sexual adjustment of cardiac patients. Br J Sex Med 1(3):17–22, 1974
441. Wallin JEW: Changing Emphasis On Mental Retardation. Address to lay and professionals, Delaware State Dept of Public Instruction, Special Education & Mental Hygiene, 1968
442. Walter SD: Sex predetermination and epidemiology. Soc Sci Med 9:105–110, 1975
443. Walters L, Gaylin W: Sterilizing the retarded child. In Veach RM: Case Studies in Bioethics, Case #538. Hastings-on-Hudson, NY, Hastings Center Report, 1976, pp 13–17
444. Webb L: Children With Special Needs In The Infant's School. Great Britain, London Collins Fontana Book, 1972, p 131
445. Westoff CF, Rindfus RE: Sex preselection in USA—some implications. Science 184(5):633–636, 1974
446. Westoff LA: Sterilization. New York Times Magazine, September 29, 1974, pp 30–31, 80–82
447. Westoff LA: Kids with kids. New York Times Magazine, February 22, 1976, pp 14–15, 63–65
448. Wickesham Voluntary Sterilization Service: A Brief Guide To Voluntary Sterilization. Voluntary Contraceptive Sterilization. The Abortion Information Guide. Booklets 1975, Association For Voluntary Sterilization, New York, NY
449. Winik J, Robbins G: Physical and psychologic adjustment to mastectomy. Cancer 39(2):478–486, 1977
450. Winter ST: The male disadvantage in diseases acquired in childhood. Devel Med Child Neuro 14(4):517–520, 1972
451. Wise T: Effects of Chronic Illness. Speech at Annual Meeting of National Sex Educators. Tape casette of Organic Conditions Program available from AASECT, Washington, DC, 20005
452. What's Happening, publication #1517, 1975. Emory University School of Medicine, Dept OBS, Family Planning Program, Atlanta, GA (#1517 Booklet)
453. WHO experts hold fetus under 22 weeks can't survive at present. Today's Child 23(6):3, 1975
454. Wolfe P: Biological and Psychological Determinants—Symposium on The Violent Child. New York University Medical Center, March 19, 1976
455. Women Over Forty Warned Against Pill. Column, Ideas & Trends, Review Of The Week Section, New York Times, Sunday July 23, 1976
456. Wright BA: Worth pondering—problems and prospects of mutual aid groups. Rehabil Psychol 19(4):180–183, 1972
457. Zackler J, Branstadt W (eds): The Teenage Pregnant Girl. Springfield, IL, C C Thomas, 1975, 323 pp
458. Zella RF: Half his body was cut away. Accent On Living 22: 58–62, Spring 1977
459. Zellweger H: Chromosomal aberrations. In American Academy for Cerebral Palsy: Syllabus of Instructional Courses. New Orleans Annual Meeting, 1971, pp 96–71
460. Zelnick M, Kantner JF: Sexual & contraceptive experience of young unmarried women in US 1976 & 1971. Family Plan Perspectives 9(2) March/April 1977
461. Zlotnick P: Chrome-plated femininity. Accent On Living 19(3):42–45, Winter 1974

INDEX